What Is Conservatism?

What Is Conservatism?

EDITED BY FRANK S. MEYER

64-11014 edit.

320.973

Holt, Rinehart and Winston   New York   Chicago   San Francisco

In memoriam

RICHARD M. WEAVER

pioneer and protagonist of the
American conservative consensus

Acknowledgments

THIS book would have been impossible without the support, financial and moral, of the Intercollegiate Society of Individualists and its president, E. Victor Milione, whose understanding and patience have sustained the undertaking from its beginnings.

The introductory essay, "Freedom, Tradition, Conservatism," which was first published in *Modern Age*, was reprinted by ISI in a brochure. The concept of a book based on the issues raised in that essay was developed in conversations with Mr. Milione, and ISI under his presidency has sponsored it at every stage.

I am also grateful to the University of Chicago Press for permission to publish F. A. Hayek's "Why I Am Not a Conservative," which originally appeared in his *The Constitution of Liberty*.

—F.S.M.

Contents

What Is Conservatism?

Introduction

CONSENSUS and divergence in contemporary American conservative thought are the themes of this book. That there is a contemporary American conservative movement, which looms larger and larger on the political scene, no one will deny. Nor is it difficult to designate the general political principles by which this movement is delimited, in contrast to the prevailing national tendency of the past three decades, the tendency which we call "liberalism." American conservatives are united in opposition to the growth of government power—of what is known as the welfare state—and to the centralization of that power in the Federal executive; they are opposed to the characteristic leveling egalitarianism of the time, an egalitarianism they see expressed on every level—political, social, economic, intellectual—of our national life; they reject what they consider the presently established national policy of appeasement and retreat before Communism, and they stand for firm resistance to its advance and for determined counterattack as the only guarantee of the survival of the American Republic and of our institutions generally.

This consensus on the practical political level rests upon a general consensus (at least so far as it is contrasted with the "liberal" outlook) on the nature of men and their relations to government and society. To discuss that consensus in detail would, however, be to anticipate the content of the book. Suffice it to say that, by and large, it is parallel in modern circumstances to the consensus of the men who founded the Republic and conceived the Constitution.

Within this consensus, however (as within the consensus of the Founders of the Republic), distinct differences of emphasis exist. Yet the consensus also exists; and it is the aim of this book to examine this apparent paradox of consensus and divergence and to suggest the ground of its resolution. Specifically, the deepest element of divergence arises from the opposed emphases of those conservatives who stress the concepts of tradition and authority and those who stress the concept of freedom. Consideration of this divergence receives the major attention of the book, although in its course other problems manifest themselves, as does the overarching consensus.

In the first chapter, "Freedom, Tradition, Conservatism," Frank S. Meyer establishes the fundamental elements of this major divergence and tentatively projects some of the aspects of its resolution within the general conservative consensus. Russell Kirk and Willmoore Kendall, each from a different point of view, champion the anti-libertarian emphasis of conservative thought, while Wilhelm Röpke, F. A. Hayek, and M. Stanton Evans reply in the name of emphasis on freedom. Father Stanley Parry breaks through the discussion to speak on another level, proposing what can only be called a prophetic view of the problems of contemporary civilization. Stephen J. Tonsor and Garry Wills attempt to move towards political principles that will embrace both the traditionalist and the libertarian emphases. Examining some concrete issues, John Chamberlain, Stefan T. Possony, and William F. Buckley, Jr. bring the discussion into the area of practical relevance as they consider respectively the economy, military policy, and specific problems among conservatives. In the concluding chapter, Frank S. Meyer analyzes the preceding discussion in terms of its contribution to the resolution of divergences and the firmer establishment of consensus.

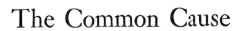
The Common Cause

CHAPTER ONE

Freedom, Tradition, Conservatism

FRANK S. MEYER

THE intellectual bankruptcy of the collectivist Liberalism which has dominated American thought for the past half century becomes every day more obvious. The imagination, the verve, the spiritual passion that once characterized it in its days of movement towards power have long since been replaced by a tired repetition of slogans empty of content and sustained only by the weight and inertia of bureaucratic power.

Power, Liberalism still has beyond doubt; but power has only the next to the last word in the affairs of men—not the last word. Power is wielded by men, controlled by men, divided by men, limited by men, as they are guided and inspired by their intellectual and spiritual understanding. There may be a gap of years, of decades, between the onset of the impotence of a false world-view, and the decay and defeat of the power structure which has arisen upon the foundations of that world-view. But its defeat is, given time, the necessary result of the re-emergence of truth in the consciousness of those who are concerned with matters of the intellect, with matters of the spirit, of those who—though they may have little control over material power at the moment—determine the foundations of the future.

The last half dozen years have seen an intellectual revolt, unparalleled in a century, against the concepts upon which Liberal collectivism is based. It is ironic, although not historically unprecedented, that such a burst of creative energy on the intellectual

level should occur simultaneously with a continuing spread of the
influence of Liberalism in the practical political sphere, to the
point where it has now captured the decisive positions of power in
the Republican as well as in the Democratic party. But ironic or
not, it is the case. For the first time in modern America a whole
school of thought has consciously challenged the very foundations
of collectivist Liberalism; two intellectually serious journals, *Modern
Age* and *National Review*, have established themselves integrally
in the life of the nation; and an increasing number of the
newer generation of undergraduates, graduate students, and young
instructors in the universities openly range themselves against the
prevailing Liberal orthodoxy. Most important, perhaps, an intense
and far-reaching discussion has been taking place among the enemies
of Liberalism on the meaning and matter of their position
in the circumstances of mid-twentieth-century America.

It is to this discussion that I want to address myself, with the hope
of helping to clarify some of the issues which divide counsels and
hinder the growth of intellectual understanding among the opponents
of collectivism. Semantic difficulties are added to substantive
difficulties in any such discussion, and I ask the indulgence of my
readers in accepting the word "conservative" as an over-all term
to include the two streams of thought that in practice unite to
oppose the reigning ideology of collectivist Liberalism. I believe
that those two streams of thought, although they are sometimes
presented as mutually incompatible, can in reality be united within
a single broad conservative political theory, since they have their
roots in a common tradition and are arrayed against a common
enemy. Their opposition, which takes many forms, is essentially
a division between those who abstract from the corpus of Western
belief its stress upon freedom and upon the innate importance of
the individual person (what we may call the "libertarian" position)
and those who, drawing upon the same source, stress value and
virtue and order (what we may call the "traditionalist" position).

But the source from which both draw, the continuing consciousness
of Western civilization, has been specifically distinguished by
its ability to hold these apparently opposed ends in balance and tension,
and in fact the two positions which confront each other today
in American conservative discourse both implicitly accept, to a

large degree, the ends of the other. Without the implicit acceptance of an absolute ground of value, the pre-eminence of the person as criterion of political and social thought and action has no
philosophical foundation, and freedom would be only a meaningless excitation and could never become the serious goal of a serious
politics. On the other hand, the belief in virtue as the end of men's
being implicitly recognizes the necessity of freedom to choose that
end; otherwise, virtue could be no more than a conditioned tropism.
And the raising of order to the rank of an end overshadowing and
subordinating the individual person would make of order not what
the traditionalist conservative means by it, but the rule of totalitarian authority, inhuman and subhuman.

On neither side is there a purposeful, philosophically founded
rejection of the ends the other side proclaims. Rather, each side
emphasizes so strongly the aspect of the great tradition of the West
which it sees as decisive that distortion sets in. The place of its
goals in the total tradition of the West is lost sight of, and the
complementary interdependence of freedom and virtue, of the
individual person and political order, is forgotten.

Nevertheless, although these contrary emphases in conservative
thought can and do pull away from each other when the proponents of either forsake one side of their common heritage of belief
in virtue as man's proper end *and* his freedom under God as the
condition of the achievement of that end, their opposition is not
irreconcilable, precisely because they do in fact jointly possess that
very heritage. Extremists on one side may be undisturbed by the
danger of the recrudescence of authoritarian status society if only
it would enforce the doctrines in which they believe. Extremists
on the other side may care little what becomes of ultimate values
if only political and economic individualism prevails. But both
extremes are self-defeating: truth withers when freedom dies, however righteous the authority that kills it; and free individualism
uninformed by moral value rots at its core and soon brings about
conditions that pave the way for surrender to tyranny.

Such extremes, however, are not the necessary outcome of a
dialectic between doctrines which emphasize opposite sides of the
same truth. Indeed, a dialectic between different emphases based
upon the same fundamental understanding is the mode by which
finite men have achieved much of the wisdom contained in tradi-

tion. Such a dialectic is in the highest degree necessary today between the libertarians and the traditionalists among conservatives. It cannot fail to achieve results of the greatest significance, if only the protagonists, in pressing that aspect of the truth which each regards as decisive, keep constantly in their consciousness other and complementary aspects of the same truth.

The tendency to establish false antitheses obstructing fruitful confrontation arises in part from an inherent dilemma of conservatism in a revolutionary era, such as ours. There is a real contradiction between the deep piety of the conservative spirit towards tradition, prescription, the preservation of the fiber of society (what has been called "natural conservatism") and the more reasoned, consciously principled, militant conservatism which becomes necessary when the fibers of society have been rudely torn apart, when deleterious revolutionary principles ride high, and restoration, not preservation, is the order of the day. For what the conservative is committed to conserve is not simply whatever happen to be the established conditions of a few years or a few decades, but the consensus of his civilization, of his country, as that consensus over the centuries has reflected truth derived from the very constitution of being. We are today historically in a situation created by thirty years of slow and insidious revolution at home and a half century of violent open revolution abroad. To conserve the true and the good under these circumstances is to restore an understanding (and a social structure reflecting that understanding) which has been all but buried; it is not to preserve the transient customs and prescriptions of the present.

It is here that the dilemma of conservatism affects our present doctrinal discussion. The need in our circumstances for the most vigorous use of reason to combat the collectivist, scientistic, amoral wave of the present tends to induce in the libertarian an apotheosis of reason and the neglect of tradition and prescription (which he identifies with the prevailing prescriptions of the present). The traditionalist, suspecting in this libertarian tendency the same fever to impose upon men an abstract speculative ideology that has characterized the revolution of our time—as well as the French Revolution and its spiritual forebears—tends to recoil and in his turn to press a one-sided position. Too often he confounds reason and principle with "demon ideology." Rather than justly insisting upon the limits of reason—the finite bounds of the purview of any one man or any one generation, and the responsibility to employ reason in the context of continuing tradition—he seems sometimes to turn his back on reason altogether and to place the claims of custom and prescription in irreconcilable opposition to it.

Both attitudes obscure the truth; both vitiate the value of the dialectic. The history of the West has been a history of reason operating within tradition. The balance has been tenuous, the tension at times has tightened till it was spiritually almost unbearable; but out of this balance and tension the glory of the West has been created. To claim exclusive sovereignty for either component, reason or tradition, is to smirch that glory and cripple the potentialities of conservatism in its struggle against the Liberal collectivist Leviathan.

Abstract reason, functioning in a vacuum of tradition, can indeed give birth to an arid and distorting ideology. But, in a revolutionary age, the qualities of natural conservatism by themselves can lead only to the enthronement of the prevailing power of the revolution. Natural conservatism is a legitimate human characteristic, and in settled times it is conducive to good. It represents the universal human tendency to hold by the accustomed, to maintain existing modes of life. In settled times it can exist in healthy tension with the other equally natural human characteristic, the dynamic impulse to break beyond accepted limits in the deepening of truth and the heightening of value. But this is only possible before the fibers of society have been loosened, before the "cake of custom" has been broken. Then these two human tendencies can be held in just proportion, since men of all conditions believe, each at the level of his understanding, in the same transcendent Ground of truth and value. But when, through whatever cause, this unity in tension is riven, when the dynamic takes off into thin air, breaking its tension with the perpetual rhythms of life—in short, when a revolutionary force shatters the unity and balance of civilization— then conservatism must be of another sort if it is to fulfill its responsibility. It is not and cannot be limited to that uncritical acceptance, that uncomplicated reverence, which is the essence of natural conservatism. The world of idea and symbol and image has been turned topsy-turvy; the life stream of civilization has been cut off and dispersed.

This is our situation. What is required of us is a *conscious* conservatism, a clearly principled restatement in new circumstances of philosophical and political truth. This conscious conservatism cannot be a simple piety, although in a deep sense it must have piety towards the constitution of being. Nevertheless in its consciousness it necessarily reflects a reaction to the rude break the revolution has made in the continuity of human wisdom. It is called forth by a sense of the loss which that cutting off has created. It cannot now be identical with the natural conservatism towards which it yearns. The world in which it exists is the revolutionary world. To accept that, to conserve that, would be to accept and conserve the very denial of man's long-developed understanding, the very destruction of achieved truth, which are the essence of the revolution.

Nor can the conscious conservatism required of us appeal simply and uncomplicatedly to the past. The past has had many aspects, all held in measured suspension. But the revolution has destroyed that suspension, that tradition; the delicate fabric can never be re-created in the identical form; its integral character has been destroyed. The conscious conservatism of a revolutionary or post-revolutionary era faces problems inconceivable to the natural conservatism of a prerevolutionary time. The modes of thought of natural conservatism are not by themselves adequate to the tasks of a time like this. Today's conservatism cannot simply affirm. It must select and adjudge. It is conservative because in its selection and in its judgment it bases itself upon the accumulated wisdom of mankind over millenia, because it accepts the limits upon the irresponsible play of untrammeled reason which the unchanging values exhibited by that wisdom dictate. But it is, it has to be, not acceptance of what lies before it in the contemporary world, but challenge. In an era like ours the existing regime in philosophical thought, as in political and social actuality, is fundamentally wrong. To accept is to be not conservative, but acquiescent to revolution.

Situations of this nature have arisen again and again in the history of civilization; and each time the great renewers have been those who were able to recover true principle out of the wreck of their heritage. They were guided by reason—reason mediated, it is true, by prudence, but in the first instance reason. Like Socrates, Plato, Aristotle, confronting the chaos in the body politic and in the minds of men created by the overweening pride of the Athenian *demos*, we do not live in the happy age of a natural conservatism. We cannot simply revere; we cannot uncritically follow tradition, for the tradition presented to us is rapidly becoming—thanks to the prevailing intellectual climate, thanks to the schools, thanks to the outpourings of all the agencies that mold opinion and belief— the tradition of a positivism scornful of truth and virtue, the tradition of the collective, the tradition of the untrammeled state.

The conservative today, like the conscious conservative of all revolutionary eras, cannot escape the necessity and the duty to bring reason to bear upon the problems that confront him. He has to separate the true from the false, applying basic principle to the task of cutting through the tangled mass of confusion and false-hood; he has the responsibility of establishing in new circum-stances forms of thought and institutional arrangements which will express the truth of the great tradition of the West. Respectful though he is of the wisdom of the past and reverent towards precedent and prescription, the tasks he faces can only be carried out with the aid of reason, the faculty which enables us to dis-tinguish principle and thus to separate the true from the false.

The projection of a sharp antithesis between reason and tradition distorts the true harmony which exists between them and blocks the development of conservative thought. There is no real antag-onism. Conservatism to continue to develop today must embrace both: reason operating within tradition: neither ideological *hubris* abstractly creating Utopian blueprints, ignoring the accumulated wisdom of mankind, nor blind dependence upon that wisdom to answer automatically the questions posed to our generation and demanding our own expenditure of our own mind and spirit.

Closely related to the false antithesis between reason and tradi-tion that distorts the dialogue between the libertarian emphasis and the traditionalist emphasis among conservatives is our historical inheritance of the nineteenth-century European struggle between classical liberalism and a conservatism that was too often rigidly authoritarian. Granted there is much in classical liberalism that conservatives must reject—its philosophical foundations, its tendency towards Utopian constructions, its disregard (explicitly, though by no means implicitly) of tradition; granted it is the source of much that is responsible for the plight of the twentieth century; but its championship of freedom and its development of political and economic theories directed towards the assurance of freedom have contributed to our heritage concepts which we need to conserve and develop, as surely as we need to reject the utilitarian ethics and the secular progressivism that classical liberalism has also passed on to us.

Nineteenth-century conservatism, with all its understanding of the pre-eminence of virtue and value, for all its piety towards the continuing tradition of mankind, was far too cavalier to the claims of freedom, far too ready to subordinate the individual person to the authority of state or society.

The conservative today is the inheritor of the best in both these tragically bifurcated branches of the Western tradition. But the division lingers on and adds to the difficulties of conservative discourse. The traditionalist, although in practice he fights alongside the libertarian against the collectivist Leviathan state of the twentieth century, tends to reject the political and economic theories of freedom which flow from classical liberalism in his reaction against its unsound metaphysics. He discards the true with the false, creating unnecessary obstacles to the mutual dialogue in which he is engaged with his libertarian *alter ego*. The libertarian, suffering from the mixed heritage of the nineteenth-century champions of liberty, reacts against the traditionalist's emphasis upon precedent and continuity out of antipathy to the authoritarianism with which that emphasis has been associated, although in actuality he stands firmly for continuity and tradition against the rising revolutionary wave of collectivism and statism.

We are victims here of an inherent tragedy in the history of classical liberalism. As it developed the economic and political doctrines of limited state power, the free-market economy, and the freedom of the individual person, it sapped, by its utilitarianism, the foundations of belief in an organic moral order. But the only possible basis of respect for the integrity of the individual person and for the overriding value of his freedom is belief in an organic moral order. Without such a belief, no doctrine of political and economic liberty can stand.

Furthermore, when such a belief is not universally accepted, a free society, even if it could exist, would become licentious war of all against all. Political freedom, failing a broad acceptance of the personal obligation to duty and to charity, is never viable. Deprived of an understanding of the philosophical foundations of freedom and exposed to the ravening of conscienceless marauders, men forget that they are fully men only to the degree that they are free to choose their destiny, and they turn to whatever fallacy promises them welfare and order.

The classical liberal as philosopher dug away the foundations of the economic and political doctrines of classical liberalism. But however much he may thereby have contributed to our misfortunes, he himself continued to live on the inherited moral capital of centuries of Christendom. His philosophical doctrines attacked the foundations of conscience, but he himself was still a man of conscience. As Christopher Dawson has said: "The old liberalism, with all its shortcoming, had its roots deep in the soul of Western and Christian culture." With those roots as yet unsevered, the classical liberal was able to develop the theories of political and economic freedom which are part of the conservative heritage today.

The misunderstanding between libertarian and traditionalist are to a considerable degree the result of a failure to understand the differing levels on which classical liberal doctrines are valid and invalid. Although the classical liberal forgot—and the contemporary libertarian conservative sometimes tends to forget—that in the *moral* realm freedom is only a means whereby men can pursue their proper end, which is virtue, he did understand that in the *political* realm freedom is the primary end. If, with Acton, we "take the establishment of liberty for the realization of moral duties to be the end of civil society," the traditionalist conservative of today, living in an age when liberty is the last thought of our political mentors, has little cause to reject the contributions to the understanding of liberty of the classical liberals, however corrupted their understanding of the ends of liberty. Their error lay largely in the confusion of the temporal with the transcendent. They could not distinguish between the *authoritarianism* with which men and institutions suppress the freedom of men, and the *authority* of God and truth.

On the other hand, the same error in reverse vitiated the thought of nineteenth-century conservatives. They respected the authority of God and of truth as conveyed in tradition, but too often they imbued the authoritarianism of men and institutions with the sacred aura of divine authority. They gave way to the temptation to make of tradition, which in its rightful role serves as a guide to the operation of reason, a weapon with which to suppress reason.

It is true that from their understanding of the basis of men's moral existence, from their reverence for the continuity and precedent that ties the present to the past, contemporary conservatism has inherited elements vital to its very existence. Yet we can no more make of the great conservative minds of the nineteenth century unerring guides to be blindly followed than we can condemn out of hand their classical liberal opponents. Sound though they were on the essentials of man's being, on his destiny to virtue and his responsibility to seek it, on his duty in the moral order, they failed too often to realize that the *political* condition of moral fulfillment is freedom from coercion. Signally they failed to recognize the decisive danger in a union of political and economic power, a danger becoming daily greater before their eyes as science and technology created apace immense aggregates of economic energy. Aware, as the classical liberals were not, of the reality of original sin, they forgot that its effects are never more virulent than when men wield unlimited power. Looking to the state to promote virtue, they forgot that the power of the state rests in the hands of men as subject to the effects of original sin as those they govern. They could not, or would not, see a truth the classical liberals understood: if to the power naturally inherent in the state, to defend its citizens from violence, domestic and foreign, and to administer justice, there is added a positive power over economic and social energy, the temptation to tyranny becomes irresistible, and the political conditions of freedom wither.

The tendency of the traditionalist conservative to insist that the crystallization of a conservative outlook today requires only that we carry on the principles of those who called themselves conservatives in the nineteenth century oversimplifies and confuses the problem. That the conservative is one who preserves tradition does not mean that his task is arid imitation and repetition of what others have done before. Certainly in ultimate terms, upon the basic issue of human destiny, truths have been given us that we cannot improve upon, that we can only convey and make real in the context of our time. Here indeed the conservatives of the nineteenth century played a heroic part, in preserving in the teeth of the overwhelming tendency of the era the age-old image of man as a creature of transcendent destiny.

In the political and economic realm, however, these truths establish only the foundation for an understanding of the end of civil society and the function of the state. That end, to guarantee freedom, so that men may uncoercedly pursue virtue, can be achieved in different circumstances by different means. To the clarification of what these means are in specific circumstances, the conservative must apply his reason. The technological circumstances of the twentieth century demand above all the breaking up of power and the separation of centers of power within the economy itself, within the state itself, and between the state and the economy. Power of a magnitude never before dreamed of by men has been brought into being. While separation of power has always been essential to a good society, if those who possess it are to be preserved from corruption and those who do not are to be safeguarded from coercion, this has become a fateful necessity under the conditions of modern technology. To the analysis of this decisive problem and to the development of political and economic solutions of it, classical liberalism contributed mightily. If we reject that heritage, we should be casting away some of the most powerful among our weapons against socialism, Communism, and collectivist Liberalism. The traditionalist who would have us do so because of the philosophical errors of classical liberalism, like the libertarian who rejects tradition because it has sometimes been associated with authoritarianism, seriously weakens the development of conservative doctrine.

The historical fact is—and it adds to the complexity of our problems—that the great tradition of the West has come to us through the nineteenth century, split, bifurcated, so that we must draw not only upon those who called themselves conservatives in that century but also upon those who called themselves liberals.

The economists of the liberal British tradition, from Adam Smith through and beyond the vilified Manchesterians, like the Austrian economists from Menger and Böhm-Bawerk to Mises and Hayek, analyzed the conditions of industrial society and established the principles upon which the colossal power that it produces can be developed for the use of man without nurturing a monstrous Leviathan. Without their mighty intellectual endeavor, we should be disarmed before the collectivist economics of Marx, Keynes, and Galbraith. And in the sphere of political theory, who has surpassed the nineteenth-century liberals in their prophetic understanding of the looming dangers of the all-powerful state? Conservatives today can reject neither side of their nineteenth-century heritage; they must draw upon both.

Differences of emphasis between libertarian and traditionalist cannot be avoided and should not be regretted. Conservatism has no monolithic party line. Our task is to overcome the nineteenth-century bifurcation of the Western tradition in fruitful dialogue, not to perpetuate it by refusing to understand the breadth and complexity of our heritage, out of a narrow historicism that unearths outworn party emblems.

I am well aware that what I have been saying can be criticized as eclecticism and attacked as an effort to smother principle. But it is not the laying aside of clear belief, either by the libertarian conservative or by the traditionalist conservative, in order to present a front against contemporary collectivist Liberalism, that is here conceived. Rather it is the deepening of the beliefs which each holds through the development of their implications in a dialectic free of distorting narrowness. That deepening—and the development of a common conservative doctrine, comprehending both emphases—cannot be achieved in a surface manner by blinking differences or blurring intellectual distinctions with grandiose phraseology. It can only be achieved by a hard-fought dialectic —a dialectic in which both sides recognize not only that they have a common enemy, but also that, despite all differences, they hold a common heritage.

As Americans, indeed, we have a great tradition to draw upon, in which the division, the bifurcation, of European thought between the emphasis on virtue and value and order and the emphasis

on freedom and the integrity of the individual person was overcome, and a harmonious unity of the tensed poles of Western
thought was achieved in political theory and practice as never before or since. The men who created the Republic, who framed
the Constitution and produced that monument of political wisdom,
The Federalist Papers, comprised among them as great a conflict
of emphasis as any in contemporary American conservatism. Washington, Franklin, Jefferson, Hamilton, Adams, Jay, Mason, Madison—among them there existed immense differences on the claims
of the individual person and the claims of order, on the relation
of virtue to freedom. But their dialectic was conducted within a
continuing awareness of their joint heritage. Out of that dialectic
they created a political theory and a political structure based upon
the understanding that, while truth and virtue are metaphysical
and moral ends, the freedom to seek them is the political condition
of those ends—and that a social structure which keeps power
divided is the indispensable means to this political end. The debate
from which our American institutions arose is a fitting model for
our debate.

That debate will the more rapidly and the more profoundly
develop the energy and the fruitfulness and the eventual understanding that are intellectually inherent in the opposed emphases,
if we constantly keep in mind the vision of life against which we
are jointly engaged in fateful combat: the Liberal collectivist body
of dogma that has pervaded the consciousness and shaped the
actions of the decisive and articulate sections of society over the
past half century or more.

In opposition to this image of man as neither free nor inspired
by a transcendent destiny, the differences between libertarian and
traditionalist are thrown into their true perspective: differences of
emphasis, not of underlying opposition. In the light of it, libertarian
and traditionalist, as they deepen their understanding in a commonly based dialogue, can maintain a common front and a common struggle. The desecration of the image of man, the attack
alike upon his freedom and his transcendent dignity, provide
common cause in the immediate struggle. As with our ancestors
who laid the foundations of the Republic, the challenge to our
common faith inspires us, without surrendering our differences of
stress, to create a fundamental unity of doctrine within which

libertarian and traditionalist, respecting each other, can mutually vindicate the true nature of man, free and responsible, against the arid, mechanistic, collectivist denial of man's nature which transitorily prevails.

Emphasis on Tradition and Authority

CHAPTER TWO

Prescription, Authority,

and Ordered Freedom

RUSSELL KIRK

CIVILIZED man lives by authority; without some reference to authority, indeed, no form of human existence is possible. Also man lives by prescription—that is, by ancient custom and usage, and the rights which usage and custom have established. Without just authority and respected prescription, the pillars of any tolerable civil social order, true freedom is not possible.

For some time it has been fashionable to deride authority and prescription—though a good many people have been experiencing a change of heart recently. "Authority," in the vocabulary of what has been called "the Freudian ethic," has meant arbitrary restraint; and prescription has been equated with cultural lag and superstition. But the consequences of these emancipated notions have been unpalatable. A generation of young people reared according to "permissive" tenets has grown up bored, sullen, and in revolt against the very lack of order which was supposed to ensure the full development of their personalities. And a world lulled by slogans about absolute liberty and perpetual peace has found itself devoured by thoroughgoing tyranny and increasing violence. If men are to exist together at all, some authority must govern them; if they throw off traditional authority, the authority of church and precept and old educational disciplines and parents, then very soon they are compelled to submit to some new and merciless authority. "If you will not have God—and he is a jealous God—" Mr. T. S. Eliot observes, "then you should pay your respects to Hitler or Stalin." Authority and prescription lacking, order cannot subsist. If the authority is unjust, and the prescription merely the decree of some new domination, then the social order will have small place for freedom. Genuinely ordered freedom is the only sort of liberty worth having: freedom made possible by order within the soul and order within the state. Anarchic freedom, liberty defiant of authority and prescription, is merely the subhuman state of the wolf and the shark, or the punishment of Cain, with his hand against every man's.

So if people really desire genuine freedom, they need to know genuine authority. "Authority" is not the policeman's baton. "Conscience is an authority," Newman writes in his essay on John Keble; "the Bible is an authority; such is the Church; such is Antiquity; such are the words of the wise; such are historical memories, such are legal saws and state maxims; such are proverbs; such are sentiments, presages, and prepossessions." Authority, in fine, is the ground upon which prudent action must be performed. If a man acknowledges no authority, he sets himself up as Cain, and before long he is struck down by nemesis, which follows upon *hubris.*

Political authority, the claims and powers of a legitimate state, though an important part of this complex of authority which rules our lives, is no more than a part. Sometimes authorities conflict; indeed, most of the great disputes of history have been, in essence, controversies over the higher source of authority. And such debates never are wholly and finally resolved. Now and again, for instance, the authoritative claims of church and state cannot well be reconciled, and then great trouble results. Similarly, the authority of faith and the authority of reason collide from age to age. In such clashes, the conscientious man endeavors, according to what light is given him, to determine what representatives of authority have claimed too much; but he is foolish if, despairing, he forsakes authority altogether.

Human nature being irremediably flawed, so that all of us in some degree rebel against the people and the institutions to which we owe most, there is in every man a certain impulse to make himself God: that is, to cast off all authority but his own lust and whim. From this vice comes the corrupting influence of total power upon even the best of natures. The rebellion of Lucifer is the symbol of this ancient anarchic impulse—the passion for over-throwing the just authority of God, that upon the vacant throne of authority the rebel may make himself absolute. Yet the doom of such risings is as sure as Lucifer's. For a grown man to rebel against all authority is as ludicrous as for a three-year-old child to defy his parents: whether they are good parents or bad, he can live scarcely a day without them.

From its beginnings, the liberal movement of the nineteenth century had within it this fatuous yearning for the destruction of all authority. Liberalism also possessed some good qualities; but it never has recovered from this congenital defiance of authority and prescription. The early liberals were convinced that once they should overthrow established governments and churches, sup-planting them by rational and egalitarian and purely secular insti-tutions, the principal problems of the human condition would be near solution. Poverty, ignorance, disease, and war might then be terminated, once enlightened self-interest, popular suffrage, and utilitarian public policies had triumphed. One had only to fight clear of the Bad Old Days and the dead weight of supersti-tion. Abolish the old Authorities, and sweetness and light will reign.

Yet the triumph of liberalism endured little more than half a century; by the 1880's, the individualism of the early liberals was being transmuted into socialism, a process easily traced in the life of John Stuart Mill. Liberalism had begun, defying authority and prescription, by breaking all sorts of ancient ties and obligations, but the latter-day Liberal, in Santayana's phrase, relaxes no bond except the marriage knot. Increasingly, though implicitly, Liberals came to accept a new authority, that of the omnicompetent wel-fare state; they continued to repudiate authority only in the sphere of private life.

Just how archaic and unreal, politically, latter-day Liberalism has become is sufficiently illustrated by a conference of the English Liberal Party in the summer of 1961. Three principal resolutions were proposed: to abolish the monarchy, to abolish the hereditary element in the House of Lords, and to expand the welfare state.

Though the first proposal was defeated after discussion, the other two were adopted enthusiastically; and so the conference adjourned, its members satisfied that they had shown the English nation how to solve its difficulties in the twentieth century. To anyone but a Liberal ideologue, it is clear enough that abolition of the British monarchy would accomplish nothing but to destroy the symbol of justice and order in Britain; that to destroy the hereditary element in the House of Lords would only injure the most serious deliberative body in the world; and that to extend the British welfare state would do no less than to finish Liberalism altogether, since that would mean certainly complete socialism, and probably the end of the British constitution and of British prosperity. So much for the eccentricities of a dying party.

Though they have abandoned nearly all their original political program, still the Liberals of the twentieth century cling to their general detestation of authority; but this detestation has shifted from the political sphere to the moral and social. The writings of an American latter-day Liberal, a disciple of J. S. Mill, Mr. David Riesman, illustrate this. Professor Riesman recognizes the decay of authority among us and is confusedly disturbed by it. He gives up for lost the "tradition-directed individual"—that is, the man with some respect for authority and tradition—and sheds few tears at his passing. What worries Mr. Riesman more, the "inner-directed individual"—that is, the typical active nineteenth-century liberal—also seems to be not long for this world. So there remain the "other-directed"—that is, the modern masses who take for their norms whatever their neighbors seem to be doing—and some scattered and harebrained dissidents, "anomics," masterless men who meaninglessly and futilely defy the great tendencies of their time. Mr. Riesman's only hope is in the possibility of a number of "autonomous" men, uncontrolled by tradition, liberal "inner direction," or the fads and foibles of the hour: rootless persons who somehow, by wishing it, may become superior to the crowd of other-directed about them. No hope could be more ridiculous than this last. Also Mr. Riesman would like to see women "deprivatized" —that is, more footloose—and to see all who would be autonomous spend much time upon "consumership" and other diversions.

One may as well laugh as cry. To such an intellectual and moral bankruptcy have come even the most intelligent of twentieth-century Liberals. Having denied the very existence of sound and just authority, having scoffed at the wisdom of our ancestors, Liberalism is altogether cut loose from such moorings as once it had. Without some principle of authority, life becomes meaningless, and political and intellectual factions slip into the dust-bin of history.

If authority, then—however unfashionable in recent years—remains ineluctable for civilization and for any truly human existence, how do men find such authority? In a number of ways; but of these, the means for most men is what we call prescription or tradition.

Prescription, socially and politically speaking, means those ways and institutions and rights prescribed by long—sometimes immemorial—usage. Tradition (a word until the end of the eighteenth century applied almost exclusively to Christian beliefs not set down in Scripture) means received opinions, convictions religious and moral and political and aesthetic passed down from generation to generation, so that they are accepted by most men as a matter of course. I have discussed the nature of tradition and prescription at some length in my book *Beyond the Dreams of Avarice*.

Fulbert of Chartres and Gerbert of Rheims, those two grand Schoolmen, said that we moderns are dwarfs standing upon the shoulders of giants. We see so far only because we are elevated upon the accomplishment of our ancestors; and if we break with ancestral wisdom, we at once are plunged into the ditch of ignorance. All that we have and know is founded upon the experience of the race. As Burke put it, "The individual is foolish, but the species is wise." Men have no right, Burke said, to risk the very existence of their nation and their civilization upon experiments in morals and politics; for each man's private capital of intelligence is petty; it is only when a man draws upon the bank and capital of the ages, the wisdom of our ancestors, that he can act wisely. Without resort to tradition and prescription, we are left with merely our vanity and the brief and partial experience of our evanescent lives. "What shadows we are, and what shadows we pursue!"

G. K. Chesterton expressed much the same truth when he wrote of "the democracy of the dead." When we decide great questions

in our time, he held, we ought to count not merely the votes of
our contemporaries, but the opinions of many generations of men
—and particularly the convictions of the wise men who have pre-
ceded us in time. By trial and error, by revelation, by the insights
of men of genius, mankind has acquired, slowly and painfully,
over thousands of years, a knowledge of human nature and of the
civil social order which no one individual possibly can supplant
by private rationality.

This is true especially in matters of morals, politics, and taste;
but in considerable degree it is true also even in modern science
and technology. Once a student objected to me that surely enlightened modern man could work out rationally a much better
system of morals and politics than the hodgepodge we have inherited from blundering ancestors. But I asked this student if,
without consulting senior technicians, books, and authority generally, he thought he could construct, unaided, an automobile—
if, indeed, he thought that he personally, even with all sorts of
advice, could make an automobile at all. He confessed that he
could not; and it began to be borne in upon him to construct,
carte blanche, a system of morals and politics that really would
work might be an undertaking more difficult still.

So even the most gifted of men, and always the great mass of
human beings, must fall back upon tradition and prescription if
they are to act at all in this world. At the very least, it saves a
great deal of time. It is conceivable that, if I set myself to it, I
might calculate for myself the circumference of the earth, quite
independently of previous calculations. But since I have no strong
mathematical gifts, it is improbable that my calculations would
be more accurate than those of the present authorities; and it seems
almost certain that my result would be quite the same as the present
calculation of the earth's circumference; so I would have spent
months or years of a brief life in trying to gain what I could have
had for the asking. If we are to accomplish anything in this life,
we must take much for granted; as Newman said, if one had to
make the choice, it would be better to believe all things than to
doubt all things. In the matter of the earth's circumference, nearly
all of us are much better off if we simply accept the "traditional"
or "authoritative" calculation.

This is even more true of moral and social first principles. Only through prescription and tradition, only by habitual acceptance of just and sound authority, can men acquire knowledge of the norms for humanity. Authority tells us that murder is wrong; prescription immemorially has visited severe punishments upon murderers; tradition presents us with an ancient complex of tales of the evil consequences of murder. Now a man who thinks his private petty rationality superior to the wisdom of our ancestors may undertake experiments in murder, with a view to testing these old irrational scruples; but the results of such experiments are sure to be disagreeable for everyone concerned, including the researcher; and that experimenter has no right to be surprised if we hang him by the neck until he is quite dead. For if men flout norm and convention, life becomes intolerable. It is through respect for tradition and prescription, and recourse to those sources of knowledge, that the great mass of men acquire a tolerable understanding of norms and conventions, of the rules by which private and social existence is made tolerable.

A norm is an enduring standard. It is a law of our nature, which we ignore at our peril. It is a rule of human conduct and a measure of public virtue. The norm does not signify the average, the median, the mean, the mediocre. The norm is not the conduct of the average sensual man. A norm is not simply a measure of average performance within a group. There exists law for man, and law for thing; the late Alfred Kinsey notwithstanding, the norm for the wasp and the snake is not the norm for man. A norm has an objective existence: though men may ignore or forget a norm, still that norm does not cease to be, nor does it cease to influence men. A man apprehends a norm or fails to apprehend it, but he does not create or destroy norms.

The sanction for obedience to norms must come from a source other than private advantage and rationality—from a source more than human, indeed. Men do not submit long to their own creations. Standards erected out of expediency will be demolished soon enough, also out of expediency. Either norms have an existence independent of immediate utility, or they are mere fictions. If men assume that norms are merely the pompous fabrications of their ancestors, got up to serve the interests of a faction or an age, then every rising generation will challenge the principles of personal and social order and will learn wisdom only through agony. For half a century, we have been experiencing the consequences of a moral and social neoterism.

"Goodnatured unambitious men are cowards when they have no religion." So, in *Back to Methuselah*, writes Bernard Shaw. "They are dominated and exploited not only by greedy and often halfwitted and half-alive weaklings who will do anything for cigars, champagne, motor cars, and the more childish and selfish uses of money, but by able and sound administrators who can do nothing else with them than dominate and exploit them. Government and exploitation become synonymous under such circumstances; and the world is finally ruled by the childish, the brigands, and the blackguards." (One may acknowledge the acuteness of this insight without subscribing to the curious religion, or quasi-religion, which Shaw sets forth—half soberly, half facetiously—in *Back to Methuselah*.)

As a gloss upon this, one may say also that the average good-natured unambitious man is a coward also if he lacks—even though retaining some religious feelings—"that wise prejudice" by which "a man's virtue becomes his habit," in Burke's phrase. If his life is regulated, almost unconsciously, upon certain received opinions concerning justice and injustice, charity and selfishness, freedom and servitude, truth and falsehood, he will behave habitually with some degree of resolution and courage; but if he is all at sea in a latter-day Liberalism and moral relativism, in which any point of view or mode of conduct has something to be said for it, then he will be unnerved when the test comes. Acting customarily upon tradition and prescription, he will not feel alone; the democracy of the dead will endorse him. But acting without norms, he must be, ordinarily, either a coward or a brute in any personal or civic crisis.

A man who accepts tested authority, and acknowledges the beneficent influence of prescription and tradition, is conventional; but he is not servile. Conventions are the means by which obedience to norms is inculcated in society. Conventions are compacts by which we agree to respect one another's dignity and rights. A high degree of respect for convention is quite consonant with a high development of individual personality, and even of eccentricity. Many of the great "characters," indeed, are the great champions of convention; the names of Samuel Johnson and Benjamin Disraeli, of John Adams, John Randolph, and Theodore Roosevelt may suffice for illustration. There exists no necessary opposition between strong outward indifference to foible and strong inward loyalty to norms. A man of strong character who accepts just authority and its works will be meek—but meek only as Moses: that is, obedient to the will of God, but unflinching against human tyrants.

The good citizen is a law-abiding traditionalist: so the politics of Virgil have been summed up. If men are courageous or virtuous, ordinarily this is because they are persons of good moral *habits*: that is, they act habitually, and almost unthinkingly, upon certain premises they have learnt from infancy, through force of example and through formal instruction. This is what Burke meant when he wrote that prejudice is the wisdom of unlettered men. They draw their strength from acceptance of tradition and prescription.

Now it does not follow that an unquestioning acceptance of received opinions and long-established usage will of itself suffice to solve all personal and public problems. The world does change; a certain sloughing off of tradition and prescription is at work in any vigorous society, and a certain adding to the bulk of received opinion goes on from age to age. We cannot live precisely by the rules of our distant forefathers, in all matters. But, again to employ a phrase of Burke's, the fact that a belief or an institution has long been accepted by men, and seems to have exerted a beneficent influence, establishes in its favor "a legitimate presumption." If we feel inclined to depart from old ways, we ought to do so only after very sober consideration of ultimate consequences. Authority, prescription, and tradition undergo in every generation a certain filtering process, by which the really archaic is discarded; yet we ought to be sure that we actually are filtering, and not merely letting our heritage run down the drain.

Similarly, the general principles and valuable institutions which we have inherited from past generations must be applied and utilized with prudence; there the exercise of right reason by the leaders of any society sets to work. We possess moral norms, the Decalogue, for instance, but the way in which we observe those norms must be determined in our time by the circumstances in which we find ourselves, so that wise men in our age must reconcile exigency and enduring standard. We possess tested political institutions; but for those institutions to endure, now and then reform is essential, lest the institutions atrophy. Thus Burke's model of a statesman is one who combines with an ability to reform a disposition to preserve.

Prescription and tradition, then, cannot stand forever if the living do not sustain them by vigorous application and prudent reform. But it is equally true that lively action and ingenious reform are mere ropes of sand, unless linked with the wisdom of the ages.

One instance of the abiding value of inherited convictions—beliefs that have their origin both in the experience of the race and in the reasoning of men of genius, but have acquired through subtle processes the status of popular prejudices—is the idea of justice, as expressed by Plato and Cicero. The great classical philosophers of politics argued that justice resides in this: to each his own. Every man, ideally, ought to receive the things that best suit his own nature. Men's talents and appetites vary greatly from individual to individual; therefore a society is unjust which treats all men as if they were uniform, or which allots to one sort of nature rights and duties that properly belong to other sorts of human beings.

This concept of justice has entered deeply into the ethics, the jurisprudence, and even the imaginative literature of what is called "Western civilization." It still is a profound influence upon many men and women who never have read Cicero or Plato. It creates a prejudice against radical egalitarianism, which would reduce all men to a single mode of existence. It has inculcated a sound prejudice in favor of *order*: that is, a society marked by a variety of rewards and duties, a commonwealth in which, as Burke said, all men "have equal rights; but not to equal things." This theory underlies, for example, the British and American constitutions.

Nowadays this classical idea of justice is challenged by the Marxist doctrine that order should be abolished: all human beings should be treated as identical units, and compulsory equality of condition enforced. When the average American or Englishman is brought face to face with Marxist demands for the overthrow of prescriptive order and the establishment of a society without demarcations, he may not be able to meet the Marxist propagandist with a privately reasoned defense of variety and constitutionalism;

but he resists the Marxist doctrine out of a feeling that what the Communist proposes somehow is fundamentally unjust. The average American or Englishman remains a law-abiding traditionalist, even in this day of giddy technological and industrial alteration; he takes it for granted that we were not born yesterday; that we have no right to cast away our tested civil social order; that monotonous uniformity of condition is contrary to deep ancient human aspirations; that Communism flies in the face of the nature of things. And because he is the heir to a great tradition, he knows something of the character of justice, and he is resolute despite the threats and seductions of the radical innovator.

"The great mysterious incorporation of the human race" is, as Burke said, a contract of sorts: but a contract between the divine and the human natures, and among the dead, the living, and those yet unborn. We know something of the terms of that eternal contract of society through traditions and prescriptions. Our obedience to norms, to true and just authority in morals and politics, keeps that immortal contract alive. And that obedience secures us all in ordered freedom.

Government is instituted to secure justice and order, through respect for legitimate authority; and if we ask from government more than this, we begin to imperil justice and order. It is one of the saddest illusions of the Liberal era, the notion that political manipulation can make men happy. But some forms of government can succeed in making men miserable. So I venture to suggest here the general lineaments of the kind of government which seems reasonably consonant with the general welfare. I think that here we need to refer to two principles. The first principle is that a good government allows the more energetic natures among a people to fulfill their promise, while ensuring that these persons shall not tyrannize over the mass of men. The second principle is that in every state the best possible—or least baneful—form of government is one in accord with the traditions and prescriptive ways of its people. Beyond these two general principles, there is no rule of politics which may be applied, uniformly and universally, with safety.

Even Mr. Riesman has rediscovered the old truth that men are not created equal; they are created different. Variety, not uniformity, gives any nation vigor and hope. Thus my first principle of good government—for which I am much indebted to Professor Eric Voegelin—has a hearing once more, though the overmastering tendency of the past century and a half has been social egalitarianism. "One man is as good as another, or maybe a little better": this secular dogma has done mischief to the preservation or establishment of good government. Equality in political power has tended to lead to equality of condition. "Everybody belongs to everybody else"—this is the motto of society in Huxley's *Brave New World*; and that society is a life in death. For these assumptions are thorough falsehoods. One man is not as good as another, and everyone does not belong to everyone else. The first fallacy is the denial of Christian morals, the second the denial of the Christian idea of personality.

Aye, men are created different; and a government which ignores this law becomes an unjust government, for it sacrifices nobility to mediocrity; it pulls down the aspiring natures to gratify the inferior natures. This degradation injures humanity in two ways. First, it frustrates the natural longing of talented persons to realize their potentialities; it leaves the better men dissatisfied with themselves and their nation, and they sink into boredom; it impedes any improvement of the moral, intellectual, and material condition, in terms of quality, of mankind. Second, it adversely affects the well-being, late or soon, of the mass of men; for, deprived of responsible leadership and example, the innumerable men and women destined to walk in the routine ways of life suffer in the tone of their civilization, and in their material condition. A government which converts into a secular dogma the Christian mystery of moral equality, in short, is hostile towards human existence.

Remember that there are two parts to this political principle: not only should a just government recognize the rights of the more talented natures, but it should recognize the right of the majority of men not to be agitated and bullied by these aspiring talents. The prudent statesman endeavors to maintain a balance between these two claims. There have been ages in which the aristocracy, natural or hereditary, has usurped the whole governance of life, demanding of the average man a tribute and an obedience which deprive the majority of their desire to live by custom and prescription and often damage their material interests. Such a regime, indifferent to the welfare of the majority, is as bad a government as a domination indifferent to the claims of the talented minority. But nowadays the danger is not that the stronger natures—and I refer to moral and intellectual qualities, not merely to domineering and acquisitive abilities—will lord it over an abused majority; rather, the curse of our time is what Ortega called "the revolt of the masses," the threat that mediocrity may trample underfoot every just elevation of mind and character, every hopeful talent for leadership and improvement. Therefore the sagacious statesman of our age must be more acutely concerned with the preservation of the rights of the talented minority than with the extension of the rights of the crowd.

A domination which confounds popular government with equality of moral worth, equality of intellect, or equality of condition is a bad government. For a good government respects the claims of extraordinary character. It respects the right of the contemplative to his solitude. It respects the right of the practical leader to take an honest initiative in the affairs of the commonwealth. It respects the right of the inventor to his ingenuity, the right of the manufacturer or merchant to the rewards of his industry, the right of the thrifty man to keep his savings and bequeath them to his heirs. It respects such claims and rights, this good government, because in the enjoyment of these rights, and in the performance of the duties to which these rights are joined, men fulfill themselves; and a considerable measure of justice—"to each his own"—is attained.

Today the balance between the claims of the unusual natures and the ordinary natures, in some ages overthrown to the advantage of aspiring talents, is injured rather by the extortionate demands of a doctrinaire egalitarianism. Communist Russia is the most thorough example of the triumph of this degradation of the democratic dogma. I am aware that Soviet Russia is governed by a clique of party intriguers and successful administrators, paying little more than lip service to their own secular dogma of egalitarianism; yet this does not alter the fact that, obedient to the ideology of dialectical materialism, the Soviets have suppressed the claims of the nobler natures to do the work natural to them. What we see in the new élite of Communism is not a predominance of the higher natures, but a domination of Jacobin fanatics, devoid, nearly all of them, of high moral endowments. This is the regime of a host of squalid oligarchs. Among them are no prophets, and no poets; the only qualification for entry into this èlite is ruthless cunning in the struggle for pure power. Not the higher natures, but the lower, in terms of moral attainment and independence of mind, are recognized and rewarded by the Soviets.

Now it is not American "democracy," as such, that stands at the antipodes from the Soviet undertaking; American moral and political tradition, rather, and American constitutionalism are the forces of resistance. A political democracy may attain a tolerable balance between the rights of the talented natures and the claims of the average natures. But it also is possible for a monarchy to achieve that balance, or an aristocracy, or some other frame of government. Respect for natural and prescriptive rights is peculiar to no single set of political institutions.

Yet the kind of government which seems most likely to appreciate and defend the claims of either interest in the commonwealth is what Aristotle called a "polity," a balancing and checking of classes in society. The United States remain, in considerable degree, a polity; *pure* democracy was not intended by the founders of this Republic, and it has not yet triumphed among us. It ought not to triumph. For the good government does not grow up from mere protection of entrenched property, nor yet from the victory of the proletariat.

A prudent government, within the bounds set by decency and good order, leaves every man to consult his own humor. It does not attempt to force the happiness of the statistical Bentham upon the romantic Coleridge; for one man's happiness, even among the talented natures, is another man's misery. By a salutary neglect, this government allows private happiness to take care of itself. One may call this prudent and tolerant government "democracy," if one wishes, though I think that is twisting the word. I call it simply a government which prefers principle to ideology, variety to uniformity, balance to omnipotence.

Now for my second principle of good government: that a government should accord with the traditions and the prescriptive ways of a people. This is the view of Montesquieu and of Burke. A good government is no artificial contrivance, no invention of coffeehouse philosophers, got up upon *a priori* abstractions to suit the intellectual mood of an hour. Governments hastily designed upon theories of pure reason ordinarily are wretched dominations. The longest-lived of these poor governments has been that of modern France, which never has recovered from the hacking and chopping that the constitution of French society received at the hands of rigid metaphysicians from 1789 onward. Much more evanescent, because they had a smaller reservoir of tradition to exhaust, were the artificial governments set up in central and southern Europe after the First World War. Now the good government, very different from these, is the growth of centuries of social experience. It has been called organic; I prefer the analogy "spiritual." Trusting to the wisdom of our ancestors and the experience of the nation, it puts its faith in precedent, prescription, historical trial and error, and consensus of opinion over the generations. Not infatuated with neatness, it prefers the strength and majesty of the Gothic style. The government of Britain, because of its age and success, is our best example of this type. And the government of the United States is nearly as good an instance of the triumph of this principle that society is an august continuity and essence, held together by veneration, prescription, and tradition.

Nominally, of course, we Americans created our Federal Constitution by deliberate action, within the space of a few months. But in actuality that formal constitution, and our state constitutions, chiefly put down on paper what already existed and was accepted in public opinion: beliefs and institutions long established in the colonies, and drawn from centuries of English experience with parliaments, the common law, and the balancing of orders and interests in a realm. Respect for precedent and prescription governed the minds of the Founders of the Republic. We appealed to the prescriptive liberties of Englishmen, not to *liberté, egalité, fraternité*; and the philosophical and moral structure of our civil order was rooted in the Christian faith, not in the worship of Reason.

The success of the American and British governments, I am suggesting, is produced by their preference for growth, experience, tradition, and prescription over a closet-metaphysician's grand design. The great lessons of politics are taught a people through their historical experience; no nation can sever itself from its past and still prosper, for the dead alone give us energy; and whatever constitution has been long accepted in a nation, that constitution—amended, perhaps, but essentially the same—is as good as a people can expect. True, that constitution may be improved, or restored; but if it is discarded altogether, like wastepaper, every order in society suffers terribly.

The American and British constitutions have worked well; but, being living essences, they cannot easily be transplanted to other states. One of the cardinal errors of the French revolutionaries was their endeavor to remake France upon the model of what they thought English politics to be. Though any people have something to learn from the experiences of any other, still there exists no single constitution calculated to work successfully everywhere. For the political institutions of a people grow out of their religion, their moral habits, their economy, even their literature; political institutions are but part of an intricate structure of civilization, the roots of which go infinitely deep. Attempts to impose borrowed institutions upon an alien culture generally are disastrous, though some decades, or even generations, may be required for the experiment to run its unlucky course. Randolph of Roanoke, in opposing Clay's design for encouraging revolutions upon the American pattern, cried out in his sardonic way, "You can no more make liberty out of Spanish matter than you can make a frigate out of a bundle of pine saplings." Though this is somewhat hard upon the Spaniards, it remains true that parliamentary government, Anglo-American style, rarely has been secure in Spanish lands; Spaniards' liberty, when they enjoy it, is secured by different institutions and customs.

Yet still our political theory and our foreign policy are plagued by the delusion that some domination of American constitutions and manners will be established universally—the American Liberal's conviction, in Santayana's sentence, that "the nun must not remain a nun, and China shall not keep its wall." This fond hope never will be realized. For individuals, as Chesterton said, are happy only when they are their own potty little selves; and this is as true of nations. To impose the American constitution upon all the world would not render all the world happy; to the contrary, our constitution would work in few lands and would make many men miserable in short order. States, like men, must find their own paths to order and justice and freedom; and usually those paths are ancient and winding ways, and their signposts are Authority, Tradition, Prescription. Without the legal institutions, rooted in common and Roman law, from which it arose, the American constitutional system would be unworkable. Well, take up this constitutional system, abstractly, and set it down, as an exotic plant, in Persia or Guinea or the Congo, where the common law (English style) and the Roman law are unknown, and where the bed of justice rests upon the Koran or upon hereditary chieftainship— why, the thing cannot succeed. Such an undertaking may disrupt the old system of justice, and may even supplant it, for a time; but in the long run, the traditional morals, habits, and establishments of a people, confirmed by their historical experience, will reassert themselves, and the innovation will be undone—if that culture is to survive at all.

The Asiatic or African who attempts to convert himself and his nation, abruptly and wholesale, to Western ways must end disillusioned; we will be fortunate if he does not end in violent reaction. Like the Lebanon Arab in Cunninghame-Graham's story *Sidi bu Zibbula*, he will crouch upon his dunghill, saying, "I have seen your Western cities; and the dung is better."

Good government is no mass-produced article. Order and justice and freedom are found in divers ways, but they cannot be divorced from the historical experience of a people. Theory divorced from experience is infinitely dangerous, the plaything of the ideologue, the darling dagger of the energumen. Though their social functions may be similar, the justice of the peace cannot supplant the *cadi*; and no James Mill, however learned, can rightfully make laws for India.

I am saying this: far from being right to revolt against the past, a people are fortunate if their political order maintains a tolerable degree of freedom and justice for the different interests in society. We are not made for perfect things, and if ever we found ourselves under the domination of the "perfect" government, we would make mincemeat of it, from sheer boredom. From just authority, from respect for our cultural and moral and political heritage, comes genuine civil freedom. It was something of this sort, I suppose, that St. Paul meant when he declared, "The powers that be are ordained of God." With authority and prescription, a people may work their way towards the freedom of the true polity. Without authority and prescription, they are afflicted by the devastating "freedom" of the Congo.

CHAPTER THREE

The Bill of Rights
& American Freedom

WILLMOORE KENDALL

Let me begin by setting down a few easily confirmable but perhaps not very well-known facts:

I

1. The Convention that drew up the Constitution of the United States voted down unanimously a proposal (by Colonel Mason) that the Constitution be made to include a declaration or bill of the natural rights of man.

2. Proposals for such a declaration or bill of rights became, in short order, the major rallying points in the several States for opponents of ratification of the Philadelphia Constitution.

3. In the controversy over ratification, as it went forward in the so-called ratifying conventions, no clear distinction was drawn by the opponents of ratification between the two issues: (a) Will the new Federal government be "too powerful" in the sense that it will threaten the integrity and sovereignty of the *States*? and (b) Will it be "too powerful" in the sense that it will threaten the natural rights of the *individual citizens of the States*?

To put it otherwise: We know that a very considerable percentage of the opponents of ratification were primarily concerned about what was going to happen to the States in the new Federal union. This is the objection to ratification that is uppermost in the minds of the authors of the *Federalist*, so that Hamilton's attack on the very idea of a bill of rights appears at a relatively late date in the series, too late to affect the controversy. But *this* animus, which would have produced a demand not for a bill of individual rights but for something roughly equivalent to the Tenth Amendment—some barrier to the expansion of Federal power at the expense of State power—never expresses itself very clearly in the course of the controversy, somehow gets absorbed into the demand for guarantees of individual rights.

Here is one of the curiosities of the whole business; one might have expected, for example, a concerted attack by the States'-rights men on the "necessary and proper" clause, which was—one is tempted to say "obviously"—*the* threat in the Constitution to the powers of the States. But the major rallying point of opponents of ratification becomes, I repeat, and becomes at an early date, the demand for guarantees of personal liberty; they apparently do not see that a bill of individual rights will in no way, or at least no direct way, protect the "sovereignty" of the States. I leave to one side, as unresearchable, the "cynical" explanation, namely: that those who opposed ratification out of concern for the States embraced the bill of individual rights in the fond hope of saving the States by defeating the Constitution altogether. The Federalists often made this charge, which we may call the "phony issue" charge. But I do not see how, even if it were true, it could possibly be substantiated; that is, I see no scholarly alternative to taking the participants in the controversy at their word and assuming that the bill-of-rights men wanted what they are reputed to have got, namely, a bill of rights.

4. The controversy was in many respects a curious one; properly speaking, perhaps, we should not speak of *a* controversy but of the *several* controversies in the several States: neither the Federalists nor the anti-Federalists ever threw up anything much in the way of a union-wide organization; the Federalists in each state merely took on their local anti-Federalists. (Let me stress the point, because it will assume considerable importance in a few minutes.) Letters and documents were exchanged; strategies were no doubt

affected, within a given State, by influences coming from outside; but that was about it. Another curiosity is that the controversies were not (to some extent no doubt for the reason just mentioned) over *the* Bill of Rights, but rather over *a* bill of rights, which nobody ever took the trouble to draw up, so that what the controversies were in fact over was Bill of Rights X, where X, as in algebra, was an unknown. This, too, will assume importance below, so let me stress it: Madison, when he finally came up tails on the issue, had an extremely free hand in preparing the first draft.

5. It is *not true*, though many historians would like us to think so, that nobody bothered to draw up a draft because "everybody knew" what provisions the future bill of rights, if incorporated in or added to the Constitution, would "have" to contain; this remained a great uncertainty right down to the moment when *the* Bill of Rights was finally voted in the First Congress. Or rather let me respond to the stirrings of scholarly caution and say: Everybody perhaps knew certain things it would contain, namely, the common-law rights that do in fact make up the bulk of *the* Bill of Rights. Indeed I have come to the conclusion that if a draft *had* been prepared and adopted by a nation-wide anti-Federalist organization, and *if* that draft had limited itself to the common-law rights, there need have been no controversies. The Federalists would have said, would have *had* to say, "Ah! If *that* is all you mean, let us by all means have your bill of rights." They were not going to take the public position that they wished the new government to have the power to make unreasonable searches and seizures, or to force witnesses to testify against themselves, or to try accused persons a second time for one and the same offense.

To put it still otherwise: *if* a draft had been prepared, and *if* it had confined itself to the substance of Amendments II through X, the only point on which the Federalists might have felt tempted to take exception was that of jury trials in civil cases. The Framers had had their reasons, rather honorable ones in point of fact, for excluding civil cases from the guarantee of jury trial in the Constitution, and their animus on that matter might well have perpetuated itself, in the hearts of the Federalists, into the hypothetical situation I envisage.

But *that* solution was out of the question, we can see in retrospect, for two reasons: First, the anti-Federalists, as we learn from the so-called "recommendatory" amendments that went forward to the First Congress from the ratifying conventions, were not of one mind even as to which of the II-X rights were "essential"; such rights appear in the most remarkably spotty fashion in the recommendatory amendments. But, second, and this brings us closer to the heart of the matter, there was the grave and potentially divisive matter—potentially divisive as between the two sides *and* potentially divisive on each side—of what rights (apart perhaps from freedom of petition and of peaceable assembly) should "go in" relating to the area we today identify with the First Amendment.

Even if *arguendo* we were to concede the point, Yes, there was consensus concerning the substance of Amendments II-X, no one could possibly argue, for reasons to which I shall give due attention a little later, that there was consensus or potential consensus about the provisions of Amendment I. To put this otherwise: I now feel sure, after careful study of the documents and long meditation, that (a) the anxieties that led the Federalists to oppose a bill of rights must have related *mainly* to what the framers of the future Bill of Rights might do in what we may now begin to call the Hugo Black area and (b) the fervor of the anti-Federalists for a bill of rights can be explained only in terms of their determination that it must say this or that in the Hugo Black area. But I stress again: one must not think of the anti-Federalists as agreed about what a bill of rights should say in that area. (Many were concerned exclusively with what it should say about *religious* freedom, but even these meant different things by religious freedom. Many were concerned mainly about freedom of the press.) To which I must now add: This is above all the area in which debate was never joined between the Federalists and anti-Federalists; nearly everyone, as one reads the records, seems to be avoiding the problem, precisely, perhaps, because it *is* so controversial. For the Federalists it is easier just to oppose a bill of rights, and so postpone the problem. For the anti-Federalists it is easier, if I may put it so, just to raise hell in favor of this or that provision that *must* "go in." The "fight" is analogous to one between two men, each convinced that the other threatens something sacred in his existence, groping blindly for one another in a pitch-dark cellar, but each avoiding contact when he senses the other's approach.

At the risk of stating it over-graphically, I offer the following thesis: The First Amendment had already become, long before it was ever written, *the* potentially—I am tempted to say unavoidably—explosive problem of the American Republic. With only minor exceptions (such as whether wire tapping is an unreasonable search or seizure or whether the self-incrimination provision of Amendment V extends to the House Un-American Activities Committee), the problem of the Bill of Rights and American freedom is and has been, ever since Mason made his motion at Philadelphia, the problem of the First Amendment and American freedom. Perhaps someone will say I should have entitled this essay "The First Amendment and American Freedom." But I couldn't: the controversies, articulately, were over a bill of rights, and we must start out from there.

6. There is some little talk in the literature on the Bill of Rights about the First Congress having "had" to enact such a bill because, variously, it was under what amounted to a "mandate" from the state ratifying conventions to do so; or the Federalists had in those conventions "committed themselves," that is, promised, to go along on the bill-of-rights issue; or (those considerations apart) there was overwhelming popular pressure, too insistent for the Congress to ignore, in favor of such a bill. None of the three notions, however, will hold water. The sentiment in favor of a bill of rights in the ratifying conventions was, in each case, a *minority* sentiment; in no case were the bill-of-rights men able (though they tried) to make the ratification voted conditional on subsequent adoption of a bill of rights; they just plain got licked all the way along the line. The Federalists, in case after case, "conceded" on the matter of "recommendatory amendments"—that is, they agreed that ratification should go forward with proposals for amendments that the First Congress might take under advisement; but one gets the strong impression that the Federalists in each convention are "conceding" not because they have to, but in the hope that the majority in the final vote shall be as large as possible, thus giving the new Constitution a broader basis of support than it would otherwise have had.

The main points to grasp are (a) that no one was in position to speak for the Federalists union-wide and (b) that, in any case, the ratifying conventions, even assuming the concessions in question to be properly speaking additive, were not in position to lay down a "mandate" to the First Congress, which would evidently be responsible to its constituents not to the conventions. The most that the conventions could do was what they did, namely, make recommendations. The majority in each case, having won on ratification *and* against conditionality (ratification to be conditional on the holding of a second convention, on the subsequent adoption of such and such amendments, on the adoption of a bill of rights) simply agreed to send along to the First Congress recommendations reflecting the views of the minority.

As for the third point, alleged popular pressure on the First Congress, the proofs are even less convincing; the anti-bill-of-rights men won the elections hands down, and so completely dominated the First Congress. Apart from the elections there existed, of course, no avenue through which such pressure could make itself felt effectively and convincingly. And, finally, nothing could be clearer to us, as we read the history of the First Congress, than this: if such pressure existed, only Madison seems to have been much aware of it or anything properly describable as sensitive to it.

Madison's problem, from the beginning, is to get attention— even a modicum of attention—from his fellow legislators to the bill-of-rights matter; *they* think there is vastly more important business to transact; in the parlance of a later era, they "stall," "drag their feet." But let me not overstate the point; there *is* satisfactory evidence of widespread minority sentiment in favor of some sort of step to assure "separation" of "church" and "state," to assure "freedom of conscience." And Madison had *promised* his own constituents in Virginia that he would try to get them a bill of rights. But that is all you can get out of the account of the matter by Rutland, who is not uneager to make the adoption of the Bill look as "democratic" as possible. I conclude: no Federalist commitment, no mandate, no overwhelming popular pressure. We cannot hope to understand what happened until we get these false notions out of our heads. The problem narrows down, in an astonishing manner, to Madison. He is indeed the "father" of the Bill of Rights, and doubly so because he begat it on the body of so reluctant a mother.

7. Back now to the "controversies" in the ratifying conventions. Astonishingly little attention has been paid to the Federalist case

against a bill of rights, though the arguments they used—now on the floor of the conventions, now in the public print, above all of course in the *Federalist*—are perhaps not unworthy of attention. Permit me, in the briefest possible manner, to summarize them, and then, also briefly, to attempt the rather unorthodox exercise of listing a few arguments they *might* have used if (to repeat my earlier language) the issue had ever got joined and they had seen themselves obliged to pull out all the stops. The overt arguments were:

a. A bill of rights is unnecessary; the new government is a government of merely delegated powers, could not possibly do the things a bill of rights would forbid it to do.

b. A bill of rights would be ineffective, unenforceable; so, the Federalists argued, bills of rights had proven themselves to be in the States, even in that great primitive mother of American bills of rights, the State of Virginia. The barriers a bill of rights imposes are, in Madison's classic phrase, "parchment barriers"; the legislature will, in a given situation, go ahead and do, *pace* the bill of rights, what seems to be called for. Only Madison and Jefferson were sufficiently prescient to envisage possible enforcement by the courts, and they did not press the point. Hamilton's discussion of unenforceability in the *Federalist* shows clearly that, whatever dreams he may have dreamed about judicial review, *he* was not thinking of future clashes between the Supreme Court and Congress over the rights to be embalmed in a bill of rights; there is not a whiff of such a suggestion in No. 84.

c. As a limitation on the powers of the new Federal government, a bill of rights would be self-defeating; it would have the effect of expanding not diminishing them. As Hamilton puts it, in effect, in No. 84, to tell the new Federal government that it must not impair freedom of the press is to create a presumption, not present in the Constitution as it came from Philadelphia, that its power somehow does extend to such matters; erect the dam, so to speak, and the water of Federal power will flow right up to it, where otherwise it would remain right back where the fifty-five at Philadelphia had left it.

This time, however, I cannot proceed without a word or two of comment: That argument, even in Hamilton's hands, would be on the face of it disingenuous without the "necessary and proper" clause, with which Hamilton was presumably familiar. The new government was, notoriously, to act directly on the citizens; it would in due course, to go no further, be called upon to wage war; Hamilton and his fellow citizens had just had some experience of the impossibility of waging war, even under a constitution without a "necessary and proper" clause, without curbing freedom of the press. Did he really believe that in some future war the sort of dam he was opposing would *pull* Federal power harder than the "necessary and proper" clause would *push* it? It is one of the misfortunes of the whole matter that the anti-Federalists were not sufficiently adroit to smoke Hamilton out, force him to face the real problem.

On the other hand, viewing the argument from the point of vantage of 1963, what a piece of prediction! I say prediction, not prophecy, because it proceeds in terms of *analysis*, and the shrewdness of the analysis is surely validated by the accuracy of the prediction. For have things not fallen out *just* as Hamilton said they would? As Hugo Black never wearies of pointing out, and Alexander Meiklejohn before him, Federal power has indeed flowed down to the dam of the First Amendment freedoms. Owing largely perhaps to the kind and capable ministrations of the United States Supreme Court, the question long ago ceased to be "Can the Federal government abridge freedom of speech, press, association, assembly, petition, etc.?", since everybody knows the answer to that question is, "Yes, it can, and does, and in the opinion apparently of most of us *must*." Rather the question is: "In what circumstances? Clear and present danger? The existence of a proper governmental interest that must be 'balanced' against our interest in enforcing the First Amendment?" I don't say it wouldn't have happened that way anyhow under the "necessary and proper" clause (though it might, mercifully, have done so without the verbal and logical saltimbankery of the decisions that make Mr. Justice Black so furious); I do say that Hamilton had himself quite a point and that we should be proud of him for it.

d. No bill of rights should be adopted because natural rights are as safe as you can make them in the hands of the people acting through their elected representatives; you can trust the people and —this overlaps, of course, the "parchment barriers" argument—in point of fact have no alternative *but* to do so. As Rousseau had put it a while before, if the people wills to do itself harm, who is to say it nay? But let us speak only of an overlap; the two points are distinct, and those who have been brought up on J. Allen Smith and his epigones may find it difficult to grasp at first that it was the Federalists not the anti-Federalists who used the "democratic" argument, the put-your-confidence-in-the-people argument, in the controversies over a bill of rights. And the argument is already prefigured in the way the *habeas corpus* provision of the Philadelphia Constitution is worded. No attempt is made to place *habeas corpus* once and for all beyond the power of Congress; rather circumstances are frankly envisaged when the "public safety" may require suspension of the right.

A pretty convincing case, in the opinion of this writer, and, insofar as convincing, let me add, as convincing a case for repealing the First Amendment as ever it was against adopting it. Yet one suspects, as one canvasses it, that it does not reveal very fully the Federalist state of mind on the bill-of-rights issue. So I now ask, how then, without injustice to Federalist political thought as we know it across the decades, can we round it out? What arguments can we add? At the risk of appearing impudent, I am going to attempt to add a few as the Federalist spokesmen *might* have put them:

a. The anti-Federalists, beginning with Colonel Mason and his statement on the floor at Philadelphia that a committee could draw up a list of the natural rights of men in "three hours," show a "temper" that is inappropriate to the genius of the Constitution drawn up at Philadelphia (and defended in the *Federalist*). That Constitution envisages the *self*-government of America by the "deliberate sense of the community," which must extend, *inter alia*, to the making of decisions from situation to situation and moment to moment as to what is called for by the purposes set forth in the Preamble. No, no, no; the issue is *not* whether men have natural rights or whether those rights should be respected by government; the issue is whether our generation, by contrast with scores of preceding generations that were also deeply committed to the idea of natural rights, has any particular reason for claiming that it can now make a "list" of them and, having done so, seek to impose them, forever and a day, on future generations. The issue is not whether men have natural rights, but whether those rights can at any moment be specified once and for all.

We might make an exception here of the common-law rights—which, however, precisely do not, in detail, have their origin in a list that some person or persons sat down and "drew up"; they have been hammered out in the courts of law over long centuries and reflect the accumulated experience of the English-speaking peoples with the vexed question of how to prevent miscarriages of justice. Probably we confuse matters by calling them "natural rights" at all. In any case, we suspect you, having seen these recommendatory amendments of yours, of wishing to go far beyond—how far, nobody knows—a mere statement of the common-law rights. We suspect you of wishing to venture where the wisest of our ancestors (none of whom ever attempted to draw up a "list") have feared to tread; there is even talk among you—not much, but enough to give us pause—of writing into your bill of rights something new and unheard-of called "freedom of speech," of writing it in as a right which government must in *no* circumstances abridge. Well, we do not think such a right is ultimately compatible with orderly government, much less with *free* orderly government. Gentlemen, let us be sensible!

b. We are not clear as to the status your bill of rights would enjoy if we did adopt it. You speak of "amendments," to be accomplished under the procedures laid down in Article V. But the Article V procedures envisage amendments that, once ratified, will enjoy *equal* status with the main body of the Constitution, and it may be that is what you seriously intend. That, however, is going to raise some very serious problems to which, honestly, you do not seem to have given much thought. There's the whole question of how and by whom your bill of rights is to be enforced the day Congress, or Congress and the President, or Congress and the President and the Federal Courts wish to set aside this provision or that one. It is hardly too much to say that if you are going to expect equal status for your bill of rights, equal with the main body of the Constitution, you are going to have to do more than just tack on a bill of rights; you are going to have to get back into the main body of the Constitution and reword it so as to take care of the enforcement problem. Otherwise you are going to create a great confusion of responsibilities; over here the Constitution will seem

to say that the deliberate sense of the community, as expressed
through the republican principle of majority rule, is to prevail;
over there the Constitution will seem to say, No, there are these
and these absolutes that the deliberate sense of the community
must stay inside of, must deem itself bound by, and let the chips
fall where they may. The system looks to us, with all candor,
downright unworkable; either your bill of rights will, as a barrier
on the power of Congress, become a dead letter, unenforceable on
the face of it, or machinery is going to have to be developed *for*
enforcing it. And we cannot imagine what shape that machinery
might take.

c. We have still another anxiety about all this. It now seems likely
that the main body of the Constitution will go into effect backed
up by a very high degree of consensus. That, we believe, is good;
we as a nation made it clear as long ago as the Declaration of Independence that we believe in government by the consent of the
people. Now, let us concede, *arguendo*, that you could embody the
common-law rights in a series of amendments, perhaps even embody in such an amendment the provision some of you speak of
about reserving to the States all powers not expressly delegated,
and still hope for a high degree of consensus. Such provisions might
well be *self*-enforcing, and so get you around the enforcement
problem we mentioned a moment ago; because all Americans believe in these guarantees, there is good reason to suppose they
would be respected. But once you go beyond that—to freedom of
speech, or freedom of press, or freedom of conscience—we doubt
whether forms of words could be devised that would command
any general agreement. Look at the wide variation in the State bills
of rights in this area. To put it otherwise: once, in your listing of
rights, you go beyond the common-law rights, you kiss good-bye
to the sanction of tradition; as a people we *have* no tradition of free
speech, or free press, or freedom of conscience—not even a tradition of having no established church. Gentlemen, you wish to
launch us on uncharted seas, and we will have none of it!

d. To go back to the status of your future bill of rights, perhaps
you do not, if only because of the apparently insoluble enforcement problem, intend it to have equal status with the main body
of the Constitution. It is well-known, for instance, that the Virginia Declaration of Rights is not regarded as part of the constitu-

tion of that State but rather as—how shall we put it—a statement of ideals that the citizens are understood to entertain in common but know not to be immediately applicable. Well, if that is the sort of thing you have in mind, we shrink from the idea of your using amendments to the Constitution as your vehicle. The Constitution is intended to be a *law*, the supreme law of the land; it is not a proper locus for high principles that we might get around to applying, if all goes well, at some moment in the indefinite future. If Congress, when the "public safety" requires, or in the interests of justice or liberty, is to set the Constitution, or any one of its provisions, aside as it sees fit, that is to undermine the very notion of law, to encourage disrespect for law. And that, Gentlemen, as you surely know, no nation can do with impunity. Or, failing that, it is to encourage verbal games, with which you persuade yourselves that you are not really violating the law although it is obvious that you are, not really setting aside the principle when you clearly are setting it aside. And no nation can do that with impunity, either.

8. One thing is certain and cannot be overemphasized: At no point in the struggle over a bill of rights, and so far as I have been able to learn at no point in that First Congress which enacted the Bill of Rights, was the question "up" whether the American society of the future was to be, should be an "open society." The rights the future bill of rights would embody, the guarantees it would vouchsafe, were to be rights and guarantees against merely the new Federal government. Paradoxically, the anti-Federalists would have been the last to wish for them any broader scope than that. The anti-Federalists were States'-rights men, not prepared to put the new Federal government into the business of enforcing such rights and guarantees against the State governments, or to alter in any significant way a state of affairs which we may define roughly as follows: the quality and intimate detail of the ordinary citizen's freedom would be determined, through an indefinite future, by the laws and policies and actions of the governments of the several States. The anti-Federalist talk of a bill of rights that would embody those natural rights that man "holds back" from "government"—and there was a great deal of such talk—represents, from this point of view, an unfortunate confusion. It suggests that the anti-Federalists were somewhat confused themselves, and it is

an inexhaustible source of quotes by which our own contemporaries confuse the meaning which, at its problematical maximum, the Bill of Rights and, most especially, of course, the First Amendment, could have had for *anybody*, Federalist or anti-Federalist, at the time of its enactment. But of that, more in a moment.

9. Finally, the procedures that brought the First Congress into existence were, from first to last, in accordance with the "republican principle"—were, that is to say, "majoritarian," and not characterized by majority submission to minority dictation or blackmail. That is true not merely of the elections that actually produced the First Congress, which involved no sort of flirtation with the so-called unanimity principle; and not merely of the post-electoral situation, in which apparently it was clearly understood on all hands that the Federalists—or as John Roche prefers to call them, the Constitutionalists—having won their majority, would rightfully dominate the scene in the new "national" legislature. It is true also of the State ratifying conventions, where the final decision went by majority vote (one State, I believe, did require an extraordinary majority, but that is still not the unanimity principle). It is true, finally, of the Philadelphia Convention, where, apart from "withdrawees" like Yates and Lansing, the minority, once it saw that further talk was futile and that it was outvoted, "went along" with the majority—the one exception here being the Great Compromise between the large and small States, where, according to Roche, Madison had the votes but decided not to press his advantage lest the Convention go to pieces. There the minority was able to prevent a majority decision that it disliked, but not—even Roche does not claim that—to "dictate," merely to force an accommodation. (Even within the State delegations—witness poor Alexander Hamilton—decisions as to how to cast delegation votes went by the majority principle.)

II

So much, I say, is not very well-known but easily confirmable fact, all of it, I believe, sorely necessary for any approach to my central topic, which is:

Justice Black assures us, with three Justices already concurring, that the Founders of the American Republic intended the First

Amendment freedoms to be "absolute"; that is, intended that they should not be set aside in any circumstances whatever; that, therefore, any infringement of those freedoms, on this ground or that, militates towards a drastic change in the basic character of the American Republic. Is he or is he not talking "good" history? Put otherwise: Did the First Amendment, as passed by Congress and ratified by the States, declare the American Republic an "open society" and put in motion machinery that would make it an "open society"? Put still otherwise: Can we properly argue, as Justice Black does, from the "plain language" of the First Amendment to the "intentions" of the majority that voted it in the First Congress and the majorities that ratified it?

These are questions, I believe, that can only be answered by recurring to facts that are even less well-known than those I have been canvassing and that are, in the nature of the case, far more difficult to confirm, partly because we do not by any means have at our disposal the data we should like to have and partly because the data we do have are, many of them, open perhaps to different interpretations. For the key questions become, in my view: First, what are we to make of Madison's course in the matter? And second, what significance are we to attach to the favorable vote he finally midwifed for his Bill of Rights out of his fellow M.C.'s?

I do not, obviously, pretend to "settle" either of these questions in this essay. But I do hope to show that there are great difficulties about Black's position in the matter. (He himself, for the most part at least, contents himself with consulting, apart from the "plain language" of the First Amendment, secondary sources.) And I hope to show that these difficulties are sufficiently great to suggest that the whole Black and Co. interpretation of the intention of the Founders is, quite simply, a *myth*, rooted ultimately in the airy fancies of J. S. Mill (who somewhat postdates the Founders). The two questions are, let me say by way of further preliminary, simultaneous, and I shall not take them up *seriatim*, but shall proceed rather by pointing to certain considerations that would, I have concluded from my researches, have to be taken into account in order for them to be answered fully and definitively.

Item. The story, as I have already intimated, narrows down in an astonishing manner to Madison (just as the Bill of Rights problem, again as I have already intimated, almost narrows down to the

First Amendment, or if you like the First and the Tenth Amendments; almost but not quite, because of a little-noticed dimension that I shall speak of below). Madison is the *sine qua non*, the necessary, though not of course sufficient, condition of the Bill of Rights as we have it. The accounts, whose authors are *not* eager to convey that impression, leave one convinced that (a) if Madison, over against the indifference and delaying tactics of his fellow Congressmen, had given up on a bill of rights, the First Congress would not have sent one forward to the States, and (b) those constituents of his in Virginia, to whom he had made his famous promise to work for a bill of rights (in order to defeat James Monroe for his House seat), would at an early moment have had to agree that he had done on its behalf all that could in good conscience be demanded of him. Yet he persevered and in the end—Rutland's chronological account of the relevant legislative events is punctuated by the word "finally"—won.

The question arises: Why? Not, one gathers, because he had changed his mind with respect to the major Federalist arguments against a bill of rights. Not only is the *Federalist* to be handed down to posterity, with his signature, as an *anti*-bill-of-rights book, but also Madison is to take steps later to make sure that his role in writing it is not underestimated (he remains, to go no further, the source of the contemptuous term "parchment barriers"). The most he is willing to commit himself to, even off at the end, is in effect: A bill of rights will (as I have put it earlier) do no harm—or, to use now his exact phrase, would not "endanger the beauty of the Government in any one important feature, even in the eyes of its most sanguine admirers." It is characteristic of the "debate" to which we owe our Bill of Rights that no one effectively calls upon him to say why, to square his new position on the matter with his old one, to meet the Federalist arguments against.

Yet an answer to our "Why?" does emerge, even from relatively stingy accounts of the matter, and, as far as it takes us (which is *not* all the way), we can be fairly sure of it, namely: somewhere along the line Madison changes the *état de la question*, ceases, if I may put it so, to be interested in the merits of a bill of rights and becomes interested primarily in the merits of *passing* a bill of rights. A single sentence of his seems to put that much in the clear: the proposed Amendments will make "*the Constitution better in the*

eyes of those who are opposed to it, without weakening its frame
or abridging its usefulness, in the judgment of those who are attached to it [;] . . . we act the part of wise and liberal men who
make such alterations as will produce that effect." Madison, in
other words, takes it into his head that the new Constitution must
have behind it, to all intents and purposes, a 100 per cent consensus;
that the last opponent and objector must be silenced; and that he is
prepared to pay, and persuade others to pay (as he proceeds to do),
whatever price be necessary for accomplishing that objective. And
that is the argument with which he appears to have fetched the
necessary majorities in House and Senate—that plus the tacit in-
ducement: pass my Bill of Rights and I'll leave you in peace.

He calls on his Federalist friends (never mind that he is already
in the process of crossing the floor of the House; they are still his
friends, else he would never have got those majorities) to change
the rules of the constitutional game, at the very moment when they
have won a clear victory under them. He calls on them to set
aside that "republican principle" of majority rule that has, from
first to last, governed the proceedings up to now, and to move
suddenly for unanimity *on the terms of the defeated minority*—
that is, by giving the minority its way not merely on the first of
the two big issues that have been at stake (a bill of rights) but on
the second as well (whether something further should be done to
"nail down" State "sovereignty").

The question of the *merits* of a bill of rights promptly goes
under water and has not, so far as I have been able to learn, sur-
faced until today. The Federalist M.C.'s, though they must have
been well-schooled in the Federalist arguments, seem to have dismissed them overnight, so to speak, from their minds. Unlike the
King of France, they had *fought* their troops up the hill, not merely
marched them; but like the King of France, they were content to
march them down again. Why? —which plunges us (pending a
great deal of research on just that point, which does *not* seem to
have engaged the fancy of our historians), into the realm of the
truly speculative. I shall content myself with saying merely this:
Concede everything you like to Madison's "prestige," which was
undoubtedly great. Concede everything you like, too, to the point
that Madison's fellow-M.C.'s could get him off their backs only
by going along with him on the bill-of-rights issue (the brevity,

peremptoriness even, of the sessions devoted to the Bill of Rights does suggest that the Congressmen and Senators were eager to get on with other things). But the mind does not rest satisfied with these answers and is, therefore, driven to seek another.

The two possibilities that seem to cry up at you are (a) Madison's fellow Congressmen themselves suddenly changed their minds on the merits of a bill of rights, which seems improbable, or (b) Madison must have been mighty convincing in the cloakrooms, not only on the consensus point but also on the point that the Bill of Rights would not "endanger the beauty of the Government," would not "weaken its frame or abridge its usefulness." Now, we find ourselves wondering, *did* he argue these points? What did he mean by them? And once again, I think, the possibilities are confined to a fairly narrow range. Either he argued (a) that the Bill of Rights, in the absence in the Constitution of any effective means of enforcement, would remain a dead letter save to the extent that the representatives of the people—ultimately, of course, Congress —chose *to enforce it upon themselves;* or (b) that the Federal judiciary would in due course put forward a claim to "guardianship" of the Bill of Rights *and make it good* (that is, that the other two branches would in fact acquiesce in that claim, and permit the judiciary to have the "last say" as to what the Bill of Rights forbids and what the Bill of Rights allows); or (c) that the Bill of Rights was of such a character that—the people over the decades, the future congressmen, presidents, and judges being all, or in their generality, of one and the same mind about such matters—no troublesome problems would ever arise.

No fourth possibility, it seems to me, presents itself. Of the three before us I offer it as my opinion that (b) the judiciary, with Congress and the Executive acquiescing, will enforce the guarantees, can safely be eliminated, just plain on the grounds that had this been Madison's rationale it would have kicked up enough fuss for us to have heard about it. As for (c), that, after all, these are matters on which we all agree and are sure to keep on agreeing, one can imagine Madison's having used it with great effect as regards the Second, Third, Fourth, Fifth, Sixth, Seventh, and Eighth Amendments as we now know them; also as regards the Ninth; conceivably, even, if we may suppose both him and his listeners to have forgotten all about the "necessary and proper" clause, as regards the Tenth; but not as regards the First.

Returning now to our distinction between *a* bill of rights and *the* Bill of Rights, it seems safe to say that Madison had a remarkably "free hand" as to what "went in," and what didn't, what sources to draw on, and what "status" the bill he introduced would, so to speak, seem to claim for itself. At one point, we are told, he receives congratulations from a friend for the excellent choice he has made among the myriad proposals that had come in from the several ratifying conventions for guarantees of rights over against the new government. He drew heavily, we are told further and more frequently, on the original Virginia Declaration of Rights. But the first of these notions must be sacrificed to Occam's razor; except for the one nearly incredible "surprise"' in his original draft, it seems to be a culling from a single document and, to come to the second notion, *not* from the original Virginia Declaration of Rights but from the recommendatory amendments sent forward by the ratifying convention in Virginia (though it might well be argued that *its* authors drew heavily on the original Virginia Declaration). Those recommendations, or rather the document in which they are embodied, is from the standpoint of modern constitutional theory a very curious affair, and for two reasons that are of considerable interest for our purposes.

First, it urges numerous guarantees for the future bill of rights that are, on the face of them, already taken care of in the *main body* of the Constitution (the guarantees, for example, that the military shall be subordinate to the civil, that legislative and executive officers shall from time to time return to their private stations); one keeps asking oneself as one reads it: "Have the authors not taken the trouble to read the Constitution they propose to amend?" and asks oneself, at the margin, "Do they or do they not take this business seriously?" (Madison, in any case, eliminates all that sort of thing out of hand; if there are objections from Virginia he can make the obvious, and unanswerable, answer.) But secondly, the document is made up, like the original Virginia Declaration, of statements of "principle," statements as to what "ought" to be done and "ought" not to be done, as contrasted with "rules of law." Both points seem to me to have an important bearing upon our topic, because they suggest that the people Madison was putatively trying hardest to please, the opponents of the Constitution in his own State of Virginia, got in Madison's draft, on one side at least, rather *more* than less than their thinking on the matter to date prompted them to ask for.

Madison does two things out of hand that have, perhaps, been insufficiently noticed. First, he confines his draft (apart from Amendments IX and X) to matters appropriate to a bill of rights as, say, Mr. Justice Black understands a bill of rights, thus *already* setting his draft apart from any "mere" statement of principles analogous to the original Virginia Declaration. But second, he transforms each provision that he adopts into a rule of law; that is, into unambiguously mandatory (as Austin would put it) *commands*. Both, evidently, were things that would have *had* to be done in order for subsequent claims as to the status of the Bill of Rights, as a series of genuine and enforceable limitations on the power of Congress, to make any sense; yet neither change seems to have been hauled out into the open for discussion, or even mentioned. No one, that is to say, seems to have noticed that the bill was so stated as to be enforce*able* and as, therefore, to invite some thought about *how* it was to be enforced. Indeed, the complaints from Virginia, when they come in, are complaints to the effect that Madison's bill did not go far enough towards guaranteeing natural rights! Add to that what I have just called Madison's Big Surprise, namely, inclusion in his draft of a provision that would have forbidden the *States* to infringe trial by jury in criminal cases, or the rights of conscience, or freedom of speech or of the press, and we begin to see the complexity of the question. What *was* Madison up to? (Of course that provision was, as Madison must have known it would be, duly struck out in the Senate; on Madison's own showing, the idea of a bill was to please the objecting minority, who were above all anti-consolidators, anti-centralizers, States' righters.)

But it is the *First* Amendment that really wants looking at from the standpoint of the Virginia recommendations. Here the Virginian text had read: (a) "That the people have a right to freedom of speech, and of writing and publishing their sentiments, *but* [my italics] the freedom of the press [the very "freedom" on which Hamilton sets his sights in Number 84] is one of the great bulwarks of liberty and ought not to be violated"; (b) "That the people have a right peaceably to assemble together, or to instruct their Representatives; and that every freeman has a right to petition or apply to the legislative for the redress of grievances"; and, finally, (c) "That religion" [promptly defined, if you please, as the "duty we owe to our Creator"] and "the manner of discharging it can be directed only by reason and conviction, not by force or violence, and therefore all men have an equal, natural, and unalienable right to the free exercise of religion according to dictates of conscience, and that no particular religious sect ought to be favored or established by Law in preference to others."

The evolution under these topics is indeed interesting to watch. The draft that goes to the Senate moves from the verbose principle on religious freedom that I have just quoted to virtually the form of guarantee we presumably live under: "Congress"—but note the shift, characteristic only and for no obvious reason of the First as contrasted with the remaining Amendments—"Congress shall make no law establishing Religion [not "a religion" but "Religion"] or prohibiting the free exercise thereof, nor shall the free rights of Conscience be infringed." "Free rights of Conscience" disappears before the final draft, never to be heard of again (though some such guarantee had been recommended by *several* States); "no law establishing Religion" becomes "no law respecting an establishment of religion," and "the equal, natural and unalienable right to the free exercise of religion" becomes a prohibition against "prohibiting the free exercise [of religion]. . . ." The Virginia provision "That the people have a right to freedom of speech, and of writing and publishing their sentiments, etc." becomes first "The freedom of speech, and of the press . . . shall not be infringed" and then, in the Bill of Rights itself, "Congress shall make no law . . . abridging freedom of speech, or of the press"—again with the new emphasis on Congress, and the small shift from "infringe" to "abridge." As for the right of assembly, it moves from "the people have a right to peaceably assemble together" to, first, "the right of the people peaceably to assemble, and consult for their common good, shall not be infringed," to "Congress shall make no law . . . abridging . . . the right of the people peaceably to assemble." And, finally, we move from "That every freeman has a right to petition or apply to the legislative for redress of grievances" to, in the House draft, "Congress shall make no law . . . abridging . . . the right of the people . . . to petition the Government for a redress of grievances."

Madison, except for narrowing it down to what *Congress* "shall not" do, merely pares and gives the "sound of law" to the Virginia text. The qualifying phrases disappear. The effect achieved is one of austere simplicity, but by the time he has done—remember, we are concerned primarily with how he could have persuaded the Federalists to vote for it—we are, so to speak, a long way from Virginia, yet not so far from Virginia that the men of Virginia can take much exception. And, *pace* Mr. Justice Black, what has suffered most, as far as the "plain language" of the First Amendment is concerned, is precisely what all the argument was about, namely, "rights," of which, indeed, according to the "plain language," we are left with only two, the right of peaceable assembly and the right to petition for redress of grievances. The "right to freedom of speech, and of writing and publishing their Sentiments," is gone, and we have only that Congress shall make no law abridging *the* freedom of speech; the idea that "the freedom of the press is one of the great bulwarks of liberty" is gone, for we have only that "Congress shall make no law abridging *the* freedom of the press." The "equal, natural and unalienable right to the free exercise of religion" is gone (along with, we might notice, the notion that the "Religion" whose "free exercise" the Congress must not "prohibit" is a "duty" we "owe to our Creator"), and we have only "Congress shall make no law prohibiting the free exercise of religion"; most particularly, the "according to the dictates of conscience" is gone ("freedom of conscience," incidentally, had turned up in several of the sets of recommendations from the State ratifying conventions, and the House draft speaks specifically of "the rights of Conscience" as one of the things that are not to be "infringed"). Finally, the most curious change of all, the Virginia pronouncement that "no particular religious sect or society ought to be favored or established by law in preference to others" becomes simply "Congress shall make no law *respecting* an establishment of religion." [My emphasis]

All very minor changes, you say, and why all the fuss? I answer, Yes, minor in the sense that Madison, final draft in hand, can reasonably say to his constituents in Virginia: "I got you what you asked for." Or, if you like, minor in the sense that the Virginians, if they look hard enough, can "see" in the First Amendment what they had been demanding. But not minor at all from the standpoint of Justice Black's question, which is whether the First Amendment embodies a decision to make the United States an open society, and not, we may I think be fairly sure, as regards picking up Federalist votes in Congress and out in the future process of ratification. For to begin with, we see that, translated into the language and concepts of the time, what the First Amendment in effect does (through the emphasis on Congress) is to recognize laws respecting an establishment of religion, or prohibiting the free exercise thereof, or abridging the freedom of speech or of the press, or abridging the right of the people to assemble peaceably and petition for redress of grievances as a *monopoly of the State governments;* that is, what it precisely does *not* do is to "take a stand" on the matters Mr. Justice Black now sees as being at stake in it. Not only is no "right" to freedom of speech asserted, rather it is also expressly avoided; no right to freedom of the press is asserted, rather it is expressly avoided; no right to the free exercise of religion, no "rights of conscience" are asserted, rather they are expressly avoided; no right to live in a land where no religious sect or society is favored or established by law in preference to another is asserted, but rather expressly avoided.

All that is left in the way of "rights," I repeat, are peaceable assembly and petition for the redress of grievances, both of which, we may note in passing, were traditional, both to a greater or less extent recognized by the common law, *unlike* any supposed right to free speech or nonestablishment or free exercise of religion. Read in the context of the times and of the document from which they were midwifed, in fine, the major provisions of the First Amendment are conspicuous precisely for the *absence* of overtones to the effect that the "freedoms" involved are "rights" and so, in Black's favorite phrase, "absolute." They are merely the Tenth Amendment (and the basic theory of the Constitution) restated in terms of speech, press, and religion, and Madison can indeed say, by the time he has done, that they will not mar the beauty of the frame of government devised at Philadelphia, that, in the language I have imagined his using, they are so worded that they are certain, as limitations on the power of Congress, to remain dead letters. Why, in view of their "plain language" after Madison has done, should any Federalist vote against them? Do they not leave the content of the freedom of speech and press and exercise of religon to be determined as, according to the *Federalist*, they ought and must be determined, namely, by the deliberate sense of the community, which must be expressed through that very Congress which the Amendment forbids to abridge them? And Madison drives the point home, one might say, by simultaneously forcing his fellow Congressmen through the (surely predictable) symbolic step of eliminating a provision that would have forbidden the States to infringe trial by jury, the rights of conscience, the freedom of speech, or the freedom of the press.

Two further points, and *I* shall have done.

First, unpleasant as it may be for some of us to contemplate, Madison has turned out, *operatively speaking*, to be quite right (though only because, as we have seen, the First Amendment does *not* say what it might have said) about the Bill of Rights not doing any "injury" to the "beauty" of the Philadelphia frame of government—as, incidentally, all those Federalist arguments against a bill of rights may be seen, in retrospect, to have been pretty good political theory. Nearly two centuries have passed since the ink dried on Madison's Bill of Rights, but the showdown that he and Jefferson expected and that his recasting of the Virginia document seemed to invite—the showdown between a Congress bent on invading a natural right and a Federal court system, armed with a declaration of rights elevated to the status of enforceable law, saying (as what else can it do given the "plain language") "No" to it—has yet to occur in the area that, as all Americans know and seem always to have known, is the dangerous one, namely, that of the First Amendment. *To this day, the Supreme Court has never declared an enactment of the Congress of the United States unconstitutional on grounds of the First Amendment.*

Opinions may, to be sure, differ as to whether "natural rights" have thrived or suffered in consequence; that is, as to whether "natural rights" would, as the Federalists insisted, be safer with the people, which is where the Philadelphia Constitution left them, than they could be made by any alternative scheme the bill-of-rights men might end up devising. But Madison's Bill of Rights, correctly read (as I believe myself to have read it here) and read as we as a people have in fact ended up reading it, also leaves the natural rights, in the areas that Justice Black correctly regards as crucial, subject to the general Federalist principles that the deliberate sense of the American community is to be trusted, and that any attempt to put parchment barriers in its way will as a matter of course be ineffective. That is perhaps not the American political system as we describe it in our civics textbooks or our Fourth of July orations; it is certainly not the American system as, for example, Jellinek describes it and has taught other Europeans to describe it; but it is the American political system as it has worked to date, and it is high time we begin to recognize it as that. Again as Rousseau put it long before the Federalists put forward their arguments: If the people wills to do itself hurt—or, we may safely add, good either—who is to say it nay? And the answer, for the American system, would appear to be: in the crucial area, nobody.

Emphasis on Freedom

CHAPTER FOUR

A Conservative Case for Freedom

M. STANTON EVANS

IF THERE is one point upon which contemporary philosophers seem to be agreed, it is that American society has somehow lost its bearings. Critics of all persuasions relentlessly inform us that our nation has strayed from the values which once made it strong and informed it with purpose. As to what those values are, or were, there is considerably less agreement.

Those who have been most vocal in decrying our fallen state have usually been identified as conservatives. Even this subdivision of social and political criticism has failed to reach an agreed analysis of what ails us. Some conservatives fix on one thing and some on another, so that the net effect is not clarification but compounded obscurity.

This confusion is joyfully augmented by the forces which error has thrust into power. Those who benefit from the prevailing tendencies have no desire to see those tendencies corrected; thus the ruling collectivists and Liberals, so called, have assiduously tried to conjure the conservative protest movement out of existence.

A whole school of literature has developed, attempting to define present-day conservatism either as a *revenant* classical liberalism, or else as a form of mental disorder. In either case, the point is to dispose of it as something too silly to be of much account. The more damaging of these criticisms, because the one more nearly containing a suggestion of truth, is the identification with classical liberalism. All those objecting to the growing dominance of gov-

ernment power and the contraction of individual freedom are
lumped together as descendants of Spencer and Sumner, and thus,
presumably, disposed of. While labeling someone a classical liberal
is not necessarily an insult, it must be pointed out that today's
conservatives, although opponents of statism, are generally not
Manchesterians. There are, to be sure, some classical liberals in the
conservative camp, just as there seem to be some Metternichian
strong men. There are still other conservatives who are neither
statists nor Manchesterians. This three-way babel of ideas, now
and again punctuated by a helpful shout from the far left, has
sundered conservative effort and diffused its strength.

Such theoretical confusion is highly unfortunate. Before they
enmesh themselves in it, most American conservatives operate in
terms of an instinctive consensus; it is only when abstract sanctions
are sought that the sectarians take over and begin compartmentaliz-
ing everyone into the suggested factions. Working unity is then
dissipated in ideological feuding. The position set forward in this
essay is not that such feuding is practically disadvantageous (although this is true enough), but that it shares a fault common to
most attitudinizing at the first level of sophistication—that those
who have set about to fragment the consensus offer us a doctrine
less coherent than the instinctive wisdom they attack.

The fundamental disagreement among conservative theoreticians
occurs over the problem of man and his nature: specifically,
whether the imperatives of individual freedom can be reconciled
with the Christian conception of the individual as flawed in mind
and will, with its demand for individual subordination to an objective, nonsecular order. Critics of the protest movement delight in
pointing to what they consider an insoluble dilemma. They are
joined by sectarians within the movement itself, urging on the one
hand that we abandon our insistence on individual freedom, on the
other that we give up our Christianized view of man. The two, we
are repeatedly informed, are simply not compatible. For the purposes of this essay, I shall call those who choose the first alternative
"authoritarians," those who choose the second "libertarians."[1]

The authoritarian believes in the objective order and is generally
ready to limit individual freedom to follow its prescriptions. He
prefers a hierarchical to a fluid society, conceiving some men as

destined to rule, others to obey—all ordained by the objective order. The libertarian finds the idea of such an immobile society repugnant and rejects the principles which have been used to sanction it. Each has been transfixed by a single aspect of the contemporary crisis and insists that this aspect alone must absorb our full attention. The libertarian sees the power of the state increasing by leaps and bounds, while the power of the individual correspondingly diminishes. He demands that all other considerations, including the structure of traditional values, yield to the task of confronting this terrible challenge. The authoritarian sees moral standards crumbling and traditional values being ignored, and demands that all other considerations, including, if need be, the cause of freedom, yield to the task of restoring a due regard for virtue.

Both positions rest on a form of illicit conversion. In the view of this writer, they have not properly related first principles and conclusions. Patient inquiry will disclose, I think, that affirmation of a transcendent order is not only compatible with individual autonomy, but the condition of it; and that a skeptical view of man's nature not only permits political liberty but demands it. An attack on traditional values, after the libertarian fashion, will not check the growth of state power but contribute to its increase. An assault on individual freedom, in the authoritarian manner, will not restore us to virtue because virtue cannot be legislated. Freedom and virtue have declined together and must rise together. They are not opposites; they are not even, in the American context, separate matters to be dealt with independently. They are complementaries which flourish or wither in a direct and dependable ratio.

The problem can best be examined if we divide it in two: first, the question of freedom as related to the existence of objective value; second, the question of freedom as related to the nature of man.

I

The libertarian, or classical liberal, characteristically denies the existence of a God-centered moral order, to which man should subordinate his will and reason. Alleging human freedom as the single moral imperative, he otherwise is a thoroughgoing relativist, pragmatist, and materialist. He puts considerable emphasis on economics. Man and his satisfactions, the libertarian maintains, are themselves the source of value—and other values cannot be imposed from without. Because the free economy best serves man and best supplies his material needs, it is moral. It works.

There seem to be a number of reasons for libertarian devotion to these views. One no doubt is that some present-day libertarians are genuine descendants of Mill and Spencer, and proceed—logically, as they believe—from relativist premises to a vindication of freedom. But I believe the more common occurrence is that other considerations, largely unspoken, incline the libertarian to his particular brand of relativism. Many attacks on the idea of a transcendent order can be traced to fears about the uses to which any particular affirmation of truth may be put. The libertarian suspects that commitment to this or that ethical judgment will imply the need for having it enforced by the political authorities. Yet that step, as we shall see momentarily, is neither necessary nor desirable for those concerned to nourish a regime of virtue.

Additionally, there seems to be considerable confusion between *value*, as received from tradition and the counsels of religious teaching, and *conformity*, imposed by the pressures of the group. The two may of course coincide—specifically, when group pressures aim at enforcing traditional value. But the fact that they may appear in conjunction does not mean they are the same; and in a time of triumphant revolution, inability to make the distinction constitutes failure at the most elementary level of analysis.

The problem is akin to that created by obscurantists of the "New Conservative" variety, who tell us that since conservatives are opposed to change, they should be in favor of the New Deal. This argument empties conservatism of all value content and makes it simply a matter of technique. But conservatives who wish to conserve value generally have some particular value in mind and must oppose any particular *status quo* which denies it. The libertarian falls into the converse error. Because he is opposed to the *status quo* of New Dealism, he determines that he must not be a conservative and battles those who so call themselves.

It is hard to believe, however, that anyone interested in conserving historic American institutions could become reconciled to the patchwork collectivism of the last twenty-five years. Our tradition, after all, running back through Adams and Madison and Dickinson and Otis to Coke and the British common law, is a tradition of imposing limitations upon the arbitrary exercise of power. The conformity of statism represents a radical break with that tradition; those who wish to affirm the values embodied in the tradition must oppose blatant violation of it, even when that violation has become settled and comfortable, and takes extraordinary effort to dislodge. They must perforce be nonconformists and rebels, ready to brave the censure of the group. Moreover, it is only if they are motivated by deeply cherished values that they can manage to do so. So far are "value" and "conformity" from being identical that the second can rise to its current distasteful height only when the first declines. A man without the interior armor of value has no defense against the pressures of his society. It is precisely the loss of value which has turned the "inner-directed" citizen of nineteenth-century America into the "other-directed" automaton of today.

Man, Ortega wrote, "is a being forced by his nature to seek some higher authority. If he succeeds in finding it of himself, he is a superior man; if not, he is a mass-man, and must receive it from his superiors." To exist in community, men must harmonize their desires; some kind of general equilibrium has to prevail. Men who lose the "inner check," as Babbitt called it, must therefore submit to an outer one; they become mass men, ruled by their "superiors."

The erosion of value is doubly destructive. As it promotes statism by creating the need for an external force to order conflicting desires, it simultaneously weakens the individual's ability to withstand the state. Men without values are more than willing to trade their freedom for material benefits. That the loss of moral constraint invites the rule of power is surely one of the best-established facts of twentieth-century history. Indeed, a number of quite unconservative witnesses have pointed out that the vigor of civilization is dependent on people who are guided by some internalized system of value and who are thus capable of initiative and self-reliant behavior. This is the burden of David Riesman's celebrated study, *The Lonely Crowd* (in which the terms "inner-directed" and "other-directed" were coined), and the message of such critics of modern society as Pitirim Sorokin, William H. Whyte, and Richard LaPiere.

The authoritarian, like the libertarian, believes that value and enforcement go hand in hand; unlike the libertarian, however, he accepts both. He merely wants to be the person doing the enforcing. The conservative, as I conceive him, rejects this common analysis. He does not share the authoritarian's readiness to coerce his fellow men into virtue, but neither does he share the libertarian's commitment to freedom at virtue's expense. The conservative believes man should be free; he does not believe being free is the end of human existence. He maintains that man exists to form his life in consonance with the objective order, to choose the Good. But "choice" of the Good can take place only in circumstances favoring volition. Freedom is thus the political context of moral decision; it is the modality within which the human mind can search out moral absolutes. In the conservative view, then, right choice is the terminal value; freedom, an instrumental and therefore subsidiary value.

To the conservative, economic and political freedom *per se* is not "moral"; only willed human actions have moral content, and freedom dictates no particular actions. A freely acting man may or may not be moral, depending on what he does. But while freedom is morally neutral, the possible alternatives, i.e., varying forms of coercion, are not. By their nature, all coercive systems require certain actions which we hold immoral: the arbitrary exercise of power over men by other men. The Western ethic holds murder and theft are wrong, because they are abrogations of divine law and of the integrity of the human personality. And it is historically demonstrable that, when total power is invested in the state, murder and theft tend to become official and impregnable. The free economy permits morality but does not guarantee it; the coerced economy guarantees immorality. This formulation may prove distasteful to authoritarians accustomed to identifying all defenders of economic freedom as Manchesterians. Yet I can conceive of no other which can maintain the conditions of moral choice. It may prove equally distasteful to libertarians, accustomed to seeing all "true believers" as enemies of liberty. Yet I can conceive of no other that will insure the sanctity of freedom. If there is no value system with which we may rebuke the pretensions of despots, what is to prevent the rule of force in the world? If there are no objective standards of right and wrong, why object to tyranny? If murder and theft are *not* immoral, why object to them either singly or in the mass?

The last argument needs to be taken a step further. The Manchesterians allege that man's self-interest, which flourishes under a regime of freedom, is sufficient sanction to keep liberty intact. But that calculus of desires is too subtle for most of mankind. It is the immemorial habit of man to be unable to see his long-term interest when a short-term one appears before him. When he thinks he can achieve an immediate benefit, he is willing to give up some of his freedom to obtain it. As F. A. Hayek puts it: "Because of the restricted capacities of our minds, our immediate purposes will always loom large, and we will tend to sacrifice long-range advantages to them." Surely the entire trend of modern politics has demonstrated this point with disturbing finality. Only when there is widespread adherence to a consensus of value, and only when that value is one which sanctions the continuance of freedom, can freedom endure. As freedom is the condition of value, so is value the guarantor of freedom.

II

When we have examined the question of value to determine whether or not freedom is desirable, we must turn to the problem of man's nature to decide what political arrangements offer the best promise of sustaining it. Metaphysically, freedom is the context of choice, the ground of decision where man seeks to break through to transcendence. Politically, it is a physical condition existing between and among men. In conventional discourse, "freedom" usually means the absence of constraint by one man upon another. Since some form of constraint is necessary to let men live together, the degree to which it can be relaxed and the conflict of what are variously defined as "freedoms" are problems for which there are almost as many answers as there are theorists.

But whatever our difficulties in defining it, freedom is obviously a product of the way men behave towards one another. If we want to maximize freedom, we can begin to do so only after examining the motives of human behavior; and the first task in the pursuit of political freedom is therefore to reach a reasoned position about the nature of man.

Again, there is a division of opinion on the Right. The libertarian, or classical liberal, affirms the natural goodness, or, in the more scientistic forms, the non-evil of human nature. He views government as the source of evil, the unfettered individual as the source of good. He has considerable faith in "progress" as the natural creation of free men and tends to believe that material success and moral virtue are closely akin, if not identical. For all of these reasons, he concludes that government should let people alone to employ their natural goodness. In his extreme form, the modern-day libertarian is a philosophical anarchist, a free-enterprise Utopian.

The authoritarian holds precisely the opposite view. He believes people in their natural state are not good, but evil. Viewing human will as perverse and human reason as limited, he does not believe in automatic "progress." He also rejects the Darwinian equation of morality and economic prosperity, with its subordination of value to the observable relation of forces. Like Henry Adams, he thinks things more probably than not are tending to unravel, which is only to be expected if the natural direction of human choice is downward. For all these reasons, the authoritarian believes in strong government. Because man is feckless, he needs aristocratic guidance to force him to be good.

The conservative, again, believes the two schools have reached their positions through a shared mistake in analysis; they fail to relate the question of man's nature to the problem of government. Concretely, they fail to see that government cannot be treated as something apart from "men"—in the one case as the source of evil, in the other as the source of moral guidance. For what is government, after all, but men in the exercise of power? In the case of the libertarian, if men are naturally good, whence comes the evil of government? In the case of the authoritarian, if men are fundamentally evil, how does government become a force for virtue?

The conservative agrees with the authoritarian that men are not to be trusted, and his constant concern is to restrain the destructive tendencies he discerns in a fallen humanity. But he does not agree that such a judgment means man should be ruled by an aristocracy. For if men are evil, then potential aristocrats are evil, too, and no man, logically, can be said to have a commission to coerce another. "Absolute monarchs," in Locke's phrase, "are but men" and, as such, heirs to the same weaknesses of the human kind as are their subjects. Moreover, their ability to inflict evil on others obviously increases with the amount of power they wield. Among kings, aristocrats, and commoners, John Adams said, "there is no reason to believe the one much wiser or much more honest than the other;

they are all of the same clay; their minds and bodies are alike. . . .
As to usurping others' rights, they are all three equally guilty when
unlimited in power." The conservative wants political freedom
precisely because he fears the fundamental nature of man. James
Madison, in *Federalist* No. 51, gives us the classic statement of the
matter: "It may be a reflection on human nature, that such devices
should be necessary to control the abuses of government. But what
is government itself, but the greatest of all reflections on human
nature? If men were angels, no government would be necessary.
If angels were to govern men, neither internal nor external controls
on government would be necessary."

I concede there is little difference between what I call the conservative philosophy on this point and the views of a number of
men sometimes thought of as classical liberals, Adam Smith, Lord
Acton, De Tocqueville. The position of this "liberal" school, if
such it be, is best suggested by Hayek's characterization of himself
as an "old Whig." Such "liberals" fear government because they
fear man—and on the technical point of the relation between man's
nature and the kind of government appropriate to him are indistin-
guishable from the conservatives.

Hayek divides the people we think of as classical liberals into
two camps: the "true" and the "false" individualists. "True" individualism may or may not come coupled with the deeper moral
affirmations of the conservative position, but it is a far cry from the
alternately sentimental and mechanistic notions about man which
convert themselves so easily to the uses of collectivism.

"The cultivated man," said Renan in a celebrated flight of false
individualism, "has only to follow the delicious incline of his inner
impulses." This was the kind of fatuous self-love which prompted
Jacob Burckhardt to reflect that mankind was losing its conception
of the need for external standards, "whereupon, of course, we
periodically fall victims to sheer power." The "true" individualist
sides not with Renan, but with Burckhardt. His chief concern in
seeking freedom is not to liberate the "natural goodness" of man,
but to localize as much as possible man's tendencies towards evil.
"It would scarcely be too much to claim," Hayek says of Adam
Smith, "that the main merit of the individualism which he and his
contemporaries advocated is that it is a system under which bad
men can do the least harm."

The mutual regard that existed between Smith and Edmund Burke is, of course, a matter of record. The similarity of their ideas suggests that, on the point of fearing man and his behavior in power, the camp of "true individualism" and conservatism are indeed one; and this *rapprochement* suggests, in turn, that a view of freedom as compatible with mistrust of human nature is recommended by a broad tradition as well as by the homely counsel of clear thought.

The conservative's task, then, is to insure that enough governmental authority exists to suppress criminal outcroppings of human weakness, but at the same time to insure that no man, or group of men, is vested with too much political power. This has proved down the centuries to be a troublesome undertaking. There is little difficulty in establishing either the authoritarian's ideal of a strong government, or the libertarian's contrary ideal of complete (if therefore temporary) freedom. The great problem is to set up a system of government providing both order and freedom, and as Burke said, "to temper together these opposite elements of liberty and restraint in one consistent work requires much thought, deep reflection, a sagacious, powerful and combining mind."

This was, as it happened, the very problem which preoccupied the Founders of the American nation, and the problem which achieved its highest resolution in the compact on which the United States was based. The dilemma of government, as the Framers of our Constitution saw it, was to restrain power in the very act by which it was granted, to establish an authority which could be used for certain limited purposes, but for those only, an authority which would be hedged about by alternative centers of decision, jealous of their own prerogatives, and by constitutional proscription. The object was for power to be so diffused and equilibrated that each source of authority would limit and restrain the others, while having sufficient strength to perform the tasks appropriate to it.

In a word, the model answer to the dilemma of free government is the American Constitution, founded in the counterpoise of interests of colonial North America and fused in the sagacious, powerful, and combining mind of James Madison. It is noteworthy that neither the "authoritarian" ideas of Hamilton nor the "libertarian" notions of Jefferson dominated the Constitution. Instead, the great conceptual balance struck by Madison prevailed in that document and, for a time, in the nation. "The great desideratum of government," Madison said, "is such a modification of sovereignty as will render it sufficiently neutral between the different interests and factions, to control one part of the country from invading the rights of another, and at the same time sufficiently controlled itself, from setting up an interest adverse to that of the whole society." And, again quoting Madison: "In framing a government which is to be administered by men over men, the great difficulty lies in this: You must first enable the government to control the governed; and in the next place oblige it to control itself."

It is noteworthy that Madison and Adams and their compatriots accepted, as a matter of course, the dual emphasis we have been discussing, combining a conservative mistrust of human nature with a libertarian desire to extend and nurture human freedom. Their answer to both problems was the classic Anglo-Saxon reliance upon limited government.

Being itself a product of fallible men, and administered by others still more fallible, the Constitution of Adams and Madison has of course achieved less than perfection. But it has maintained a shifting equilibrium, and it is testimony to the Founders' intentions that they are even today the center about which our political controversies revolve. Certainly, whatever its imperfections and whatever its current ravaged condition, the American Constitution has proved that the practice of conservatism, beginning from a profound mistrust of man and of men panoplied as the state, can well serve the ends of freedom.

CHAPTER FIVE

Education in Economic Liberty

WILHELM RÖPKE

I

SOME years before Benedetto Croce's death I had the honor of participating in a very significant discussion with him. I was rather appalled that even vis-a-vis such a towering spirit I had to defend the idea that our economic system should reflect the political and spiritual principles ruling our society, wherefore we cannot admit any possibility of coexistence between a collective economy based on compulsion and a social order based on liberty.

The economy is freedom's first line of defense. Accordingly, the modern economist above all others has the difficult and glorious task of defending the values of liberty and personality, together with a state based on justice and law and on that kind of morality which can only be bred by liberty; and in order to do this, he must focus his thinking on the central problem of how to maintain an essentially liberal economy even under the difficult conditions of our modern industrial society and how to ensure it against the assault of collectivism in its daily infiltrations. Though Croce's answer to this was that the organization of our economic life is only a question of workability and of no concern to the philosopher (who in the political and spiritual field may be an advocate of freedom whereas in the economic field he may well be an advocate of collectivism), it is hardly necessary to prove how grave and dangerous an error his views represent.

This error, however, seems to be thoroughly rooted, especially among philosophers who are strangers to the strict reasonings of political economy. In this connection I am loath to enter into polemics with an excellent woman, but I cannot help noting that Hannah Arendt has the same misconception as Benedetto Croce when in *The Hungarian Revolution and Totalitarian Imperialism* (Munich, 1958, p. 49) she claims that "the object of economy is nothing more than working and consuming, i.e., activities which apparently belong to the lowest sphere of human life where men are anyway under compulsion, though not under a political one." Owing to this misconception, which she shares with many others, she does not consider economic liberty to be an essential feature of the free world nor the lack of it a characteristic of the unfree world.

From all this we can draw the following conclusion: If economic liberty is of such decisive importance for liberty as a whole, the best way to educate men to accept it is obviously to convince them of its importance. We should not start, therefore, by showing the undoubted economic advantages and material productivity of economic freedom but point to the supreme immaterial values expressed by the very idea of liberty. It is, of course, rather important that a greater abundance of goods should result from the market economy than from the collective economy; nonetheless we must first make it clear that economic liberty is an integral part of freedom as such, and that we ought to prefer it even if it were less advantageous from a material point of view. Freedom is such a precious good that we ought to be ready to sacrifice everything for it, possibly even prosperity and abundance, should we be compelled to do so by the necessities of economic freedom. Then we can point out that, luckily for us, an economic system based on liberty— without which liberty itself cannot exist—is at the same time infinitely more productive than a system of controlled economy.

We should avoid luring men into acceptance of economic liberty by holding out to them the candy of material abundance; our educational efforts should instead be made on the high level of social philosophy and should appeal to the last and supreme values. We should impress upon people that one cannot deny freedom in the economic field and grant it in the remaining sectors of human activity, and we should summon the whole strength of logical argument and of experience to render this idea convincing.

It should be noted that there is a very serious question as to whether there are not powerful forces at work within the modern Jacobin mass democracy which are anything but favorable to freedom as such and which are most definitely hostile to economic liberty. It must, in fact, be remembered that the market economy in Germany, whose revival has proved to be a great blessing, was not a legitimate child of democracy, because in 1948 no modern democracy existed. It was rather an illegitimate child which was adopted only later on, after ever increasing signs of affection, by the German democracy—*legitimatio per subsequens matrimonium.* Attempts to restore a free market had much less success in Italy, notwithstanding Einaudi's efforts, and still less in France, where the reinstatement of economic liberty and of monetary discipline, which is its inseparable companion, has become a possibility only under the authoritarian government of De Gaulle.

Germany's example makes it particularly clear that experiencing the extreme contrast to economic freedom, i.e., collectivism and inflation, represents a rather brutal but otherwise very effective way of educating people to accept economic liberty along with monetary discipline. After all Erhard and Vocke have done only what was popular from the very beginning, even before the huge success of combining the free market with monetary discipline became apparent; they did what was popular because it meant a change in an extremely hateful state of affairs.

II

We will now consider some particular aspects of our efforts to educate in economic freedom. First, we repeat the compelling arguments of which such an education has to make use: the appeal not only to the technical and material superiority of an economic system based on freedom, but above all the emphasis that economic liberty is an extremely important part of freedom as such, and must be recognized as such by the social philosopher also. What economic liberty actually means becomes obvious when we state that the contrary of it is compulsion. Every limitation of economic liberty, every state intervention and every single act of planning and directing, contains some constraint. It is this constraint which, together with compulsory state taxation, takes away from us bit by bit that genuine freedom which is so dear to us all.

The more economic freedom is limited, the higher rises the flood of compulsory measures and the narrower becomes the space for freedom. To educate people to accept economic freedom means, therefore, to teach them to consider every increase of compulsion with the gravity it deserves, including every extension of the so-called welfare state, to which compulsion is so essential that for the sake of clarity one should rather call it the "compulsory welfare state." This compulsory character is the really hateful thing in all economic systems lacking freedom, the planned economy as well as the welfare state and fiscal socialism. It is surprising, therefore, that this point is so seldom mentioned, though people are in general agreement that compulsion is unworthy. Doubtless it is an unpleasant and hideous fact; those who are willing to accept compulsion as part of an economic system and of economic policy have an interest in distracting us from it.

The skillful effacing of important distinctions is such an attempt to distract us. Is not compulsion an indispensable element of any social order? Would not the lack of it result in anarchy? And does not the economy, too, require certain firm rules, the observance of which has to be enforced by the state? Where must we draw the line? Why then do we pathetically refuse to accept any kind of compulsion?

It becomes obvious at once what such questions are aiming at. The intention is to blot out border lines and to lure us into trespassing lightheartedly. It is therefore all the more necessary to give clear answers in order to be saved from such seduction.

First, it ought to be stated that compulsion is, if anything, a necessary evil, which means that we must try to manage things with a minimum of it and not let it increase to the maximum characteristic of collectivism. It means further that the burden of proving its necessity lies always with those who ask for more compulsion and that we must be extremely exacting towards their proofs because any further increase of constraint will certainly have the most serious repercussions.

It is, however, not only a question of how much compulsion is being exerted but of making a very clear distinction between the various kinds of coercive measures which can be adopted in economic life. It goes without saying that compulsion is the indispensable mortar of social and political order within every state system and that its monopolization in the hands of government defines the state as such. Looking at the question from this angle, it is certainly wrong to say that power as such is evil and that "all power corrupts."[1] Even the freest economic system cannot do without compulsion and without the power of the state, because under all circumstances two things are necessary, namely, law and a monetary system, which cannot be put into effect without using constraint. It is, however, a sign of great ignorance of the workings of a market economy and of the opposite system not to see clearly that the difference between the two forms of economy lies very obviously in the kind of compulsion associated with each. Everybody ought to know by now that the market economy is an economic system where constraint, intervention, or limitation of freedom is confined to the framework, the regulations, within which economic intercourse itself is free. Collectivism, on the other hand, is marked by compulsory planning of individual economic operations themselves. If anyone fails to understand this fundamental difference or is inclined to consider it sophistic, he should be asked: Is it the same to you whether you have to stop at a traffic light as a free man at the steering wheel of your own car, or as a prisoner in a police wagon?

In a market economy the compulsory measures are of the kind that every state has to apply in order to regulate the coexistence of men; they are of a general nature and apply to everybody; they are predictable, not arbitrary, and are formulated in precise regulations. In a collectivist economy, we are confronted instead with compulsion exerted case by case; it is, therefore, of necessity arbitrary, unpredictable, and a direct limitation of freedom. Hayek has the merit of having pointed out and proved very intelligently once and for all that the first kind of compulsion characterizes the constitutional state, whereas the second kind of compulsion is contrary to the constitutional state.

Economic freedom is, therefore, to be considered an indispensable condition of the constitutional state, and its loss entails the wreckage of that very state; even the growing limitations of economic liberty endanger it more and more. The reverse also applies: the constitutional state is an indispensable condition of every economic system based on freedom, because it offers the only means to ensure safety and protection against arbitrary measures. Without that safety no decision can be made in a market economy in a really efficient way, especially as regards the future (investment and savings).

An actual case will show into what dangerous territory a conscious or unconscious blotting out of these border lines may lead. Among the strange effects produced by the radiations of the German Communist zone on the political opinions of Western Germany and of the entire West—and, of course, desired and fostered by Moscow—surely the most bizarre is the notion haunting many a head that it ought to be possible to bring together both parts of Germany in a sort of confederation, with each part maintaining its present economic system. This notion apparently stems from the idea that the two parts of Germany differ only in a higher or lower degree of economic freedom.

How mindless such a plan is and what total ignorance of all basic economic problems it reveals become evident when one bears in mind that we are not dealing with higher or lower degrees of compulsion but with two fundamentally different types of compulsion, which render the two economic systems so utterly unlike as to be completely incompatible. Notwithstanding all interventions, state-owned companies, and welfare-state activities, in West Germany we have a genuine market economy which is based on economic freedom; in Soviet Germany we have a centrally directed collectivist economy, operating under command and denying every economic liberty. Since the collective economy is completely identified with the state itself, such a state could be blended into an all-German confederation only by introducing a directed economic system in West Germany also. Otherwise it would be completely impossible to join together both parts, even in a rather loose form of confederation. Conversely, the amateurish ideas of the statesmen at Yalta, who had fancied a common administration of Germany including the Soviet Zone, were revealed as dangerous fiction when, in 1948, an economic system based on liberty was introduced in West Germany.

For the sake of completeness, a last argument should be mentioned, though it can hardly be taken seriously. It is claimed (in order to make the compulsion ensuing from the loss or limitation of economic freedom seem less hideous) that the market economy is also an economic system based on constraint in so far as it compels us to pay for all goods we desire and puts us under a com-

pulsion limiting our freedom to the extent that we are lacking
money to buy this or that. It is rather appalling that such things
are not only thought and voiced but even printed, because their
absurdity is so manifest that it is hardly a pleasure to undertake
their refutation. According to this argument, the fed prisoner
would be free but the man who has to earn his living as a free
worker would be unfree. Consequently, complete freedom could
exist only when all limitations due to shortages of goods were to
disappear; that is to say, in a fool's paradise.

All this is really very obvious. Nonetheless these nonsensical conceptions continue to crop up and are taken seriously by many
persons. We all surely remember the time when people attacked
a policy of no rationing as "rationing through the purse"; they
thereby were advocating the alternative of rationing enforced by
the police order of a compulsory economic system and at the same
time were trying to deal a blow to the market economy. Real
compulsion applied by a controlled economy is lightheartedly
put on the same level with limitations we have to endure owing
to the general shortage of goods. Even worse, those who rattle
along like this apparently prefer real compulsion, which may get
us into jail or, in totalitarian states, into concentration camps or to
the gallows, to the methods of the market economy, which adapt
demand to the scarce availability of goods without jeopardizing
freedom. Some years ago, during the austerity period under Sir
Stafford Cripps, a Roman friend of mine gave his answer to this
choice. He was invited by the British Council to give some lectures
in London, but he turned the invitation down on the grounds that
life is too short to stay even a week in a country whose government
would be giving him orders as to how to spend his money. He preferred to remain in his own country where, it is true, he had to
work hard to earn money but could spend it as he liked.

Who will fail to perceive that the famous slogan, "freedom from
want," by which Roosevelt has enriched the ammunition of the
demagogues of our time, goes back to this same thoughtless equali-
zation of true and false compulsion? This easygoing slogan means,
in fact, throwing into one and the same kettle real freedom and
false freedom, liberty in the highest ethical sense along with a
pseudofreedom that means only the absence of something tiresome
which limits perfect happiness. But the great success of such con-

fusion proves how dangerous is the sophism which we here encounter in all its different versions, and how urgent the necessity to
finish it off.

One more observation is pertinent in this connection. The more
the material limitations of our existence have in fact diminished,
with the increased production of goods in the course of the last
generation, the heavier compulsion has become throughout the
world. While, for instance, distances on the globe are shrinking
more and more, owing to the extraordinary acceleration of modes
of travel, time is increasingly lost in coping with the formalities of
the various states and fighting endless red tape—always under threat
of punishment. "En additionnant les heures qu'on passe pour pré-
parer un voyage, il faut plus de temps à un Français pour aller en
Amérique qu'au temps de Jules Verne et de Phileas Fogg."[2]

III

From these considerations we can draw the conclusion that
education in economic freedom is primarily the task of reason.
The modern economist, therefore, has the very important job of
enlightening people concerning the thoughtless absurdities and
contradictions now current.

There is still another reason for going into detail on this point.
Pierre Gaxotte, whom I have quoted above, also says: "Lorsque,
dans un pays de liberté une partie importante du peuple ne re-
connait plus comme légitime l'ordre social établi, la liberté est
condamnée à disparaitre."[3] This is obviously true, but it is necessary that the essence of this social order be generally understood.
What Lucien Romier a quarter of a century ago pointed out in his
pamphlet *Si le capitalisme disparaissait* (Paris, 1933) still applies:
no civilization can be maintained in the long run when its structure
and inner laws are no longer understood by the mass of the people
who support it. But just this very understanding of our economic
system based on freedom, which is an essential part of our civilization, is progressively weakened as its mechanism becomes more
complicated, thus making things all the easier for all sorts of
demagogues.[4] One of the most important tasks of political economy,
then, is to nurture this understanding by explaining the rudiments
of the market economy and the price mechanism, clearly indicating
the proper place of each. Economists should take pains to see that

the essential notions of their science become part of the living essence and knowledge of the civilization of our time.[5] They will thus make a most important contribution to people's education in economic freedom.

Unfortunately we cannot, in all conscience, affirm that this task is being fulfilled in a satisfactory manner; we cannot even say that it is generally recognized and acknowledged. If we may be somewhat irreverent, we might say that most of our modern economists are circulation engineers, national accountants, model cabinet makers and graph-plumbers. One might even let this pass, had not so many of them become quite insensible to the huge problems of social philosophy our time has to face, the problems which confer dignity, sense, and profundity even on the strictly theoretical work of political economy. When one takes part in a discussion among learned persons on such topics as inflation, business cycles, European integration, and the like, he is appalled to note time and again that many people lack what the French would call "doctrine." They talk as if they were indifferent to all questions of social philosophy and as if it were beneath their dignity as scientists to have an opinion on nonmaterial values, or at least to voice such opinions. They have become mere economic technicians—economocrats, experts in whose hands economics is becoming purely instrumental.

IV

It would, however, be unjust to turn the guns of our criticism only one way. Those who have clearly understood the paramount importance of economic liberty, and are therefore convinced of the necessity of educating people in it, also have sins on their doorstep. How many of them have any really clear idea about those premises of economic liberty which lie beyond the rules of supply and demand? About the significance of property and all the other anchors of existence which enable the masses to embrace economic freedom? About the damage that is done to, and the discredit that is thrown on this very economic freedom (and consequently on the economic system which is based on it) by those who sneak away through the back door as soon as they are summoned to make sacrifices in support of economic liberty, who are the first to call for state-enforced compulsory measures every time they get the worst of it under economic freedom and free competition, that is to say, by all those whom we might call the "bilkers of market economy"?

Thoughtful consideration will make it evident that education in economic freedom is inseparable from education in liberty itself in the highest moral sense. Educational efforts in both directions have to spring from a moral ground and must go back to those last mysterious sources from which the ethical impulses of men originate. We can breathe the air of liberty only to the extent that we are ready to bear the burden of moral responsibility associated with it.

We can apply to economic liberty Burke's judgment when he said that men are ready for freedom to the extent that they are willing to check their appetites, to the degree that their love of justice is stronger than their avarice, the solidity and temperance of their judgment overcomes their vanity and pretentiousness, and they prefer the counsel of the honest and judicious to the flatteries of scoundrels. Even economic liberty cannot last if we do not put a check somewhere on untamed wantonness and appetite. The less efficient this restraint is *within* men, the more it must be applied externally; and, accordingly, the less economic liberty and the less freedom as such will we have.

CHAPTER SIX

Why I Am Not a Conservative

F. A. HAYEK

> At all times sincere friends of freedom have been
> rare, and its triumphs have been due to minorities,
> that have prevailed by associating themselves with
> auxiliaries whose objects often differed from their
> own; and this association, which is always danger-
> ous, has sometimes been disastrous, by giving to
> opponents just grounds of opposition.
>
> LORD ACTON

I

AT A time when most movements that are thought to be progres-
sive advocate further encroachments on individual liberty,[1] those
who cherish freedom are likely to expend their energies in opposition. In this they find themselves much of the time on the same
side as those who habitually resist change. In matters of current
politics today they generally have little choice but to support the
conservative parties. But, though the position I have tried to define
in my book *The Constitution of Liberty*, is also often described
as "conservative," it is very different from that to which this name
has been traditionally attached. There is danger in the confused
condition which brings the defenders of liberty and the true conservatives together in common opposition to developments which
threaten their different ideals equally. It is therefore important to
distinguish clearly the position taken here from that which has long
been known—perhaps more appropriately—as conservatism.

Conservatism proper is a legitimate, probably necessary, and certainly widespread attitude of opposition to drastic change. It has, since the French Revolution, for a century and a half played an important role in European politics. Until the rise of socialism its opposite was liberalism. There is nothing corresponding to this conflict in the history of the United States, because what in Europe was called "liberalism" was here the common tradition on which the American polity had been built: thus the defender of the American tradition was a liberal in the European sense.[2] This already existing confusion was made worse by the recent attempt to transplant to America the European type of conservatism, which, being alien to the American tradition, has acquired a somewhat odd character. And some time before this, American radicals and socialists began calling themselves "liberals." I will nevertheless continue for the moment to describe as liberal the position which I hold and which I believe differs as much from true conservatism as from socialism. Let me say at once, however, that I do so with increasing misgivings, and I shall later have to consider what would be the appropriate name for the party of liberty. The reason for this is not only that the term "liberal" in the United States is the cause of constant misunderstandings today, but also that in Europe the predominant type of rationalistic liberalism has long been one of the pacemakers of socialism.

Let me now state what seems to me the decisive objection to any conservatism which deserves to be called such. It is that by its very nature it cannot offer an alternative to the direction in which we are moving. It may succeed by its resistance to current tendencies in slowing down undesirable developments, but, since it does not indicate another direction, it cannot prevent their continuance. It has, for this reason, invariably been the fate of conservatism to be dragged along a path not of its own choosing. The tug of war between conservatives and progressives can only affect the speed, not the direction, of contemporary developments. But, though there is need for a "brake on the vehicle of progress,"[3] I personally cannot be content with simply helping to apply the brake. What the liberal must ask, first of all, is not how fast or how far we should move, but where we should move. In fact, he differs much more from the collectivist radical of today than does the conservative. While the last generally holds merely a mild and moderate version of the prejudices of his time, the liberal today must more positively oppose some of the basic conceptions which most conservatives share with the socialists.

II

The picture generally given of the relative position of the three parties does more to obscure than to elucidate their true relations. They are usually represented as different positions on a line, with the socialists on the left, the conservatives on the right, and the liberals somewhere in the middle. Nothing could be more misleading. If we want a diagram, it would be more appropriate to arrange them in a triangle with the conservatives occupying one corner, with the socialists pulling towards the second and the liberals towards the third. But, as the socialists have for a long time been able to pull harder, the conservatives have tended to follow the socialist rather than the liberal direction and have adopted at appropriate intervals of time those ideas made respectable by radical propaganda. It has been regularly the conservatives who have compromised with socialism and stolen its thunder. Advocates of the Middle Way,[4] with no goal of their own, conservatives have been guided by the belief that the truth must lie somewhere between the extremes—with the result that they have shifted their position every time a more extreme movement appeared on either wing.

The position which can be rightly described as conservative at any time depends, therefore, on the direction of existing tendencies. Since the development during the last decades has been generally in a socialist direction, it may seem that both conservatives and liberals have been mainly intent on retarding that movement. But the main point about liberalism is that it wants to go elsewhere, not to stand still. Though today the contrary impression may sometimes be caused by the fact that there was a time when liberalism was more widely accepted and some of its objectives closer to being achieved, it has never been a backward-looking doctrine. There has never been a time when liberal ideals were fully realized and when liberalism did not look forward to further improvement of institutions. Liberalism is not averse to evolution and change; and where spontaneous change has been smothered by government control, it wants a great deal of change of policy. So far as much of current governmental action is concerned, there is in the present world very little reason for the liberal to wish to preserve things as they are. It would seem to the liberal, indeed, that what is most urgently needed in most parts of the world is a thorough sweeping away of the obstacles to free growth.

This difference between liberalism and conservatism must not be obscured by the fact that in the United States it is still possible to defend individual liberty by defending long-established institutions. To the liberal they are valuable not mainly because they are long-established or because they are American but because they correspond to the ideals which he cherishes.

III

Before I consider the main points on which the liberal attitude is sharply opposed to the conservative one, I ought to stress that there is much that the liberal might with advantage have learned from the work of some conservative thinkers. To their loving and reverential study of the value of grown institutions we owe (at least outside the field of economics) some profound insights which are real contributions to our understanding of a free society. However reactionary in politics such figures as Coleridge, Bonald, De Maistre, Justus Möser, or Donoso Cortès may have been, they did show an understanding of the meaning of spontaneously grown institutions such as language, law, morals, and conventions that anticipated modern scientific approaches and from which the liberals might have profited. But the admiration of the conservatives for free growth generally applies only to the past. They typically lack the courage to welcome the same undesigned change from which new tools of human endeavors will emerge.

This brings me to the first point on which the conservative and the liberal dispositions differ radically. As has often been acknowledged by conservative writers, one of the fundamental traits of the conservative attitude is a fear of change, a timid distrust of the new as such,[5] while the liberal position is based on courage and confidence, on a preparedness to let change run its course even if we cannot predict where it will lead. There would not be much to object to if the conservatives merely disliked too rapid change in institutions and public policy; here the case for caution and slow process is indeed strong. But the conservatives are inclined to use the powers of government to prevent change or to limit its rate to whatever appeals to the more timid mind. In looking forward, they lack the faith in the spontaneous forces of adjustment which makes the liberal accept changes without apprehension, even though he does not know how the necessary adaptations will be brought about. It is, indeed, part of the liberal attitude to assume that, especially in the economic field, the self-regulating forces of the market will somehow bring about the required adjustments to new conditions, although no one can foretell how they will do this in a particular instance. There is perhaps no single factor contributing so much to people's frequent reluctance to let the market work as their inability to conceive how some necessary balance, between demand and supply, between exports and imports, or the like, will be brought about without deliberate control. The conservative feels safe and content only if he is assured that some higher wisdom watches and supervises change, only if he knows that some authority is charged with keeping the change "orderly."

This fear of trusting uncontrolled social forces is closely related to two other characteristics of conservatism: its fondness for authority and its lack of understanding of economic forces. Since it distrusts both abstract theories and general principles,[6] it neither understands those spontaneous forces on which a policy of freedom relies nor possesses a basis for formulating principles of policy. Order appears to the conservatives as the result of the continuous attention of authority, which, for this purpose, must be allowed to do what is required by the particular circumstances and not be tied to rigid rule. A commitment to principles presupposes an understanding of the general forces by which the efforts of society are co-ordinated, but it is such a theory of society and especially of the economic mechanism that conservatism conspicuously lacks. So unproductive has conservatism been in producing a general conception of how a social order is maintained that its modern votaries, in trying to construct a theoretical foundation, invariably find themselves appealing almost exclusively to authors who regarded themselves as liberal. Macaulay, Tocqueville, Lord Acton, and Lecky certainly considered themselves liberals, and with justice; and even Edmund Burke remained an Old Whig to the end and would have shuddered at the thought of being regarded as a Tory.

Let me return, however, to the main point, which is the characteristic complacency of the conservative towards the action of established authority and his prime concern that this authority be not weakened rather than that its power be kept within bounds. This is difficult to reconcile with the preservation of liberty. In general, it can probably be said that the conservative does not object to coercion or arbitrary power so long as it is used for what he regards as the right purposes. He believes that if government is in the hands of decent men, it ought not be too much restricted by rigid rules. Since he is essentially opportunist and lacks principles, his main hope must be that the wise and the good will rule—not merely by example, as we all must wish, but by authority given to them and enforced by them.[7] Like the socialist, he is less concerned with the problem of how the powers of government should be limited than with that of who wields them; and, like the socialist, he regards himself as entitled to force the value he holds on other people.

When I say that the conservative lacks principles, I do not mean to suggest that he lacks moral conviction. The typical conservative is indeed usually a man of very strong moral convictions. What I mean is that he has no political principles which enable him to work with people whose moral values differ from his own for a political order in which both can obey their convictions. It is the recognition of such principles that permits the coexistence of different sets of values, that makes it possible to build a peaceful society with a minimum of force. The acceptance of such principles means that we agree to tolerate much that we dislike. There are many values of the conservative which appeal to me more than those of the socialists; yet for a liberal the importance he personally attaches to specific goals is not sufficient justification for forcing others to serve them. I have little doubt that some of my conservative friends will be shocked by what they will regard as "concessions" to modern views that I have made in Part III of *The Constitution of Liberty*. But, though I may dislike some of the measures concerned as much as they do and might vote against them, I know of no general principles to which I could appeal to persuade those of a different view that those measures are not permissible in the general kind of society which we both desire. To live and work successfully with others requires more than faithfulness to one's concrete aims. It requires an intellectual commitment to a type of order in which, even on issues which to one are fundamental, others are allowed to pursue different ends.

It is for this reason that to the liberal neither moral nor religious ideals are proper objects of coercion, while both conservatives and socialists recognize no such limits. I sometimes feel that the most conspicuous attribute of liberalism that distinguishes it as much from conservatism as from socialism is the view that moral beliefs concerning matters of conduct which do not directly interfere with the protected sphere of other persons do not justify coercion. This may also explain why it seems to be so much easier for the repentant socialist to find a new spiritual home in the conservative fold than in the liberal.

In the last resort, the conservative position rests on the belief that in any society there are recognizably superior persons whose inherited standards and values and position ought to be protected and who should have a greater influence on public affairs than others. The liberal, of course, does not deny that there are some superior people—he is not an egalitarian—but he denies that anyone has authority to decide who these superior people are. While the conservative inclines to defend a particular established hierarchy and wishes authority to protect the status of those whom he values, the liberal feels that no respect for established values can justify the resort to privilege or monopoly or any other coercive power of the state in order to shelter such people against the forces of economic change. Though he is fully aware of the important role that cultural and intellectual elites have played in the evolution of civilization, he also believes that these elites have to prove themselves by their capacity to maintain their position under the same rules that apply to all others.

Closely connected with this is the usual attitude of the conservative to democracy. I have made it clear that I do not regard majority rule as an end but merely as a means, or perhaps even as the least evil of those forms of government from which we have to choose. But I believe that the conservatives deceive themselves when they blame the evils of our time on democracy. The chief evil is unlimited government, and nobody is qualified to wield unlimited power.[8] The powers which modern democracy possesses would be even more intolerable in the hands of some small elite.

Admittedly, it was only when power came into the hands of

the majority that further limitation of the power of government was thought unnecessary. In this sense democracy and unlimited government are connected. But it is not democracy but unlimited government that is objectionable, and I do not see why the people should not learn to limit the scope of majority rule as well as that of any other form of government. At any rate, the advantages of democracy as a method of peaceful change and of political education seem to be so great compared with those of any other system that I can have no sympathy with the antidemocratic strain of conservatism. It is not who governs but what government is entitled to do that seems to me the essential problem.

That the conservative opposition to too much government control is not a matter of principle but is concerned with the particular aims of government is clearly shown in the economic sphere. Conservatives usually oppose collectivist and directivist measures in the industrial field, and here the liberal will often find allies in them. But at the same time conservatives are usually protectionists and have frequently supported socialist measures in agriculture. Indeed, though the restrictions which exist today in industry and commerce are mainly the result of socialist views, the equally important restrictions in agriculture were usually introduced by conservatives at an even earlier date. And in their efforts to discredit free enterprise many conservative leaders have vied with the socialists.[9]

IV

I have already referred to the differences between conservatism and liberalism in the purely intellectual field, but I must return to them because the characteristic conservative attitude here not only is a serious weakness of conservatism but tends to harm any cause which allies itself with it. Conservatives feel instinctively that it is new ideas more than anything else that cause change. But, from its point of view rightly, conservatism fears new ideas because it has no distinctive principles of its own to oppose to them; and, by its distrust of theory and its lack of imagination concerning anything except that which experience has already proved, it deprives itself of the weapons needed in the struggle of ideas. Unlike liberalism with its fundamental belief in the long-range power of ideas, conservatism is bound by the stock of ideas inherited at a given time. And since it does not really believe in the power of argument, its last resort is generally a claim to superior wisdom, based on some self-arrogated superior quality.

This difference shows itself most clearly in the different attitudes of the two traditions to the advance of knowledge. Though the liberal certainly does not regard all change as progress, he does regard the advance of knowledge as one of the chief aims of human effort and expects from it the gradual solution of such problems and difficulties as we can hope to solve. Without preferring the new merely because it is new, the liberal is aware that it is of the essence of human achievement that it produces something new; and he is prepared to come to terms with new knowledge, whether he likes its immediate effects or not.

Personally, I find that the most objectionable feature of the conservative attitude is its propensity to reject well-substantiated new knowledge because it dislikes some of the consequences which seem to follow from it—or, to put it bluntly, its obscurantism. I will not deny that scientists as much as others are given to fads and fashions and that we have much reason to be cautious in accepting the conclusions that they draw from their latest theories. But the reasons for our reluctance must themselves be rational and must be kept separate from our regret that the new theories upset our cherished beliefs. I can have little patience with those who oppose, for instance, the theory of evolution or what are called "mechanistic" explanations of the phenomena of life simply because of certain moral consequences which at first seem to follow from these theories, and still less with those who regard it as irreverent or impious to ask certain questions at all. By refusing to face the facts, the conservative only weakens his own position. Frequently the conclusions which rationalist presumption draws from new scientific insights do not at all follow from them. But only by actively taking part in the elaboration of the consequences of new discoveries do we learn whether or not they fit into our world picture and, if so, how. Should our moral beliefs really prove to be dependent on factual assumptions shown to be incorrect, it would be hardly moral to defend them by refusing to acknowledge facts.

Connected with the conservative distrust of the new and the strange is its hostility to internationalism and its proneness to a strident nationalism. Here is another source of its weakness in the struggle of ideas. It cannot alter the fact that the ideas which are changing our civilization respect no boundaries. But refusal to acquaint one's self with new ideas merely deprives one of the power of effectively countering them when necessary. The growth of ideas is an international process, and only those who fully take part in the discussion will be able to exercise a significant influence. It is no real argument to say that an idea is un-American, un-British, or un-German, nor is a mistaken or vicious ideal better for having been conceived by one of our compatriots.

A great deal more might be said about the close connection between conservatism and nationalism, but I shall not dwell on this point because it may be felt that my personal position makes me unable to sympathize with any form of nationalism. I will merely add that it is this nationalistic bias which frequently provides the bridge from conservatism to collectivism: to think in terms of "our" industry or resource is only a short step away from demanding that these national assets be directed in the national interest. But in this respect the Continental liberalism which derives from the French Revolution is little better than conservatism. I need hardly say that nationalism of this sort is something very different from patriotism and that an aversion to nationalism is fully compatible with a deep attachment to national traditions. But the fact that I prefer and feel reverence for some of the traditions of my society need not be the cause of hostility to what is strange and different.

Only at first does it seem paradoxical that the anti-internationalism of the conservative is so frequently associated with imperialism. But the more a person dislikes the strange and thinks his own ways superior, the more he tends to regard it as his mission to "civilize" others[10]—not by the voluntary and unhampered intercourse which the liberal favors, but by bringing them the blessings of efficient government. It is significant that here again we frequently find the conservatives joining hands with the socialists against the liberals—not only in England, where the Webbs and their Fabians were outspoken imperialists, or in Germany, where state socialism and colonial expansionism went together and found the support of the same group of "socialists of the chair," but also in the United States, where even at the time of the first Roosevelt it could be observed: "the Jingoes and the Social Reformers have gotten together; and have formed a political party, which threat-

ened to capture the Government and use it for their program of
Caesaristic paternalism, a danger which now seems to have been
averted only by the other parties having adopted their program
in a somewhat milder degree and form."[11]

V

There is one respect, however, in which there is justification
for saying that the liberal occupies a position midway between the
socialist and the conservative: he is as far from the crude rationalism of the socialist, who wants to reconstruct all social institutions
according to a pattern prescribed by his individual reason, as from
the mysticism to which the conservative so frequently has to resort. What I have described as the liberal position shares with
conservatism a distrust of reason to the extent that the liberal is
very much aware that we do not know all the answers and that
he is not sure that the answers he has are certainly the right ones
or even that we can find all the answers. He also does not disdain
to seek assistance from whatever non-rational institutions or habits
have proved their worth. The liberal differs from the conservative
in his willingness to face this ignorance and to admit how little we
know, without claiming the authority of supernatural sources of
knowledge where his reason fails him. It has to be admitted that
in some respects the liberal is fundamentally a skeptic[12]—but it
seems to require a certain degree of diffidence to let others seek
their happiness in their own fashion and to adhere consistently to
that tolerance which is an essential characteristic of liberalism.

There is no reason why this need mean an absence of religious
belief on the part of the liberal. Unlike the rationalism of the
French Revolution, true liberalism has no quarrel with religion,
and I can only deplore the militant and essentially illiberal anti-
religionism which animated so much of nineteenth-century Continental liberalism. That this is not essential to liberalism is clearly
shown by its English ancestors, the Old Whigs, who, if anything,
were much too closely allied with a particular religious belief.
What distinguishes the liberal from the conservative here is that,
however profound his own spiritual beliefs, he will never regard
himself as entitled to impose them on others and that for him the
spiritual and the temporal are different spheres which ought not
to be confused.

VI

What I have said should suffice to explain why I do not regard myself as a conservative. Many people will feel, however, that the position which emerges is hardly what they used to call "liberal." I must, therefore, now face the question of whether this name is today the appropriate name for the party of liberty. I have already indicated that, though I have all my life described myself as a liberal, I have done so more recently with increasing misgivings— not only because in the United States this term constantly gives rise to misunderstanding, but also because I have become more and more aware of the great gulf that exists between my position and the rationalistic Continental liberalism or even the English liberalism of the utilitarians.

If liberalism still meant what it meant to an English historian who in 1827 could speak of the revolution of 1688 as "the triumph of those principles which in the language of the present day are denominated liberal or constitutional,"[13] or if one could still, with Lord Acton, speak of Burke, Macaulay, and Gladstone as the three greatest liberals, or if one could still, with Harold Laski, regard Tocqueville and Lord Acton as "the essential liberals of the nineteenth century,"[14] I should indeed be only too proud to describe myself by that name. But, much as I am tempted to call their liberalism true liberalism, I must recognize that the majority of Continental liberals stood for ideas to which these men were strongly opposed, and that they were led more by a desire to impose upon the world a preconceived rational pattern than to provide opportunity for free growth. The same is largely true of what has called itself Liberalism in England at least since the time of Lloyd George.

It is thus necessary to recognize that what I have called "liberalism" has little to do with any political movement that goes under that name today. It is also questionable whether the historical associations which that name carries today are conducive to the success of any movement. Whether in these circumstances one ought to make an effort to rescue the term from what one feels is its misuse is a question on which opinions may well differ. I myself feel more and more that to use it without long explanations causes too much confusion and that as a label it has become more of a ballast than a source of strength.

In the United States, where it has become almost impossible to use "liberal" in the sense in which I have used it, the term "libertarian" has been used instead. It may be the answer; but for my part I find it singularly unattractive. For my taste it carries too much the flavor of a manufactured term and of a substitute. What I should want is a word which describes the party of life, the party that favors free growth and spontaneous evolution. But I have racked my brain unsuccessfully to find a descriptive term which commends itself.

VII

We should remember, however, that when the ideals which I have been trying to restate first began to spread through the Western world, the party which represented them had a generally recognized name. It was the ideals of the English Whigs that inspired what later came to be known as the liberal movement in the whole of Europe[15] and that provided the conceptions that the American colonists carried with them and which guided them in their struggle for independence and in the establishment of their constitution.[16] Indeed, until the character of this tradition was altered by the accretions due to the French Revolution, with its totalitarian democracy and socialist leanings, "Whig" was the name by which the party of liberty was generally known.

The name died in the country of its birth partly because for a time the principles for which it stood were no longer distinctive of a particular party, and partly because the men who bore the name did not remain true to those principles. The Whig parties of the nineteenth century, in both Britain and the United States, finally brought discredit to the name among the radicals. But it is still true that, since liberalism took the place of Whiggism only after the movement for liberty had absorbed the crude and militant rationalism of the French Revolution, and since our task must largely be to free that tradition from the overrationalistic, nationalistic, and socialistic influences which have intruded into it, Whiggism is historically the correct name for the ideas in which I believe. The more I learn about the evolution of ideas, the more I have become aware that I am simply an unrepentant Old Whig—with the stress on the "old."

To confess one's self an Old Whig does not mean, of course, that one wants to go back to where we were at the end of the seventeenth century. It has been one of my purposes in *The Constitution of Liberty* to show that the doctrines then first stated continued to grow and develop until about seventy or eighty years ago, even though they were no longer the chief aim of a distinct party. We have since learned much that should enable us to restate them in a more satisfactory and effective form. But, though they require restatement in the light of our present knowledge, the basic principles are still those of the Old Whigs. True, the later history of the party that bore that name has made some historians doubt whether there was a distinct body of Whig principles; but I can but agree with Lord Acton that, though some of "the patriarchs of the doctrine were the most infamous of men, the notion of a higher law above municipal codes, with which Whiggism began, is the supreme achievement of Englishmen and their bequest to the nation"[17]—and, we may add, to the world. It is the doctrine which is at the basis of the common tradition of the Anglo-Saxon countries. It is the doctrine from which Continental liberalism took what is valuable in it. It is the doctrine on which the American system of government is based. In its pure form it is represented in the United States, not by the radicalism of Jefferson, nor by the conservatism of Hamilton or even of John Adams, but by the ideas of James Madison, the "father of the Constitution."[18]

I do not know whether to revive that old name is practical politics. That to the mass of people, both in the Anglo-Saxon world and elsewhere, it is today probably a term without definite associations is perhaps more an advantage than a drawback. To those familiar with the history of ideas it is probably the only name that quite expresses what the tradition means. That, both for the genuine conservative and still more for the many socialists turned conservative, Whiggism is the name for their pet aversion shows a sound instinct on their part. It has been the name for the only set of ideals that has consistently opposed all arbitrary power.

VIII

It may well be asked whether the name really matters so much. In a country like the United States, which on the whole still has free institutions and where, therefore, the defense of the existing is often a defense of freedom, it might not make so much difference if the defenders of freedom call themselves conservatives, although even here the association with the conservatives by disposition will often be embarrassing. Even when men approve of the same arrangements, it must be asked whether they approve of them because they exist or because they are desirable in themselves. The common resistance to the collectivist tide should not be allowed to obscure the fact that the belief in integral freedom is based on an essentially forward-looking attitude and not on any nostalgic longing for the past or a romantic admiration for what has been.

The need for a clear distinction is absolutely imperative, however, where, as is true in many parts of Europe, the conservatives have already accepted a large part of the collectivist creed—a creed that has governed policy for so long that many of its institutions have come to be accepted as a matter of course and have become a source of pride to "conservative" parties who created them.[19] Here the believer in freedom cannot but conflict with that conservative and take an essentially radical position, directed against popular prejudices, entrenched positions, and firmly established privileges. Follies and abuses are no better for having long been established principles of policy.

Though *quieta non movere* may at times be a wise maxim for the statesman, it cannot satisfy the political philosopher. He may wish policy to proceed gingerly and not before public opinion is prepared to support it, but he cannot accept arrangements merely because current opinion sanctions them. In a world where the chief need is once more, as it was at the beginning of the nineteenth century, to free the process of spontaneous growth from the obstacles and encumbrances that human folly has erected, his hopes must rest on persuading and gaining the support of those who by disposition are "progressives," those who, though they may be seeking change in the wrong direction, are at least willing to examine critically the existing and to change it wherever necessary.

I hope I have not misled the reader by occasionally speaking of "party" when I was thinking of groups of men defending a set of intellectual and moral principles. Party politics of any one country has not been my concern. The question of how the principles I have tried to reconstruct by piecing together the broken fragments of a tradition can be translated into a program with mass appeal, the political philosopher must leave to "that insidious and crafty animal, vulgarly called a statesman or politician, whose councils are directed by the momentary fluctuations of affairs."[20] The task of the political philosopher can only be to influence public opinion, not to organize people for action. He will do so effectively only if he is not concerned with what is now politically possible but consistently defends the "general principles which are always the same."[21] In this sense I doubt whether there can be such a thing as a conservative political philosophy. Conservatism may often be a useful practical maxim, but it does not give us any guiding principles which can influence long-range developments.

The Prophetic View

CHAPTER SEVEN

Reason and the Restoration

of Tradition

STANLEY PARRY, C.S.C.

I THE PROBLEM

THE contemporary emergence of Liberals and conservatives is basically a consequence of the crisis in the internal order of Western civilization. The two positions constitute two radically different types of response to that crisis. In an earlier paper[1] I suggested the tragic possibility that both positions misunderstand the nature of the crisis, and consequently offer only irrelevant solutions to the problem of the day. The Liberal position, unfortunately, is incurably wrong and irrelevant. A correction of it would necessitate a rejection of fundamental Liberal premises about reason, society, and freedom. The conservative position, however, can be reformulated within its own premises so that it becomes relevant. This paper attempts such a restatement of one basic premise of conservatism: its characteristic insistence on the limits of reason.

The distinction between reason and tradition is certainly basic to conservatism. Yet this distinction, however relevant it may have been to the eighteenth-century problem, cannot cope with the great problem of the twentieth century. This distinction as it comes to us from earlier conservative thought is quite misleading; it directs attention to the wrong problems and limits conservatism to the negative function of criticism and objection. Of all the variants of conservatism, the Burkean comes closest to relevance. Reason operates effectively in its own right only when it moves within the context of a healthy tradition. But in Burke this leads only to a defense of tradition against rationalistic forms of reason. He never had cause to examine the principle of limitation from another aspect: What is the function of reason when the tradition is sick? When the tradition offers no context for reason, what then are the limits of reason? The Burkean formulation, therefore, is inadequate because it is an *ad hoc* formulation whose terms were dictated by the problem of defending tradition as yet healthy. In the contemporary world, most conservatives, overly impressed by the new rationalism of the Liberals, have been content to reassert Burke's principle of limitation. They have not, therefore, faced up to the problem raised by the dissolution of the tradition. Does the dissolution of tradition liberate reason as many moderns think? Has reason been given a new function in our day?

Hitherto the dominance of gnostic forms of reason has made the debate about reason difficult. Some important progress has been achieved by the analysis of gnostic or ideological movements. But the major import of this research has been to establish that in a crisis of civilization one of the forms of crisis is that of an excessive rationalism which closes the soul of man in upon itself. As yet the occasion has not risen for a discussion of the question whether in such a crisis issues can be met by reason healthily organized and utilized. Now, however, the clear emergence of an appeal to reason on the Right makes such a discussion possible. This conservative appeal to reason is quite moderate, non-ideological, rooted in metaphysical realism, and heavily weighted with natural-law theory. It is an appeal for a recovery of tradition through reason. It has the charm and attractiveness that goes with any program of positive problem solving.

However, in its own way it misses the mark even more than the modern Burkean appeal to tradition. On the positive side this conservative position has achieved awareness of the nature of the problem. On the negative side it has attempted to meet Liberal rationalism with a more valid formulation of reason's function, but one that accepts the Liberal assumption that reason is not only the highest but also the sole instrument with which man can face the problem of order. The Burkean intuition has been lost, probably because it is so inadequately formulated by the Traditionalists. Against the Traditionalist position, the appeal to tradition must be rejected because tradition does not exist effectively in our time. This new appeal to reason must be rejected precisely because reason becomes helpless when it has no context of tradition within which to operate. This latter objection constitutes the issue of the present discussion. Such a discussion is possible precisely because the new appeal to reason has been made in such a way as to obviate a long refutation of the very conception of reason on which it bases itself.

I assume the fact of a crisis in tradition. The problem is to understand why reason is unable to solve the problem of such a crisis. The solution of this problem leads us to a clarifying critique of the assumptions behind the new appeal to reason on the Right and to a consequent deepening and reformulation of the basis for distrusting reason. Through such a critique we can then advance to a positive position that is not only relevant but which incorporates into its solution the authentic intuitions of conservatism concerning reason.

The crisis in tradition can be met only by a religious response, one that recapitulates the compact experience that gives birth to civilization: the experience of "alienation" leading to a sense of transcendence in the context of "salvation." This is, in general, the Platonic response: the philosopher, too, is but a child of his civilization; the gods must give the city its truth if it is to have any at all. In particular, since ours is a Christian civilization, the only adequate response to our crisis is an authentic revitalization of divine revelation in the soul of every man. Reason's contribution to this process is negative. It must purge itself of the arrogance that is an integral part of the crisis of tradition itself and return to a humble questing in the real world of being for whatever wisdom it may be able to wrest from that world.

II MORAL REASON AS SUBJECTIVE

The radical inability of reason to solve the problem of a crisis in civilization rests essentially on the fact that in all moral reason there is a necessary element of subjectivity. As a result of this element, the methods of persuasion, the only ones available to reason, collapse with the disappearance of the social pre-conditions necessary for the process of persuasion. Since the basic pre-condition is a commonly accepted moral order, it follows almost by definition that in a collapse of tradition, i.e., of a commonly accepted moral order, reason becomes helpless. This is essentially the argument against the appeal to reason, even as it is made by the Right. As it stands, however, it needs a great deal of elaboration before its validity becomes apparent.

The elaboration must begin with a new appreciation of the subjective element in moral reason. The ancients were fully aware of this factor in reason and of its strategic position vis-à-vis the problem of social order. But in modern times this appreciation has been lost. The basic confusion begins with the rationalistic identification of reason with speculative reason alone. In moral theory this led to the discarding of moral judgments, as men usually make them, as pure pre-rational preferences without foundation in objective reality. Thereupon the problem of moral truth became a problem of discovering the "scientific" methods whereby truly objective knowledge about man could be gained. The ideal was to formulate moral principles apart from the insights of moral man.

Against this critique two defenses emerged. In the first phase, natural-law theorists responded by working out, with at times brilliant metaphysical insights, the ontological grounds of moral reason. The identification of being and oughtness was firmly established. The existence of nature and the function of the "tendencies of nature" were grounded in solid analysis. But in this preoccupation natural-law thought tended to neglect the other aspect of moral reason, its subjectivity. So, moral reason, almost by default, was treated as though it were not essentially different from speculative reason. In other words, the defense of objectivity did not properly question the assumption of univocal reason made by the rationalists.

The price paid for this neglect has been high. Natural-law theory tends to treat every problem of social order as a problem of truth alone. It neglects the aspect of the problem which the ancients considered so central: how is the truth to be given existence as the ordering principle in a society? The reason for this centrality seems clear. The subjectivity of moral knowledge raises no problem *about* truth, but it is the central element in the problem of the *social existence* of truth.

In the second phase of the defense of moral reason, this neglect of subjectivity is being corrected. First, a vigorous critique of "scientism" in the moral sciences has been set in motion by Eric Voegelin, Leo Strauss, and many others. The dialectic of this critique stresses the true character of moral reason as having its own grounds and processes for achieving truth through a valid subjectivity. Secondly, there is a return to the ancients, especially to Plato, for a positive redevelopment of a subjectivity-conscious theory of moral knowledge. Especially important is the developing application of this theory to problems of social order within the context of a crisis of order in society. The development, however, is not yet complete. Natural-law theorists still tend to be wary of approaches based on the assertion of subjectivity. And because of this, many of them are not yet fully aware of the radical inability of reason to cope with problems of basic order. It is this point which must now be made.

The idea that moral knowledge has a subjective element derives from the fact that the knowing subject is himself a part of the moral object known at the moment of moral judgment. Because of this, the condition of the knower deeply affects the content of the moral judgment made. Judgment about right action is not rooted in knowledge about some abstract nature of man. At the moment of judgment it is a judgment about the concrete nature of the one making it. The concrete nature, moreover, is not some static, unchanging object of knowledge; it is a dynamic "locus of intelligible necessity" whose tendencies have already been extensively developed or distorted by the entire prior life of the agent. The radical consequence of this condition is that for every man the objective moral order available for his judgment is one which he himself has helped to build. Every man has formed the primitive nature originally his into something in accord with, or against, the inner tendencies of that nature. And what is there is truly there whether it is good or evil. And whatever is there is the only reality available when a moral judgment is to be made. In the inner moral world man can construct realities that are not morally true. Thus moral knowledge is acquired by a moral agent whose act affects his ability to know rightly, because his every act specifies the nature in and through which he perceives reality.

When a Glaucon looks into himself and sees a basic preference for evil, or when a Nietzsche sees only a will to power, these men see the truth about themselves. For their natures have been morally deformed. When Aristotle's *spoudaios* looks into himself and sees the order of the *Ethics*, he perceives both the truth about himself and moral truth. In our confused age the question is asked: how do we know whose reason is right? The question assumes some third reality as standard, or else triumphantly proves the relativity of moral knowledge because of the lack of standard. But there is no such third reality. The seemingly circular answer, the reason of the *spoudaios* is right because he lives rightly, is the only answer possible. For it alone combines the recognition of an objective order, existing primitively as tendencies to action, with the further recognition that every man lives either developed or distorted with regard to those basic ontological imperatives. Every man builds his own moral world. If it is a good one, he enlarges his horizons; if it is evil, he traps and blinds himself. But in either case, it is the only world he truly knows. The good man can recognize evil as a defect, but the evil man cannot recognize good.

From this basic condition certain consequences flow which are central to the argument about the limits of reason. On a practical level, we can easily explain why charges of bad will, or "refusal to recognize," are frequently made when debate centers around moral issues. If two men with notably different moral natures discuss a moral point, not much progress is made. They are reasoning from two different realities; consequently, for each the arguments of the other are unreal. When this is not recognized, each can only think that the other really sees the truth of the argument but refuses to admit it. This condition can be generalized. Between a good man and an evil man, or between men evil in different ways, no communication can exist in the moral order. Since each lives in his own reality, each can find in it the evidence only for his own ideas. Thus no argument based on another reality can possibly have any persuasiveness.

Aristotle saw quite clearly that this quality of moral reason has major implications for social order. He saw that the process of persuasion can work perfectly only in a society of *spoudaioi*. In proportion as men are imperfect they multiply exclusive realities for themselves. And common action derives more and more from force, the necessary substitute for persuasion when order is essential. In like manner basic differences in conviction about justice are traced to prior differences in the way men understand their own natures, i.e., what they have made of themselves. Plato, too, saw the impossibility of communication between good and deformed men. The people of the cave will always kill the philosopher king because he questions the order which they know to be true. This, of course, does not hold for speculative reason where the perception of truth is not tied into the moral condition of the knower as object. Here communication is always possible. But speculative reason cannot discover moral truth. Only moral reason can do that. And the necessary subjectivity of moral reason blocks communication between moral reasons rooted in different moral realities.

From this blocking of effective communication, there follows a pragmatic equality of moral judgment. The equality is, of course, entirely pragmatic. For moral judgment can be tested for truth and true judgments are superior to false ones. But this does not change the effective practical consequence, that every man must hold his judgment to be equal to, i.e., as good as, every other man's, for each has access only to the reality of his own moral world which, since it is the only reality he knows, must be treated as exclusively real. Judgments rooted in it can be compared to one another for truth as against the reality; and so among men who know or live in the same moral world, a structuring of men as superior or inferior is possible. This is true also among men whose moral world is evil in the same way. But in practice and for purposes of social action, no comparisons are possible between judgments rooted in different moral worlds. (In all this, of course, the case of a man acting against his own moral judgment is a special case.)

Thus we have come to one of the basic limits on moral reason: it cannot communicate with another moral reason that differs radically from it. The nature of this limitation should be carefully noted. It is not the limitation usually identified by conservative Traditionalists. They stress the difficulty of achieving wisdom apart from one's tradition. They argue basically that since tradition is the accumulated and tested wisdom of generations it is superior to the wisdom an individual can garner by himself. And in the case of a difference between the individual and the tradition, a *prima facie* case exists in favor of the tradition. There is implied here a limitation of reason, but not one that is spelled out in any way. No theoretical ground is developed for it. But even if we see in this position an implied theory about the limits of the power of reason to achieve wisdom, there is still no similarity between this position and the one developed here. The latter is not concerned at all with the boundaries of the truth available to moral reason. It is concerned exclusively with the limits of communication among the reasons of individual men. Likewise, the limit here identified differs basically from the limits of reason identified by the classical economic thinkers. They are preoccupied with an almost technical limit to practical reason, the inability of the human mind to understand and handle the infinite number of variables that go to make up a free economy. Consequently, it is held, any rational planning of economic activity will either suppress these variables, and so freedom, or else it will create disorder by its neglect of variables. The limit central to the argument of this paper, however, is not concerned with the power of the mind to know, but with its ability to communicate under certain conditions with other minds.

III TRADITION IN CRISIS

If these actually are the limiting conditions under which moral truth can be communicated effectively by reason, one might wonder how it can be communicated at all. Given the great divergences in the moral condition of men, it would seem that the conditions for communication are seldom present. The solution to this difficulty is found in the idea of civilization or, to use the term that stresses the moral content of civilization, tradition. It is the function of a civilization to educate its members to openness to its tradition, and so to openness and communication with each other. This point requires some development because the key stage in the unfolding argument is found precisely in the thesis that a crisis in tradition destroys this openness and so introduces a moral atomization within which reason finds communication to be impossible. The issue is not the general one, whether reason can persuade concerning moral truth. The issue is a highly specific one, whether reason can so persuade when persuasion is absolutely necessary, when, that is, tradition needs to be reconstituted after a period of crisis.

One of the ancient insights into the nature of tradition is expressed in the saying that "the laws, not the walls, make the city." The ancients also were well aware that the ambit of the city so understood constitutes the moral universe of the citizen. Moral life can be lived only within the confines of an ordered society. More than this, an ordered society, a civilization, having a common tradition, is in its basic significance nothing more than the organized moral life of the members. (Our vast technology, the massiveness of our science, and the grotesque consequences of its practical applications conceal the essentially human and therefore moral nature of a civilization from us.) We can from this point of view define a civilization as a system of intersubjective relations among the members of a multitude. Here one is tempted to cite the famous passage of Burke to the effect that society is a partnership in all of life. For if we examine any civilization in its period of health we find it to be rooted in a shared view of man's meaning and destiny. We find basic to it expectations of how men behave, agreement about the noble and ignoble, consensus about justice. In other words, in all these elements which have an essentially subjective dimension in their perception, we find agreement, communication, discourse.

We find debate also, it is true, and disagreement about specific interpretations of principle. And any society will have its loose ends: those who live outside the walls while remaining in the city. These peripheral events are irrelevant. The essential thing is that civilization is a system based on the communication of inner perceptions of the truth about man. Thus a common tradition enables men who differ widely as to actual moral achievement to live a life in common. The shared principles structure the community. The structuring is publicly organized, and normally is established by processes whose sanction lies in the fact that they do implement the view of the good held to be true by all. We can say, in brief, that a civilization exists in the first instance when a multitude of natures are open to each other for communication on the level of moral perception. Where natures are closed to each other, there is no civilization. It has fallen out of existence, even though the massive exoskeleton of buildings and technology still exists. A tradition exists as the ordering principle of a multitude precisely when it exists in the soul of each member and constitutes thereby the opening from each to every other soul. If there is no such opening, there is no tradition, even though the symbols of the tradition continue to exist and receive a formalized recognition.

This communication of moral truth through a common tradition does not meet the difficulty raised above in the case of moral reason; for a tradition is not rooted in rational speculation concerning the nature of men. Here again rationalistic speculation about the irrational in society requires a caution. Tradition constitutes the truth that the members of a society hold about man, God, and the world. It is held in a rational way. And many members of the society spend their lives analyzing that truth, in the process constructing impressive philosophical and theological systems. Within the tradition reason roams the avenues of speculation freely and with fruitful results. But the organizing principle of the tradition, its root perception, is held by way of belief, of faith, rather than by way of a ratiocinative establishment of truth.

Voegelin calls this the original compact experience that constitutes a people in the first instance and is the element of unity during the entire history of that people. It is a common sharing in this compact experience that opens the members to one another. The structuring of the society results to the degree to which the members experience this organizing belief, so that men can persuade one another concerning good and evil by argumentation which presupposes and relates to the compact experience. We are not concerned here to prove that this is so. For this we rely on the extensive work of men like Voegelin, Eliade, Wilson, Frankfurt, and others. We are concerned here to identify as precisely as possible the relation between compact experience, unfolding tradition, and communication.

If we examine the compact experience we find that it is, in its essential nature, a religious experience. Men hold it as a revelation about the truth, not as a discovery of truth in the rational sense of that term. The work of Voegelin on the concept of compact experience constitutes an interesting specification of the more general observation of Dawson that every great civilization is based on a religion. Further work on the history of religion has uncovered a vast quantity of information about the nature of this original and, we might say, constitutive compact experience. Certainly the appearance of the religious mind does not of itself constitute the emergence of civilization. Neolithic man also was religious. Here we are in the area of unproven speculation, but one can surmise that the religion of neolithic man was a part of his general movement within the rhythms of nature. And one might also surmise from the documents available that the characteristic religious experience that founds civilization occurs when men in the presence of threats from nature seek more active co-operation with the transcendent. Men then see things in terms of transcendent intention, of beginning and end, and therefore in terms of meaning and purpose in human life. Within this context they can then do something about salvation, whatever that may mean to a particular people.

We have here the foundation of any true idea of freedom: man's power to contribute to the divine purpose of his existence, man's power to co-operate with the divine. Thus the motivating experience contains in germ all the moral views that will develop as the civilization grows. Within the civilization moral discourse on any level will be persuasive in proportion as it relates itself to an application of this generally accepted compact experience. With regard to the moral nature of man, the truth about man is held as a truth about the divine purpose in making man.

Here again a distinction must be made. Human nature is certainly knowable by moral reason. In a healthy society moral reason can discover a great deal of natural law from rational reflection. In principle we can admit that this kind of knowledge is possible even in the context of a disrupted tradition. The point is that in the latter case, the one at issue, such knowledge is not communicable. At least it cannot be the basis for the re-establishment of a tradition. The point could be argued simply on the basis that a tradition is not constituted by this type of knowledge in the first place. But this would neglect the point of the radical inability of moral reason, because of its nature, to establish such a reconstruction.

The compact experience, in contrast to the concepts of moral reason, is communicable precisely because it is not rooted in persuasive rational argument. Its sanction is not derived from the reasonableness of its explanation but from its origin in a revealing divinity. The truth presented demands assent precisely because it is divine. And assent is reasonable once such truth is seen in its origins, because such truth is self-validating. The persuasion here is both complex and simple. It is complex because it involves not only a content of truth, but more deeply an experience of personal helplessness before threat, of such a nature as to induce a sense of the need for salvation. But the persuasion is also simple, for it appeals to experience rather than prior premises, and it offers a clear resolution of the problem on which it is based, a resolution that can be simple or highly elaborate, depending on the capacity of the individual. There is no need for persuasion concerning the truths of the specific elements of the resolution. By their nature these are mysterious and can be expressed only in symbols and myths. It is necessary only that the religious world-view be coherent as a whole. *Credo ut intelligam* is the only possible response to this body of explanation in any civilization.

The motivating compact experience, then, is the root of tradition. Through it the tradition communicates itself by authoritative means. It depends, however, not on the authority of reason but on the authority of the superior source of its truth. On the psychological level, this superior source is valid as long as the individual experiences the basic need to which the compact experience arises as a resolution. Every civilization has as its normal basic process an educational system ordered to communicating this tradition in its authoritative form. Formal education in the truth is but one aspect of the process. The liturgical life of the community involves, in the healthy period of the civilization, a symbolic *reliving* of the motivating compact experience.

The massive acceptance of the tradition by the people and its status as a public order constitute an educative force for each member. So, the truth of the society forms the inner life of its members. The process seems so self-contained that one wonders how it could ever falter. But we know that it does falter. And when it does the civilization experiences a basic crisis in its existence. If we examine this crisis from the point of view of common life and the communication it presupposes, we find that basically the souls of the individual members close up and lose contact with one another. The idea may seem melodramatic, but this is the phenomenon already extensively analyzed in our own crisis. Oretga y Gassett analyzed it as the "mass mind," the mind out of communication with other minds. Other writers have called it by various names: Weil, "rootless," Guardini, "without horizons." Each writer has his own vocabulary and point of departure. All analyze the same basic atomization of the civilization.

How does this closing in of natures occur? What lies behind a crisis in tradition? The answer in terms of a specific history is not enough, for the crisis has occurred over and over in different civilizations with different histories. If we look to history we find great complexity and controversy. There is debate about the time of the crisis that touches close to the question of its nature. Some hold that the crisis is built into the origins of a civilization. A few, pushing this point, see the history of a people as a history of their decline. Against this position one must insist on the fact of the growth and flowering of a civilization. It is not all decline. The strong point of the position, however, lies in its insistence that the crisis involves the compact experience on which the civilization rests. Others identify the time of troubles in a society as occurring at specific points in its history. But usually even this position can trace the origin of the disturbing factors back to the beginning of the tradition. From both positions, then, it would seem that crisis and origin are closely related. A further difficulty in analyzing crisis historically is found in the problem of distinguishing a crisis in basic form from a period of what we might call ordinary trouble. It is not always easy to identify precisely when tradition ceases to be the organizing form of a civilization. The tradition does not simply disappear; it continues in the society. Many still adhere to it and are internally formed by it. But the tradition no longer gives the whole its form. It is not authoritative for the public order. And that order writhes with the effort of retaining an order in the absence of a form bolstered by moral sanctions.

Such complexities as these are avoided if we approach the problem analytically. There are dangers in this approach, for it results in schematic outlines of a vast social process. And this in turn implies certain necessities in historical development. One can, however, avoid any theory of historical inevitability in this matter by restricting the inquiry to an analysis of the principles involved. They need not run to term in any order. But we know that civilizations have crises, and it is a legitimate question to ask whether crisis is inherent in a civilization. To this question, it seems an affirmative answer must be given. By its very nature every tradition will experience crisis. Whether one must say that every civilization must fall is another question, one not relevant to this inquiry.

It has been suggested that a civilization is rooted in an originating experience. This experience has three principal components: (1) a view of reality from the standpoint of transcendent intention, (2) an experience of danger and salvation in the face of a threatening reality, (3) the experience of religion as conferring on man the power to co-operate with the divine to meet the danger in the matter of his own salvation. A crisis of tradition is in the first instance described as a crisis of form, i.e., of the ordering principles or world-view of the civilization. But this seems to be a consequence of something else, rather than an originating cause. The form is rooted and validated in the experience of threat and salvation. And it seems that here is the crucial element in crisis. Crisis occurs when men no longer experience the need to be rescued from some cosmic dilemma that defies their own meager resources. Thus we push the question back another step. Is this loss of the compact experience the ultimate source of crisis? It would seem that crisis is in fact caused by some such loss, for the tradition collapses without the support of the experience. But it would seem further that the loss of the experience itself is explicable in the light of the third element of the experience.

In the case of Christianity there are unique elements. Yet in general there is a close relationship between religion and man's organization of his temporal life on earth, that is, his civilization; they are dependent one upon the other. This interdependence gives rise to a characteristic problem, the problem of *hubris* or pride. It would seem that the principle of pride is latent in every civilization, just as by implication the experience of humility and helplessness marks the beginning of every civilization. In other words the conflict between pride and humility is not simply a phenomenon of individual psychology or sin; it is basically a social problem—a problem both of religion and civilization. The problem is organized into the very origins of civilization by the religious experience both of being saved and of receiving the power to contribute to one's own salvation.

In proportion as a civilization is viable it develops. As it masses its achievements, it realizes more success and gains greater security for its members and greater control over its own environment and destiny. Thus, by the very process of flowering, a civilization will tend to erode the sense of need and helplessness on which it is based. It begins to think of itself as autonomous, or—the word suddenly achieves new significance—it thinks of itself as sovereign. And herein lies its time of troubles. One need not yet have immediate recourse to strictly religious explanations and say that the divine punishes man for his impudence, although it is true, "Whom the gods destroy, they first make proud." The development is understandable as an inner disruption of a compact experience. As the sense of danger and threat from a cosmos, now nicely organized, declines, the tradition emerging from this same sense and experience begins to lose its relevance to the life man now thinks he has made for himself. Not only does its relevance weaken (there is no danger), but also its sanctions grow less persuasive and authoritative. The liturgy of salvation grows more formal as the society grows more powerful. Thus the motivating compact experience breaks up. From the original sense of co-operation with divine power, men move to the idea of independence. New freedoms emerge which are not of divine origin but of natural right. Finally, the religious explanation of reality is no longer persuasive precisely because the motivating sense of need and humility has been exorcised by success, and its place taken by a proud sense of autonomous existence. When this process is completed, the civilization is in absolute crisis. When a society is no longer ordered by a tradition growing out of a compact experience, then there is no society.

With regard to the capacity of reason alone to cope with this crisis, the issue now becomes complex. In a real sense the crisis is one of reason. It is so precisely because the major element in it is found in reason's emancipation from the religious base of the society. The crisis is one of rebellion. One is tempted to describe the cure as consisting in reason's return to a right relation to the ordering principles of the society. But such a description misses the point that the rebellion, when it reaches the point of crisis, is successful. The tradition has been destroyed as an ordering principle, and so there is no pre-existing order to which reason can return. The problem is one of reconstruction, not simply of repentance. The real issue the appeal to reason raises, even when moderately put, is whether reason can reconstruct the order, i.e., restore the principles of the tradition. It should be clear always that the question, in its final precision, is whether reason working from natural moral law can achieve the reconstruction in such a way as to restore principles to their public status.

This question can now be answered in the negative. The explanation can be found in the analysis of both reason and tradition. To begin with the latter, the problem of the reconstruction of tradition is not a problem of natural law at all. It is a problem first of all of the re-experiencing of a dependence on transcendent intention for the meaning of life. Secondly, it is a problem of re-incorporating the tradition, now with the new dimension of loss and recovery, into the motivating experience. The tradition is in its root a tradition of mystery, its symbols are transparent to transcendence but will not fit completely into the narrow confines of the human mind. Natural-law philosophy is a part of that tradition, but it is almost superstructure, if a suspect term may be used. It represents the achievement of reason, but after reason has been given horizons and a meaningful universe within which to work. In it there is no experience of threat but rather an experience of order; no problem of salvation, only a problem of rectitude of behavior.

But even if the problem of crisis could be defined as a natural-law problem, reason still would be unable to cope with it. The earlier analysis of the conditions reason requires for effective intrasubjective communication precludes this. The common ground for discussion and persuasion has disappeared. Not only that; even more compelling is the consideration that the tradition does not simply disintegrate, it is attacked by reason infected with *hubris* and in the possession of a fundamentally distorted view of reality. When the crisis becomes acute, it means that *hubris* is the dominating vice of the society. As Plato analyzed the phenomenon, the souls of men are turned upside down, become sick. As modern writers analyze it, reason begins constructing alternate realities to the one presupposed by the tradition; men project the sickness of their own souls into the objective order and propose to make it the public order. It might well be that even apart from the moral evil involved in this type of crisis, the simple breakdown of a common ground of discourse would invoke the limitation reason experiences because of its subjective aspect. But the argument need not depend on this more subtle and precise point. In a crisis the full force of the inability of reason to communicate over the gap between good and evil is invoked. Thus no appeal to natural law and natural goodness could ever work that radical therapy needed in the soul of man if order is to be re-established on the basis of tradition, or on any other basis. The appeal would not even cross the threshold of the listeners' conscience.

As a *coda* to this part of the analysis, certain precisions on the argument are necessary. As it stands now, there is a possibility that the distrust of reason here proposed could be interpreted as a kind of fideism. It should be kept clear that in the discussion of reason a basic distinction is always present. We can analyze the power of reason to know the nature of man, natural law, and all the other aspects of human life. And in this analysis, we can agree that reason on its own ground and by its own inherent capacities has this power to know. It is a far different thing, however, to inquire into the existential conditions, the conditions in a sense extrinsic to the faculty of reason itself, that are necessary if reason is to exercise its powers successfully. It has been suggested, first of all, that reason cannot effectively read the law of nature unless it operates in a man who as a whole is rightly ordered. This is in fact a rather ordinary and routine truth about the operation of moral reason, but one not frequently applied to the solution of problems in our day. It has been suggested, secondly, that the moral truth reason can acquire cannot be effectively communicated to another reason unless that reason is rightly structured with regard to truth. And this proposition is in fact a simple corollary to the first one. A mind closed to moral truth as it inheres in reality cannot acquire the truth simply by being told it.

Reason has indeed a role to play in the resolution of the crisis of tradition. But before it could be suggested, it has been necessary to insist on the rigorous limits of reason with regard to this problem. The emerging appeal to reason among men not infected with the *hubris* of rationalism makes this necessary. Only recently, Father Courtney Murray, in his book, *We Hold These Truths*, seems to say that since religion is too internally dissident to achieve unity in the West, we must look to the schools for the beginnings of a return to unity. This position, which is held by an increasing number of serious men, is precisely the one which must be rejected. To all intents and purposes, it lets the rationalists continue to define problems falsely. We cannot answer the gnostic revolt against tradition by distinguishing between reason rightly and reason wrongly understood. We must redefine the problem of unity itself against the background of a true analysis of the factors in it. Then, after proposing the fundamental solution, we can define with some precision the contribution reason can make to the basic process of reconstruction.

IV   THE ROLE OF REASON

From the above analysis it follows that the restoration of tradition can be achieved only through a re-experiencing of the compact experience that sanctions tradition. With regard to this experience, reason plays a secondary role. But it does not play an unimportant one. Its specific function can be briefly described as that of turning reason out from itself towards the real world of being. The analysis of the essential incommensurability between the nature of the compact experience and the capacity of reason indicates that reason can do no more than this. But an analysis of the nature of the *hubris* that closes the mind in upon itself will show that this, if done effectively, is a major contribution towards the solution of the problem of restoration.

There is no need here to recapitulate the extensive analysis of gnostic *hubris* already available in the works of De Lubac, Danielou, Strauss, Voegelin, and others. It is clear from this work that the essence of gnosticism is a closing of reason in upon itself, a shutting up of thought within a closed system of speculation that begins with a radical rejection of the real world of being. As Voegelin observes, this gives the gnostic complete control over being, which now no longer is treated as an objective substance, but simply as a subject of speculation which exercises no control over the mind of the speculator. The closing of the mind involved here has levels to it. First, the mind is alienated from transcendence as a consequence of rejecting the tradition of the society and the experience of transcendence on which it is based. Once this occurs a number of consequences follow. The chief of these is the need to re-establish some source of meaning in the immanent world. There appears the ancient satanic desire to be like God. The desire, however, is not a desire to emulate Him but to create Him to our own likeness and

image. Once this desire is realized and the transcendence im-
manentizes, the mind must necessarily close itself even to the immanent world. For that world will not submit easily to a strange
God. It is stubborn; it keeps refusing to fit into the new categories
of meaning. The solution is to disregard it, to silence it. Camus'
tragic observation that the "universe is silent" is more a commen-
tary on the closed mind than it is on the universe. But once the
universe is silenced, then the godlike mind can speak to it in words
of command.

It is this closing up of reason that reason can help undo. In a sense
reason must purge itself of pride by becoming aware of what has
happened to it. This alone will not resolve the crisis, but it is the
praeparatio, the *via negativa* for the resolution, if such words may
be used. Although no others seem to be adequate, the use of such
terms as pride, humility, repentance is perhaps unfortunate. For
the process through which reason is reopened to reality is not moral
at all in its essence. It does not consist in exhortations to humility,
castigations of pride, calls to repentance. Rather it consists in a
quiet scholarly analysis of the alienation of the mind from its proper
object: being. The moral problem exists because one of the basic
alienations has been that of morals from ontology. The essence of
relativism is found where morals are made a function of the unre-
lated mind. When the mind is opened again, again related to the
reality around it, the problem of morals will work itself out. The
process of liberation is essentially a philosophical and metaphysical
one; the terms of its development are dictated by the conditions of
the closed or imprisoned gnostic mind.

In the first place gnosticism must be analyzed as *hubris*. This
means that the typical gnostic set of a mind must be carefully
analyzed to discover the motivating experiences from which it
grows. This is not exactly to set up a philosophical dialogue with
gnosticism, but it constitutes, perhaps, a valid pre-philosophical
dialogue, one that is not rooted in the truth of premises, but in the
examination of raw experiences that underlie thought and ways of
thinking. From this analysis one can work out a comparison of experiences whose validity depends on the experiences themselves.
This is another way of saying that the Platonic critique of sophism
must be developed again in our day. The objective of such a critique
is not to refute a philosophical system but to apply therapy to a

state of mind. To continue in Platonic terms, the objective is to re-
constitute thought on the basis of a motivating experience of need
or *eros* whose fundamental impact is to push the mind outside
itself, where need is present, into the world of being in search of
the good that can satisfy the need. This therapy alone, if successfully applied, will cure intellectual *hubris*. For the essence of *hubris*
is that reason seeks to satisfy its need, not by a humble questing in
the real world but by an arrogant imposition of order on a reality
considered to be chaotic, or absurd, or stupid, or evil. The complexity of this comparison should be well noted. The gnostic experience is compared with the true philosophical experience, not
with the religious experience of threat and salvation. The entire
process proceeds in the order of reason, or, to use a Christian term,
the order of nature. The central problem of the religious experience
is not touched. The entire objective is to heal reason.

Here again the conservative appeal to reason within the natural-
law tradition fails to cope with the problem in its existential form.
Its basic error is to appeal to nature as the source of order, precisely
when ill minds perceive nature as the source of disorder, as the dilemma from which they must save themselves. A simple counter-
assertion cannot work the therapy needed. The real problem is to
move to a perception of nature as ordered by a transcendent purpose, whose intention can be learned only by a revelation from on
high. The real solution is to move from the threat of disordered nature to the perception of the right order that has been determined
by divine intention. Within Christianity and its current crisis, this
raises specific problems of the order of nature and of grace which
cannot be discussed here. But these problems make it all the more
inappropriate to appeal to a natural order for a solution. For centuries Western man has developed a secular or natural civilization
more and more at variance with the compact experience on which
Christianity is based. To attempt to go back to nature, to the beginning of the distortion and restate the conception of nature is to
deal with abstractions almost as unreal as the gnostic ones. We must
understand that whatever may be said of the inherent order of
nature, that order is latent; it must be actualized. The existential
fact is that nature, human nature, has become disordered. And its
disorder has produced characteristic threats to human existence.
Man has distorted nature, both his own and that of the inanimate

world. And this distortion is there as a fact. Nature itself now needs to be seen afresh as coming from the creative mind of God where the pattern of its proper development is actual as intention. Men must experience right order as obedience to God, not as his contribution to the actual ordering of reality. To do this, we must start with the experience of threat, the valid experience in the mind of the gnostic.

From this experience of threat, the analysis of nature must be projected in a way that opens the mind to transcendence, not in a way that focuses it on world-immanent forms, even on legitimate ones. Here the natural law tradition has a great deal to offer, but has not yet cast it into existentially relevant form. It must be remembered that natural-law theory can be formulated in world-immanent forms; the Stoic formulation is such. In our times there are deistic ideological forms of natural-right theory that actually constitute part of the attack on ordered society.

In general, it can be said that whenever natural-law theory preoccupies itself with moral problems, it tends to world immanence. In Christianity, Augustine felt compelled to levy a deep attack on the idea that nature is a norm of action. "When therefore man lives according to himself—that is, according to man, not according to God,—assuredly he lives according to a lie." (*City of God*, XIV, 4) In Aquinas, the natural-law theory primarily reveals the congruity between nature and grace. And Aquinas is quite clear that the norms of the good life are not derived from nature but from grace. The basic assertion of Christianity against the morality derived from reason alone is that not virtue but beatitude is the end of man; i.e., grace not nature reveals the ultimate intention of God with regard to man. To propose seriously natural standards as the basis for a reconstruction of tradition is to betray the tradition itself. To propose them tactically as the only possible ones in the situation where religious thought is unpersuasive, is to miss the point that the function of reason in this order is not to persuade man of the truth but to teach him to look at nature from a point of view that is open to further Christian explication.

It is clear, however, that the therapy must have something to do with the mind's attitude towards nature as well as towards transcendence. We cannot simply say that nature is ordered, because we must admit that *de facto* nature is deeply disordered. But the disorder does not reach into the existential grounds of nature. Here one can find nature still objectively open to transcendence, not closed in on itself. And a basis is found for viewing nature, not in itself, but in the light of the paradigm of nature in the Eternal Mind. This is the therapy that will free the mind. The intellectual process is essentially metaphysical. Its essence consists in the restoration of two fundamental ways of looking at being: the way of the analogy of being and the way of participation. These ways do not claim any existential order in nature; they have to do with the transcendent ground of nature's existence. Both concepts stress the contingent and dependent quality of finite being. They open the door to the experience of the ultimate inadequacy of any explanation of meaning that is rooted in finite existence itself. Moreover, they open the mind to the quest for meaning through a dialogue with transcendence where ultimate meaning resides. These concepts do not give answers to the problem of order. But the mind that considers reality within their context, is open to transcendent meaning. Moreover, they are compatible with, and even poignantly open to, the possibility that in the human order there may at any particular time be no meaning at all. In short, they open the mind to transcendence without closing it with the answers of natural reason.

At the root of a crisis in civilization we can find the key to the solution of the crisis. There is, first, a descent into disorder. The achievements of civilization erode the sense of need on which the civilization is based. This engenders prideful intentions, mainly that of living a world-immanent life, an autonomous life where reason is the source of meaning. The disorders that flow from this distorted endeavor at first produce a disordered response. In our civilization men began constructing gnostic systems within which self-contained meaning is found. These of course further exacerbate the disorders they hope to cure. Finally man is confronted with the hopelessness of his situation. At this crucial moment, which seems to be present now, the situation itself tends to invoke the motivating experience of a need for a salvation. Man becomes aware that autonomy is simply a form of alienation. He experiences the need to be re-united with some source of meaning. As yet the responses to this experience are under the influence of the gnostic experience, producing, on the whole, collectivist experience in salvation. It may very well be that the real issue in our time is whether reason can heal itself in its own order of operation—whether, that is, it can open itself to nature, which, however disordered it may be, is still grounded in transcendence. Man must again be able to say *intelligo ut credam*. The appeal to reason, therefore, is strategic. But it must be made with a well-defined understanding of what it can achieve. Reason can restore man to his proper condition in reality where the universe is not silent but speaks incessantly to him. And if man can again acquire the ability to listen, he may once again hear the "good news of great joy" that constitutes the essence of the Christian tradition.

Towards Accommodation

CHAPTER EIGHT

The Conservative Search for Identity

STEPHEN J. TONSOR

WRITING with all the Romantic appreciation of the dialectic of opposites and polarities, Walt Whitman said, "Do I contradict myself? Very well then I contradict myself, I am large, I contain multitudes." Whitman and the Romantics expressed eloquently and frequently the profound observation that the essence of life is polarity, opposition, contradiction, and that these, when integrated, harmonized, synthesized, their warring forces harnessed by the sovereign personality, institution, or society, enrich and energize the larger context of which they are a part.

However, the organic union of opposites is not today a central intellectual concern. "Things fall apart, the center cannot hold," wrote W. B. Yeats. The stern necessities of an age of ideology demand conformity, and, locked in his preconceptions, the Liberal intellectual is impotent to do more than mourn the passing of an age in which variety and the dialectic of opposites produced a rich and dynamic society. He desires movement but refuses to pay the price for movement; he desires nonconformity and creativity but refuses to tolerate the divergences of viewpoint and the frequent eccentricity which are the price of nonconformity. He wishes creativity but is uncomfortable with the messiness of failed experiments and failed lives which creativity produces. For the organic reconciliation of opposites, which is the measure of a healthy society, he has substituted the myth of "pluralism," the dream of a multitude of mutually exclusive and hostile social units and individuals which coexist, but which fail either to stimulate to action or to enrich the common group. It is a classical age but like all classical periods it is both static and weary. It would be false to assume that, unlike Liberal thought, conservative thought has avoided the spirit of the age and that it is broader, more inclusive, more dynamic and creative than the doctrinaire Liberalism which is its counterpart. The blunt truth is that most conservatives do not know what manner of men they are; they have no clear conception of the society they wish to create, have no organic relationship either to the present or the past, hold no grand design, entertain no enduring principles, and are responsible to no whole and healthy vision either of man or society. Their discourse consists of the platitudes of political criticism, and, however salutary and necessary this may be, it is neither a substitute for principle nor a guide for action.

The tendency of conservatism is to disintegration, for the centrifugal forces are much greater in it than in contemporary Liberalism. Liberalism is a body of coherent doctrine, deductively derived from a set of central propositions, while conservatism is a synthesis of contradictory principles, the principle of authority and the principle of freedom. These principles are ever held in precarious balance by individuals and by societies; the resolution of their forces is never final; their synthesis is never complete. The drive which they impart to society is in a measure the product of their instability.

If conservatives are finally to achieve the common agreement necessary to the establishment of both principle and party, they must reconcile themselves to the dialectic of freedom and authority and must capitalize on the values of their divided heritage. They can achieve this in no better way than through an exploration of the thought of Alexis de Tocqueville (1805-1859) and Lord Acton (1834-1902). Together their lives spanned the nineteenth century, and together they elaborated the soundest and most coherent modern body of conservative thought of which contemporary conservatives may avail themselves. They reconciled, in their lives and their thinking, authority and freedom; anticipated the modern world with all of its problems; and worked towards viable and optimistic solutions. They both stood near the center of power; they both mistrusted power and spoke repeatedly of its corrupting influence. Both were active in practical politics, but both were contemplative by nature, preferring the study of power to its exercise. Both were deeply religious men, but both stood near the edge of heresy. Both suspected the worst of human nature, but optimistically hoped for the best. Both were born to an aristocratic order which was in the process of dissolution, and both met the situation, not by reaction but rather by an attempt to understand and to assimilate themselves to the new social processes which were transforming Western society. Both were ethical thinkers of the highest order who would tolerate no concession of principle to practical politics. Both combined in their thought and in their lives such a devotion to both principle and freedom as ought to distinguish the contemporary conservative.

Not only singular personalities, but history itself by slow conjunction unites the opposites which men so often find in contradiction. Providence, which has its own purposes, disposes, and wise men conform themselves to a world whose ordering was only partially theirs. It is difficult, once man accepts the basic proposition of historical purpose, to couple with this acceptance the necessity of individual and collective action. It is all too easy to assume, as others in the past have, that faith and hope make an active charity unnecessary. But it is only through historical understanding, through action, and finally through faith in God's Providence that the reconciliation of opposites becomes possible. Lord Acton and De Tocqueville understood both the necessity of faith and hope and the necessity of immediate political action. Although both were pessimists about human nature, both were optimists largely because of their belief in an overriding Providence. Acton said, "Christ is risen on the world and fails not." Tocqueville wrote, "I cannot believe that the Creator made man to leave him in an endless struggle with the intellectual wretchedness that surrounds us. God destines a calmer and a more certain future to the communities of Europe. I am ignorant of his designs, but I shall not cease to believe in them because I cannot fathom them, and I had rather mistrust my own capacity than his justice."

But both Acton and Tocqueville recognized that if it is difficult to accept the necessity of action and understanding within the framework of a world ordered by Providence, it has been, for the past two and a half centuries, even more difficult to accept the concept of Providence itself. The attack upon Providence and purpose has been the distinguishing characteristic of modern society, the abandonment of hope and of value its singular mark. Whether in Voltaire's *Candide* or in the anti-rational and anti-Providential works of the Marquis de Sade, the general conception of a creative Providence which establishes purpose and imposes meaning upon the events of history was denied by the eighteenth century. What has been described as the "revolt against the eighteenth century" was well under way before the eighteenth century was half over. It was only incidentally a revolt against reason, but reason, too, was forced to abdicate its sway, once purpose had been banished. The era of nihilism and the totally absurd begins with a doubt as to the nature and purposes of God in history. The nineteenth-century attempts at the restoration of order, the restoration of value, the restoration of purpose, all revolved around the central problem of restoring meaning to history. Even Marxism is an attempt to restore purpose, to restore ends, to restore values to history. That it restores these to history without restoring Providence is the most telling reason for its failure. It is difficult enough to reconcile God's ways to man as they reveal themselves in the ambiguities, failures, and dilemmas of history; it is impossible to justify the course of dialectical materialism as it reveals itself in its subhuman and antihuman processes.

In order to escape from absurdity man must move into the realm of order, value, purpose, and belief. By the end of the eighteenth century this had become intellectually impossible except through an appeal to authority. At the social and the political level the appeal was to the authority of the established social and economic institutions; at the religious level the appeal to authority was an appeal to orthodoxy and especially to established religious forms and institutions. The moment was anti-revolutionary and anti-rationalistic; authority was to be re-established by restoration of the throne and the altar. But note that those who sought authority from the conservative side were unyielding pessimists. De Maistre, De Bonald, Metternich, all despaired both of human nature's and God's ability to produce a better world. Skepticism had broken through the barriers of rationality; the absurd had replaced the world of meaning and purpose, nihilism and the diabolical had replaced the world of value and of beauty. There is in *Les Soirées de Saint Petersbourg* of De Maistre a terrible echo of the violence, despair, and ugliness of the vision of the Marquis de Sade. "Don't you hear the earth crying for blood?" writes De Maistre, who then proceeds to paint the most terrible picture of the struggle of life against life depicted by any Western thinker. Darwin's picture of the struggle for survival is innocent because it is natural; De Maistre's is diabolical because the struggle is metaphysical. He concludes in a dreadful pasage: "The earth, continually drenched in blood, is only an immense altar where everything that lives must be immolated endlessly, without respite, until all things are used up, the evil is extinguished and death itself is dead. . . ."

The poet De Nerval echoed the ruin which had fallen on the world when he wrote: "Seeking the eye of God, I only saw a huge black bottomless socket, whence the night that dwells in it radiates over the world and becomes ever more dense; A strange rainbow surrounds this dark pit, threshold of old chaos whose shadow is nothingness, a vortex swallowing up the Worlds and Days!"

Those contemporary "conservatives" who seek a conservatism that is not coupled to a principle, a life which is not teleological in its orientation, a history which is devoid of meaning have not studied mankind and do not know the meaning of the past. Both the Right and the Left these past 150 years have reflected the anguished efforts of men to regain the lost center, to reintroduce a principle of authority, to fathom the riddle of history. Lacking internal religious authority, society can exist only if an external secular authority is imposed. The nineteenth-century conservative alliance between the throne and the altar was a failure because neither throne nor altar retained any compelling power. Pessimism and a loss of faith is a poor beginning for conservative politics.

Writing in *Democracy in America*, De Tocqueville predicted the consequences of loss of belief:

> When the religion of a people is destroyed, doubt gets hold of the higher powers of the intellect and half paralyzes all the others. . . . When there is no longer any principle of authority in religion any more than in poltics, men are speedily frightened at the aspect of this unbounded independence. The constant agitation of all surrounding things alarms and exhausts them. As everything is at sea in the sphere of the mind, they determine at least that the mechanism of society shall be firm and fixed; and as they cannot resume their ancient belief, they assume a master.

From authority to authoritarianism is but a short step, and substitute religions of force spring up where authentic religions of love
fail. In a society where "the strong do what they can and the weak
suffer what they must," men are driven to the employment of force
and coercion in order to preserve the fabric of civilization. If John
Donne's vision be true

> And new Philosophy calls all in doubt,
> The Element of fire is quite put out;
> The Sun is lost, and th' earth, and no man's wit
> Can well direct him where to look for it.
> Tis all in peeces, all cohaerence gone;
> All just supply, and all Relation.

then indeed we are lost and must take such comfort as we can in
the absolutism of the Right or the absolutism of the Left. We will
act for good or ill in the measure in which we retain some unde-
stroyed bourgeois prejudices or some undissolved illusions . . . for
a time. And then even the human myth will weaken and the un-
contained forces of decay will complete their work.

Authority may be imposed from without for a moment; the fabric may be conserved for a time, but the life expectancy of the Empires of the absurd are rather less than a thousand years. At the
vital center of man's experience stand the Gods, and they alone can
grant immortality, purpose, and grace.

Faith, purpose, and value, while expressing themselves in social
forms, are never social in origin. It is because of this that religion
can never be legislated, and that authority can only endure when
it is the result of assent freely given. Authority and freedom are
not only contradictory in human society; they are interdependent.
No true authority exists without unqualified freedom, and individual freedom is quite impossible without assent to some generally
held set of beliefs. "For my own part," wrote De Tocqueville, "I
doubt whether man can ever support at the same time complete
religious independence and entire political freedom. And I am inclined to think that if faith be wanting in him, he must be subject;
and if he be free, he must believe."

However, the conception of the absolute inviolability of the conscience is a relatively new one. Not until the late eighteenth century

did it occur to many men that the consciences of others ought to be respected; not until the nineteenth century did men generally assume that the purpose of the state was the extension of liberty rather than the preservation of religious orthodoxy. The mission of the state was to make men both good and happy, and it defined goodness in terms of a particular Christian orthodoxy. This conception of the state was an ancient one, reaching back to the Roman imperial ideal, and it was one only reluctantly abandoned. For the vast majority of men the object of civil society has not been to make men free but rather to make them good and happy. An important part of the conservative movement, now as in the eighteenth century, conceives the role of the state in positive terms and the mission of the state as that of temporal and eternal welfare.

But to enforce orthodoxy, to establish religion, to guarantee security, to legislate happiness, forces the state to intrude itself into the consciences of individual men, to circumscribe their freedom and deny their liberty. And so, in the name of religion, freedom, the greatest gift of religion, is denied men. Authority cannot stand without assent, and throughout history men have sought to compel what they could not win. Consequently the links between political reaction and religious establishment have been constant.

However this may be, the fact is that only the internalized authority of the voice of conscience, prophetic and revolutionary, conservative and hopeful, possesses the moral and ethical energies necessary to secure religion and to extend liberty. The conscience lies outside the authority of either church or state. They can only resist it or bow to its demands.

Nevertheless, it was religion itself that slowly paved the way for the ascendency of conscience. Lord Acton in his *Lectures on Modern History* described the process in the following passage:

> Yet the most profound and penetrating of the causes that have transformed society is a medieval inheritance. It was late in the thirteenth century that the psychology of conscience was closely studied for the first time, and men began to speak of it as the audible voice of God, that never misleads or fails, and that ought to be obeyed always, whether enlightened or darkened, right or wrong. The notion was restrained on its appearance, by the practice of regarding opposition to church power as specific heresy,

which depressed the secret monitor below the public and visible authority. With the decline of Coercion, the claim of Conscience rose, and the ground abandoned by the Inquisitor was gained by the individual. When it had been defined and recognized as something divine in human nature, its action was to limit power by causing the sovereign voice within to be heard above the expressed will and settled custom of surrounding men. By that hypothesis, the soul became more sacred than the state, because it received light from above, as well as because its concerns are eternal, and out of all proportion with the common interests of government.

How important Acton thought the conception of conscience was, in relationship to the establishment of liberty, is indicated in one of the thousands of notes he made for himself:

> Importance of S. Thomas's use of the term [Conscience].
> Why then did he not apply it to religion?
> Because he denies that religious error is conscientious.
> So long, there was no liberty.
> If the state excludes all that, it does what it likes.
> Extend the domain of conscience to religious error
>   and then only is liberty possible.

And in another passage Lord Acton summarized this relationship once more:

> The Christian notion of conscience imperatively demands a corresponding measure of personal liberty. The feeling of duty and responsibility to God is the only arbiter of a Christian's actions. With this no human authority can be permitted to interfere. We are bound to extend to the utmost, and to guard from every encroachment, the sphere in which we can act in obedience to the sole voice of conscience, regardless of any other consideration.

Consequently the authority which Acton and Tocqueville and the great conservative libertarians of the nineteenth century sought was not the institutionalized authority of orthodoxy speaking in either church or state. It was the authority of conscience, a conscience which had its source in God and which was graven by Him on the human heart. "The moral law," Acton wrote, "is written on the tablets of eternity." In another place Acton quoted with approval a passage from Alexander Vinet which runs: "Conscience is not ourselves; it is against us; therefore it is something other than ourselves, what can it be but God: And if it be God, we must give it the honor due to God: we cannot reverence the Sovereign less than the ambassador."

And just as conscience was not institutionalized in the secular or religious authority, so conscience and liberty could not stand uncorrupted if either secular or religious authority possessed power to crush it. If liberty was man's highest good, then governments ought to be so constructed that men might satisfy the demands their consciences make upon them.

There was no doubt in Acton's mind that liberty was man's highest good. He wrote: "The best things that are loved and sought by men are religion and liberty, not pleasure or prosperity, not knowledge or power. Yet the paths of both are stained by infinite blood."

Governments ought to enable men to act according to their consciences. In his Inaugural Lecture, Acton noted that "duties are the cause of rights," that is to say that liberty arises from conscience. In an essay of 1861 in the *Rambler*, he wrote: "Liberty is not the power of doing what we like, but the right of being able to do what we ought." In a note to himself he added, "Liberty enables us to do our duty—unhindered by the State, by society, by ignorance and error." Where, therefore, religion or the state stands in the way of conscience they are evil and must be resisted.

But the proposition that whatever the objectives and intentions of the state, its actions frequently end in oppression and violation of the conscience, is one which has been demonstrated over and over again since the beginning of the nineteenth century. Only the conservatives of that century and the Liberals of our own century have insisted that the action of the state, whatever the circumstances and whatever its purposes, was good. Even Karl Marx knew the state for what it was, an instrument of oppression; and his utopian politics called for its withering away in the name of freedom. He saw the tendency of the centuries as the destruction of the class state which in turn would free the individual for the full development of all his potentialities. But the movement of the century did not liberate, educate, and humanize its offspring; rather it brutalized and corrupted them. The state did not wither away; rather it grew monstrously, intruding itself in the Soviet Union into every aspect of human life and thought. The revolution made in the name of conscience and against authority did not always free men but, just as the reactionary conservatives had warned, it simply led to the war of all against all. The reign of conscience and opinion led inevitably to the establishment of democracy, and democracy, unchecked by any influence and fired by the dreams of demagogues and messiahs, threatened the whole structure of society. The conception of man's relationship to the state and to authority suddenly changed, and many men found the system which they had destroyed in the name of conscience to be superior to that which took its place.

Thus, the problem of our age was to be a new one, not previously faced by men. Democracy tended to bring absolute conformity and tyranny in its wake unless it was checked by churches, constitutions, economic interests, divided powers, and decentralization and plurality of authority. The movement of the age was not, as Marx's sociology predicted, towards freedom, but towards tyranny. Acton, a wiser man and a more discerning political mind, noted:

> To reconcile liberty with an aristocratical society and a monarchical State was the problem, the striving of many centuries. To preserve it under absolute democracy is the special problem of the future. . . . [The modern danger] is state absolutism, not royal absolutism. . . . It is bad to be oppressed by a minority, it is worse to be oppressed by a majority. From the absolute will of an entire people there is no appeal, no redemption, no refuge but treason.

Nor was Acton alone in his vision of the dangers the future would hold. Tocqueville wrote in the middle of that optimistic century:

> When the state of society among a people is democratic— that is, when castes or classes no longer exist in the community and its members are nearly equal in education and in property

the mind follows the opposite direction [away from liberty]. Men are much alike, and they are annoyed, as it were, by any deviation from the likeness; far from seeking to preserve their own distinguishing singularities, they endeavor to shake them off in order to identify themselves with the general mass of the people, which is the sole representative of right and might in their eyes. The spirit of individuality is almost obliterated.

"I think," De Tocqueville wrote in *Democracy in America,* "that in the democratic centuries that are beginning, individual independence and local freedom will always be the product of art. Centralization will be the natural government."

Marx, as well as Tocqueville, knew the tendencies of his age. He studied and encouraged its centralizing tendencies; and yet his utopian expectations were completely out of keeping with his political and his sociological knowledge. He could not see that unless checks to the democratic tendencies in society were instituted, the banishment of inequality would mean the extinction of liberty.

Nor did he see that materialism provides a most inadequate base for the love and exercise of freedom. This was due, in part, to the fact that Marx saw freedom not as an end but rather as a by-product of economic and sociological process. For Acton and Tocqueville freedom was an absolute end, a primary value to which all other objects and ends in society must be sacrificed if necessary. "Liberty is so holy a thing," Acton wrote, "that God was forced to permit evil that it might exist." On another occasion he said, "Liberty is not a gift or an acquisition; not a state of rest, but of effort and growth; not a starting point, but a result, of government."

Perhaps with the destructive and anti-liberal tendencies innate in democratic society, it were better to follow the advice of those conservatives who would halt the economic and social developments which have overtaken our society and, if not set back the clock, at least prevent the further democratization of our society. Perhaps it were better to install in power, and support, class governments around the world in the hope that the tyranny of a class society would, at all odds, be less pervasive and efficient than the tyranny of a classless society.

Conservatives who think in these terms, aside from the basic immorality of the proposition, are living in a world of illusion. Conservatism, for good or for ill, is the child of change as much as it is the child of tradition. From Burke to Buckley it has combined conservative ideas with revolutionary politics and economics. Capitalism and personal freedom are the two most revolutionary ideas in modern society. And, even more important, we live in a revolutionary society which will not be deflected from the course of change. Technologically and socially we are in the grip of vast and constant changes. There is no turning back. Indeed, there has been no turning back in our dynamic Western society since the tenth century. Democracy and increasing social and economic equality are the givens of the society in which we live.

Tocqueville was quite certain of this one hundred years ago when he wrote:

> I am persuaded that all who attempt, in the ages upon which we are entering, to base freedom upon aristocratic privilege will fail; that all who attempt to draw and retain authority within a single class will fail. At the present day no ruler is skillful or strong enough to found a despotism by re-establishing permanent distinctions of rank among his subjects; no legislator is wise or powerful enough to preserve free institutions if he does not take equality for his first principle and his watchword. All of our contemporaries who would establish or secure the independence and the dignity of their fellow men show themselves the friends of equality; and the only worthy means of showing themselves as such is to be so: upon this depends the success of their holy enterprise. Thus the question is not how to reconstruct aristocratic society, but how to make liberty proceed out of that democratic state of society in which God has placed us.

And Acton, writing of William Gladstone said:

> The decisive test of his greatness will be the gap he will leave. Among those who come after him there will be none who understands that the men who pay wages ought not to be the political masters of those who earn them (because laws should be adapted to those who have the heaviest stake in the country, for whom misgovernment means not mortified pride or stinted luxury, but

want and pain, and degradation and risk to their own lives and
to their children's souls), and who yet can understand and feel
sympathy for institutions that incorporate tradition and prolong
the reign of the dead.

Just so! The question is "how to make liberty proceed out of that
democratic state of society in which God has placed us." To those
conservatives who would retreat from the tendencies of our
democratic age, to those who would stand still, the answer is the
same. To those Liberals who have asserted that there can be no
genuine American conservatism because America lacks a Tory
class, a privileged aristocracy and establishment, the answer is,
"Thank God! We have nothing to undo." Conservatives will face
the issues of their times, and their enduring concern as children of
authority and children of revolution will be that the interests of
liberty and the sanctity of the individual be preserved.

The democratic revolution which was brought about by the
introduction of the principle of conscience has changed the nature
of the problem of government. Tocqueville wrote:

> The political world is metamorphosed, new remedies must
> henceforth be sought for new disorders. To lay down extensive
> but distinct and settled limits to the action of government; to
> confer certain rights on private persons, and to secure to them
> the undisputed enjoyment of those rights; to enable individual
> men to maintain whatever independence, strength, and original
> power he still possesses; to raise him by the side of society at
> large, and uphold him in that position; these appear to me the
> main objects of legislators in the ages upon which we are now
> entering.

The concern of Acton and Tocqueville and the concern of the
legislators who would follow them was to be with the growth of
centralized authority. The state, whether dominated by liberals
or by conservatives, in the nineteenth century continued the progress to the centralization of authority and the growth of absolutism
which it had begun in the twelfth century. There was, by the
second half of the nineteenth century, no mistaking the tendency
in Western political institutions. Acton wrote: "In that society out

of which modern European States have grown, the corporation was the first thing, the sovereign State the second. But the State gradually gained ground and took into its hands what was common to all." Increasingly, as corporate rights and obligations had been assumed and discharged by the central governments, the liberties in which these rights were embedded disappeared. Moreover the many competing forces and authorities which existed within the pre-modern state limited the power and the authority of any one body. For this reason Acton warned repeatedly: "Never destroy a force. When it is not dominant it may serve to check dominion." But one by one competing authorities within the state disappeared. Churches were nationalized, assemblies decayed, and central authority grew; classes were impoverished or displaced; power shifted from status to money, and freedom increasingly was sacrificed to security. The drift of affairs was clear enough in Tocqueville's day. He wrote: "The unity, the ubiquity, the omnipotence of the supreme power, and the uniformity of its rules constitute the principal characteristics of all the political systems that have been put forward in our age. They recur even in the wildest visions of political regeneration; the human mind pursues them in its dreams."

But this tendency was absolutely inimical to liberty. So much, Acton and Tocqueville saw even without the added experience of our generation. As libertarians they both, therefore, detested any form of political organization which hastened the growth of absolutism, any form of political organization which by its very nature broke down those natural checks to absolute authority. What then of their attitude to democracy, for patently democracy paved the way to tyranny? Acton wrote:

> [In the French Revolution] the people were quite resolved to be oppressed no more by monarchy or aristocracy, but they had no experience or warning of oppression by democracy. The classes were to be harmless; but there was the new enemy, the State. . . . They were protected from government by authority or by minority; but they made the majority irresistible, and the plebiscite a tyranny.

Tocqueville and Acton recognized that democracy and the reign of opinion were but an extension of the principle of the absolute character of the dictates of conscience. Moreover, both realized that democracy was to become the dominant political form of their time, that its march was irresistible. Both believed this to be Providential. But how was democracy to be prevented from destroying liberty? How was freedom finally to be reconciled with authority?

The answer was to come from America. Acton wrote in a note to himself:

> The great revelation of America was that of a
>   revolution effected by conservative politicians.
> Hamilton and Adams and Washington.
> In our days, Deak, Cavour.
> Nobody can measure their force.

Decentralization, multiplied authorities, federalism were not only the natural checks on absolute democracy but were the basis of good government. "Centralization," Acton wrote, "means apoplexy at the center and paralysis at the circumference."

Because federalism, multiplied authorities, and decentralization were at the heart of the American constitutional system both Tocqueville and Acton hoped that in America the tendencies to tyranny implicit in democracy would be checked. Acton witnessed the first great disappointment to his hopes in the course of the American Civil War. In the course of the twentieth century more and more of these natural and constitutional checks on democracy have disappeared.

Tocqueville was minute and specific in his discussions of those aspects of American life and the American Constitution which kept democracy from fulfilling itself in tyranny. Of major importance to Acton and Tocqueville were the institutions of federalism, the separation of church and state, an educational system not wholly dominated by the central government, and a free-enterprise, market economy.

Local initiative and local authority constituted for these men the most important aspect of federalism. Charity and education, law and government, to be either effective or libertarian, must be local. Divided powers and divided authorities were no less important. Above all both Acton and Tocqueville would have been depressed

by the drift of all power and privilege to the central government
in Washington.

But even aside from the checks of federalism, there were other
important checks on democracy in the American system. It may
be true that, as Acton said, "religion and liberty are more dear to
men than prosperity or pleasure," but modern revolutions have
been made at least as often in the name of social and economic
justice as they have been made in the name of liberty. Tocqueville
wrote:

> Almost all the revolutions that have changed the aspect of the
> nations have been made to consolidate or to destroy social in-
> equality. Remove the secondary causes that have produced the
> great convulsions of the world and you will almost always find
> the principle of inequality at the bottom. Either the poor have
> attempted to plunder the rich, or the rich to enslave the poor. If,
> then, a state of society can ever be founded in which every man
> shall have something to keep and little to take from others, much
> will have been done for the peace of the world.

Lord Acton was no less certain of the necessity for a wide and
just distribution of the material resources of life. He wrote: "There
is no liberty where there is hunger. . . . The theory of liberty demands strong efforts to help the poor. Not merely for safety, for
humanity, for religion, but for liberty." Property, if it is a natural
right, must be so broadly based as to fall to all men who make a
genuine contribution to their society.

The theory of democracy requires an ever increasing degree of
equality, and unless this can be achieved through the instrumentality
of a market economy and an advanced technology, it will be
achieved by the hand of the demagogue or tyrant. Tocqueville saw
this clearly. "The foremost or indeed the sole condition required
in order to succeed in centralizing the supreme power in a democratic community is love of equality, or to get men to believe you
love it. Thus the science of despotism, which was once so complex,
is simplified and reduced as it were, to a single principle."

But complementary to this preoccupation with equality and a
wide distribution of property among the democratic masses on the
part of Acton and Tocqueville was their concern for a market

economy. Tocqueville, particularly, was worried about the impact of state capitalism upon the enterprise and free institutions of the people. There was as much to fear in the nineteenth century and the period which followed it from a state which dominated the economic life of its people as there was from the dangers of an established religion. It seems odd indeed that the contemporary Liberal who finds the thought of an established religion so disgusting because of its impact on personal liberty finds the thought of state capitalism so comforting. Both are absolutely incompatible with political liberty.

For Acton and Tocqueville it was obvious, however, that while economic and social equality were a *sine qua non* for a stable society, they were not the most important elements in that society. "Democracy," wrote Acton, "without a moral standard . . . could no more stand than a Republic governed by Marat." Tocqueville pointed up Acton's meaning by saying:

> Most religions are only general, simple and practical means of teaching men the doctrine of the immortality of the soul. That is the greatest benefit which a democratic nation derives from its belief, and hence belief is more necessary to such a people than all others. When, therefore, any religion has struck its roots deep into a democracy beware that you do not disturb it; but rather watch it carefully, as the most precious bequest of aristocratic ages.

Conservatism ought not to confuse its cause with secularism. Neither ought it to confuse its cause with those who encourage a religious establishment.

The doctrine of the separation of church and state does not and never has implied the theory of a wall of separation, and conservatism ought to do all in its power to strengthen and encourage religion. Religious education, far from being divisive in a democratic society, can only strengthen and solidify the federalism of the state of which it is a part. Tax monies ought to be employed for the support of church schools; nonsectarian religious education should be a part of the educational program of the public schools; and faculties of theology should be associated with the state university systems. They will, by taking a large part of the educational structure out of the hands of the state, insure an area of liberty and nonconformity to the popular prejudices of Liberal secularism.

But just as certainly, the coercive power of the state ought not to be employed to enforce religion's observation or intrude itself into the realm of private as distinct from public morality. The enforcement of orthodoxy, even in the seemingly benign form of "blue laws," constitutes a danger to the individual's freedom of conscience. Religion can compel through an interior command; it cannot command through an exterior force and still retain its place in men's hearts. Nor should religion seek to usurp an authority which belongs to the state or to other community bodies. Its message is an eternal one, and it ought to divorce itself from the meddle, meddle, meddle of the pious Mr. Slopes and the ecclesiastical Uriah Heep. Tocqueville wrote:

> The more the conditions of men are equalized and assimilated to each other, the more important it is for religion, while it carefully abstains from the daily turmoil of secular affairs, not needlessly to run counter to the ideas that generally prevail or to the permanent interests that exist in the mass of the people. For as public opinion grows to be more and more the first and most irresistible of existing powers, the religious principle has no external support strong enough to enable it long to resist its attacks. This is no less true of a democratic people ruled by a despot than of a republic. In ages of equality kings may often command obedience, but the majority always commands belief; to the majority therefore, deference is to be paid in whatever is not contrary to the faith.

Religion is important to the democratic state not only because it preserves the fabric of society but also because it acts as the most important power to check the aggressive, centralizing, and totalitarian tendencies of the modern state. Without a strong religion, which remains outside and independent of the power of the state, civil liberty is unthinkable. The power of the state is, in part, balanced and neutralized by the power of the church. The freedom of the individual is most certain in that realm which neither church nor state can successfully occupy and dominate.

Finally, if contemporary conservatives cast their political sentiments in terms of Acton's and Tocqueville's libertarian conservatism they will abandon pessimism for an optimistic and active faith. Acton wrote:

> End with the kingdom of God, which is liberty.
> How far from the end? Africa not begun, Asia how little
> But America and Australia, South Africa,
> Governed by the ideas of our revolution. The Ideas
>   that went out there govern the world—Their reaction
>   in Europe.

CHAPTER NINE

The Convenient State

GARRY WILLS

THE Liberal and the conservative who would sort out their differences, for some constructive purpose, encounter from the outset an unusual problem: the very things that seem to unite them are a cause of confusion and deeper cleavage. Even when we of the West fall out, we select our weapons from the same armory; and, as (in the stock jibe) the same medieval God heard the prayers of opposed armies, so Plato and Aristotle seem to hover over the ranks of every possible faction in the civilization they helped to create. Even when men undermine our citadel, they do it with our engines; and, in greatest part, unconsciously. This brings the bitterness of fratricide into the dispute over our inheritance. The conservative claims guardianship over the storehouse of Western wisdom. The Liberal contends that the genius of the West lies in its capacity for innovation, in a daring reliance on reason and a resiliency towards change.

Because these two forces share a vocabulary and, to some extent, a vision, the discovery that they are saying different things in the same words leads, on either side, to suspicion of betrayal; and the variations in meaning that the common vocabulary suffers seem to open an unbridgeable chasm. In no case is this so clear as in the allegiance of both sides to the principles of freedom and order; for neither party denies the necessity of some polarity and balance between the two. The Liberal is traditionally considered the spokesman of freedom, the conservative of order. But, even aside from the shifting maneuvers these terms have lately performed, no one ever claimed that such a simplistic division was absolute. The most partisan Liberal cannot, if he claims to speak responsibly, deny that conservatives are concerned with guaranteeing freedom. And the archest reactionary this side of insanity cannot claim that the Liberal is not trying to construct a social order. In fact, as time wears on, the stress on principles ancillary to their professed ones makes Liberals and conservatives seem to change places, so that Liberals now champion a strong central government, and conservatives speak for economic and political individualism. Is the difference between these two, then, merely accidental at any moment because it is, in the long run, only a matter of degree, the conservative laying heavy emphasis on the prescriptive, the Liberal on the spontaneous, elements in political life? Given the same set of ingredients, do the cooks simply vary their recipes? No; the shared language disguises, and so perpetuates, fundamental differences.

Freedom and order, justice and settled interests, progress and tradition . . . the words are used of different things in the different camps; and when these concepts cluster to form more complex groupings of ideas—republic, democracy, self-determination, aristocracy—the differences undergo a staggering multiplication. It is true that freedom and order will be correlates in any of the systems advanced. But this, again, impedes communication, since the varieties of meaning in the one word will exact an answering variation in the other. It is useless, therefore, to debate whether the emphasis should be on freedom or order, or to adjudicate between major political systems by discussing the *degree* of freedom desired, or the *extent* of order, as if these were constant substances varying only in quantity. The question should be *what kind* of order, *what kind* of freedom, is at issue. Our history is littered with defeated varieties of each virtue. To take an obvious case, there is the theocratic definition of freedom and order—principles which become, under this rubric, Providence and Virtue. In such a scheme, freedom is freedom to be virtuous, and order is the right to exact virtue from man as his proper attribute. At another extreme of our experience is anarchism, which (read the paradox how you will) is a system for avoiding system. It, too, has a principle of order—the removal and continued negation of political coercion—corresponding to its untrammeled freedom.

These systems are both unworkable, since virtue that is enforced is not virtue, and anarchy that is guaranteed against control is to that extent controlled. But their *ignis fatuus* has drawn men down tragic paths, and they will continue to beckon. The important thing is to see that there is no use distinguishing such schemes by *degree*, as having a different internal disposition of freedom and order. The anarchist does not err in exalting freedom over order, but in exalting the wrong kind of freedom and the wrong kind of order. It is his whole philosophical framework that is incorrectly established. He is right about the machinery of these correlates; he is only wrong about the world. To put it another way, the relation of freedom to order is a dynamic one that can manifest itself in any number of consistent programs; and a political system is therefore to be judged by its substance, not by its dynamics.

Thus Mill cripples his discourse from the start when he calls the treatise on liberty an attempt to adjudicate the ancient "struggle between Liberty and Authority,"—as if these were two things of perduring and permanent meaning, but with shifting relations, towards each other, of supremacy or subjection. The real difference, for instance, between the historically normative polities of ancient Greece and the "barbarians" was not simply one of liberty as opposed to tyranny. The ancient empires had a mystical sanction. Their art and customs show no awareness of the individualism that emerged in Hellas' statues of man. Liberty, in such a society, has another meaning than it was to take on in the debates of the Hellenes. And in the primitive societies so thoroughly scrutinized by modern anthropologists, the instruments for educating and preserving the individual, under severe disadvantages, are the very disciplines for initiation into the political order on which all life depends. In such a world, the relation of freedom to order continues to exist, but as a drastically reduced version of the religious maxim, *cui servire regnare*. A similar paradox is worked out in the Marxist dialectic, and summarized, satirically, in Orwell's "Freedom is slavery." Far from being a game of the mind, this slogan expresses the only possible approach to freedom in the Marxist world; the Communist paradox has the same consistency as the Christian language used to describe a freedom heightened to indefectible obedience in the beatific vision. The only error is trying to acclimatize heaven to the intemperate regions of practical politics. Again, men are right about the relation of freedom to order, and only wrong about the world.

Since freedom and order are correlates, an absolutism at one pole leads to an absolutism at the other. The Marxist starts from order and asserts that "freedom is slavery." The absolutists of individualism start at the other pole but end in the same contradiction. Even the most extreme libertarian must justify his position by an appeal to order. Mill, for instance, advocates a free market of ideas as the most infallible guide to certitude—enough talk automatically producing truth, triumphant over all pretenders and "self-evident." Thus freedom becomes authority and arms itself with all the instruments the Liberal state has taken to itself in order to advance man's "self-evident" rights.

But if freedom always implies order in any consistent system, why has Western civilization made freedom a separate aim and motto, so that the boast of Greece was to have invented freedom, and a war of national liberation like America's could float the banner "liberty or death?" The reason is that the Western tradition —as opposed to all others, even the most sophisticated Oriental disciplines—has exalted the individual person. This civilization, centered in the primacy of the private soul, brought a whole new ordering of society into human history. The difference is immediately apparent when Greek thought and art enter the world. Impersonal pattern, hieratic system, absorption in the eternity of the Ideal give way to the naked splendor and particularity of man; even the gods assumed those anthropomorphic forms still vital in Western imaginations. The Greek "idea" was first detached and delineated in the cult statues given various gods' names, but in reality sharing one title: Man. No longer did man achieve his manhood by religio-political initiation into secrets of order. The individual reason became the test of reality with the Greeks, and this reason asserted itself by defying the order of magic and mystery. The state religion was secularized; it sloughed off its theric elements, boasting of this liberation under the symbol of battle with centaurs and other half-human powers. The individual reason, thus exalted, ventured on the distinctive Western achievements— systematic logic and science, a philosophy freed of superstition.

The discovery of the individual's unique resources, the testing of the world against the private reason, forced the state into a new role. Formerly, man's hard-won achievements had been stored up in the authority of the community, kept under sacred leadership and symbols. But the Greek mind freed itself of this total dependence on tradition, and man's sights were set on the uncharted areas where no collective approach to mystery could lead him. The state took on a humbler function, keeping order among the individuals whose free quest gave Greek cities their divided, spontaneous, almost anarchic individuality.

Thus freedom became an assertion of the individual's right to pursue his own vision; and liberty became a prior demand for all human speculation or education. This demand did not lessen as the Hellenic world spread and was transmuted by Christianity. In fact, the Christian emphasis on the individual soul's worth, and its otherworldly goal, deepened the cleavage between man and the religious state. The Christian recognizes a divided loyalty, giving to Caesar what is Caesar's, but to God the inestimably vaster reaches of the soul that belong to God.

But if the state's order is no longer, in the Greek world, co-extensive with man's attempt to order his private world, what role is government to play? Where does the supremacy of the private person find its frontier, or verge on other claims? How do the sacred areas of each man's individuality meet and adjust to each other? It is this question that has put the problem of freedom at the center of Western political dispute. And, in a kind of slovenly philosophical shorthand, this problem has been cast as a search for the *amount* of freedom man is to enjoy. But the problem is that the Greek world introduced an entirely new conception of human life, one still novel today; a conception that runs into contradiction if pushed by a ruthless logic. The autonomy of the individual, the fight against tradition, seem to make government at worst a causeless evil, at best a necessary evil. But experience has taught that a "freedom" which travels down the road of anarchy is never seen again. Thus the problem of the Western world has been to find a new kind of order to act as foundation for its fugitive new kind of freedom. Many attempts at the solution of this problem have been short-lived, because they did not come to grips with the particular kind of freedom—with its almost impossible demands— that the West has chosen to pursue. The attempts which remain in the central line of Western experiment cluster into two main groups. These continuing schools of thought, or lines of approach, correspond in some degree with the popular division of political thinkers into Liberal and conservative. In some degree, but not exactly; and the popular terms are no longer precise. It will be better, then, to give unequivocal if unfamiliar names to the two, calling them the Order of Justice and the Order of Convenience.

I THE ORDER OF JUSTICE

If the state is not meant to initiate man into his place in the world, what is its function? The earliest and most arresting answer is Plato's: the end of the state is justice. The liberated intellect of man discerns, behind all disciplines of mystery, an order whose sole force is its claim upon the reason. This is the order of each thing's due, of justice as an Idea. But some intellects are not capable of grasping this ideal form; and so it is the task of human society to find and put in office the intellects fitted for communion with the Idea of justice. The rest of men will have to take what these rulers dispense, as they mediate the light of justice to men bewildered by shadows.

Plato wrote when the Greek adventure into individuality seemed to be reaching a suicidal point of fission. He wrote to meet the practical demand for order, and to forestall the resurgence of sheer mystery—in this case, the mystery of force—as a claim on man's obedience. He makes the claims of the state meet the challenge of reason; but the Platonic state answers this challenge so successfully that it again becomes the entire area of man's endeavor. The state brings justice into the flux of history. Theocracy has returned, and absolutism; but reason is the new deity and absolute. The assertion of the individual intellect leads to an equal assertion of the state's power as the seat of truth. Men throw off mystery, only to be ruled by Idea.

Aristotle, though he introduced empirical elements of observation and psychological realism into political theory, nonetheless based the state on metaphysical principles as two-edged as Plato's. The Greeks had advanced the boast of the individual's self-sufficiency against the hieratic absolutism of less rational civilizations. Aristotle considered the reason's own claim to autonomy with rigor and found that man, isolated, cannot meet the test of self-sufficiency, or *autarkeia*, either economically or psychologically. The smallest unit that can make a pretense at *autarkeia* is the state that is armed against foreign aggression and able to supply internal economic needs. Then, translating human dependence into logical dependence, Aristotle argues: "By the very order of things, the state is prior in right to the family, and to each of us singly, since the whole is of necessity prior to the part" (1253a19-20). Man, without the *polis* to complete him, is not even a man: perhaps an animal, perhaps a god (1253a29). Like "an isolated piece at draughts," such a man has no function aside from the action of the total set of markers. The entire business of being man, which is to be just (1253a16-18), is only fulfilled in the state, the guardian of justice: "The virtue of justice has, as its sphere, the *polis*. For the virtue of justice (*dikaiosunē*) establishes what is just (*to dikaion*), and this order of justice (*dikē*) gives men's relations their political pattern (*politikēs koinōnias taxis*)" (1253a37-39). Therefore the state alone is equipped to achieve the highest good (1252a4-6).

In his own way, Aristotle repeats the Platonic recoil of a complete individuality into a new state absolutism. Both systems tried to achieve freedom of the will through the free exercise of reason. But the reason is not free. It is an instrument for reaching an outside and objective reality, which is single under single aspects. Man can refuse to think, or think confusedly; but once the evidences of reality are received within the intellect, it is not free to think anything it pleases. Thus any attempt to base political freedom on the claims of man's intellect makes the state the center of truth—in Plato, truth as moral enlightenment; in Aristotle, truth as a set of logical imperatives—and nothing is more absolute than the claim of truth upon man.

The empirical observations of Aristotle gave origin to a certain political realism, but the authoritarian principle hidden in his definition of the state haunts us. The Christian Aristotelian could no longer take *autarkeia* as the test of man's achievement. For the Christian, man's nobility comes from the fact that he is out of place in the world, meant for another City, with a higher and lasting citizenship. There is a further problem. Aristotle wrote that the state is prior to man "by nature," or in the order of things. The Christian doctrines of Creation, the Fall, and Heaven give a range of meanings to the word "nature" that Aristotle could never have imagined. In the new scheme, "nature" can mean the proper ordination of things as intended in the pristine state of man. Or nature is *fallen* nature—the human condition weighted by tendencies towards sin; the rest of creation scarred, and subject to catastrophe, as a result of man's rebellion. Or nature can mean the evidences of original order still asserting themselves in, and adapting themselves to, the present state of man. Nature can mean the good product of God's hand or the twisted remains of man's work. It can be contrasted with "unnatural" acts, as the model of ordination; or it can be contrasted with grace, as the frustrated thing unable to rise to its goal without redemption from a supernatural source.

For the Christian, the state can no longer fill up man's failings or aim at self-sufficiency and ideal justice. The earthly order must be identified as temporal, an area of trial and transition. As Augustine posed the problem, citizens of the two eternal Cities, the heavenly and the diabolic, must live together and mix in earthly polities, the wheat and chaff growing together before the final sifting. The earthly political community must concentrate on a limited agreement to ensure tranquillity, a state of truce in which citizens of both eternal Cities work out the mystery of their salvation or damnation.

But Aquinas, after putting Aristotle's politics in a context which transmutes it entirely, in a metaphysical realism and a theological history, let the Aristotelian terms and transitions stand as a model analysis in the order of intellect. To be useful as a practical science, this analysis must be applied, in concrete instances and by the use of prudence, to a real world radically altered in the light of revelation. The trouble is that the followers of Aquinas could not or would not follow the alterations that must be made when an Aristotelian politics is put in the existential framework of Christian theology. By the same process that dehydrated the entire Thomist metaphysics, the logical terms of Aristotle were once more applied to reality without the mediation of metaphysical realism and the moral act of prudence. *Autarkeia* clashed too obviously with the Christian mentality; but "the common good" took over the content of that key term, as an ideal order perfecting the "individual good." And justice is treated as the aim of the state,

almost as simply as in Aristotle's time, by many modern Thomists.¹
As the Thomist politics was denatured, "natural law" became
the sanction of "divine right" theories of government. Here, the
Christian religion replaced reason in the Hellenic scheme, making
the ruler the source of justice for other men.² Then the "laws of
nature" were totally emptied of realistic content to become the
ideal "Nature" of the eighteenth century. The rebellion against a
monarch's "natural" legitimacy turned political union into a free
contract, arising from the insufficiencies of the "natural" condition. But Rousseau treads the same perilous circle that Plato first
traced—out from the state as mystery and back to supreme political authority in the form of reason. In the eighteenth-century
myth of a "state of nature," reason, in a vacuum, constructs a "case"
for government, draws up a contract, insists on its terms as if
they were points in logic, then consents to this invention of the
mind.

Those things which have been criticized as inconsistencies in
Rousseau—his union of extreme individualism with collective
tyranny—are actually the result of his penetrating logic. He saw
that Locke's doctrine of natural rights surrendered by agreement
leads to a state that is either absolutely just, or—when the state
fails in some particular, and tries to prevent dissolution of the
agreement by force—absolutely unjust. Society and the state are
coextensive terms. Prior to the social contract, each man is a world
apart; and the absolute autonomy of this condition can only be
surrendered to a custodian that discerns and demands absolute
right. That is why the eighteenth-century reformers had to believe that Nature's intent was clear, everywhere "self-evident," in
order to embark on their experiments. It is fascinating to watch
this antinomy at work, individualism reaching an extreme where
it is automatically transmuted into governmental absolutism:

> no more perfect union is possible, and no associate has any
> subsequent demand to make. For if the individual retained any
> rights whatever, this is what would happen: there being no com-
> mon superior able to say the last word on any issue between him
> and the public, he would be his own judge on this or that point,
> and so would try before long to be his own judge on all points.

... Each gives himself to everybody so that he gives himself to nobody.[3]

Because man's reason is not of itself free, the state based on "pure reason" only recognizes the freedom to be right; the state must, in Rousseau's famous phrase, "force men to be free":

> In and of itself, a people always wills, but does not always see, what is good; while the general will is always well-intentioned, the judgment that directs it is not always an instructed judgment. It must be brought to see things as they are. It must be brought, sometimes, to see things as they ought to appear. It must be shown the right road, which it is seeking.[4]

Since, in the purely rational world of Socrates and Rousseau, men only do wrong through some mistake in judgment or information, putting them on the right way is not forcing the will but "freeing the mind of error." Once again, the fallacy of extreme individualism, or simple democracy—society's attempt to make its circumference, or whole area, its own center—results in a reverse reading of the riddle: the center, source of truth, becomes the circumference, enclosing all human activities in a rigid rule.

The enduring attractiveness of the Order of Justice arises from its total reliance on reason. Rationalism flatters the individual; it is particularly seductive in the Western tradition, where the unfettered reason has accomplished so much; and it always produced spokesmen of the highest logical dexterity. Men of this school can invoke the great political theoreticians—Plato, Aristotle, Rousseau—though they find little support in the great political institutions of the past, in the achievements of the real order, usually wrought by slow accumulation of constitutional safeguards, or by a system of compromise and enlightened expedience.

Perhaps an even deeper source of inspiration for this view of the state is the fact that it taps moral, religious, and humanitarian enthusiasms. When a man argues that the state should not be an oracle of justice, a teacher of morals, or a dispenser of human comfort, the defenders of the Order of Justice frequently represent such a man's stand as an attack on justice itself, or a lack of moral principle, or an insensitivity to the demands of the human heart. Of course, it is precisely the state's usurpation of a religious and moral role that leads to its betrayal of freedom. Proponents of such a state always demand a hard orthodoxy of its subjects. Plato makes a grasp of ideal justice the qualification for political office. The "divine right" theories of government rest on a common profession of faith. The Enlightenment theories are based on the certitude that the "laws of Nature" are easily discernible and universally recognized. The beginnings of a Paine-Jefferson orthodoxy in America, based on these "self-evident" laws, were aborted by the religious fundamentalism of Americans and the system of compromise that effected the federalist union.[5] But modern Liberals have reintroduced an orthodoxy of self-evident rights by their positivist insistence on the universal validity and viability of certain concepts, like "democracy," "equality," and "self-determination."

It will be seen that the Order of Justice I have described corresponds, accidental usages aside, to what is generally termed the Liberal strand in Western political discourse.[6] The title arises from the initial stress, in all these systems, on reason and the free individual. But the turning of a rationalist freedom into a tyranny of intellect is not, as has so often been supposed, a mere accident or relapse of human weakness under the demands of a great ideal. The seeds of tyranny were in the ideal from the beginning. Robespierre and the Terror are the logical consequence of Rousseau and the Social Contract. When men realize this, they will cease wondering at the "inconsistencies" in Plato's or Rousseau's authoritarian state, or at the conversion of "divine right" into sheer might under a simplistic reading of the natural law. The Order of Justice is like the statue of Justice; its attributes are a blindfold, and the sword.

II THE ORDER OF CONVENIENCE

The title I have given this second form of order will strike some as frivolous; and "convenience" is, I admit, susceptible to misunderstanding. But other words that suggest themselves are even more misleading—rule by the expedient or the opportune (which now connote a lack of moral probity), government by concurrence (which gets mixed up, now, with dogmas of democratic procedure, though I would use the word in Calhoun's sense), or the principle of community (a word now dessicated by abstract definitions of the "common good"). So there is nothing for it but to choose a comparatively neutral word, at first glance trivial, and give it a specific function for this discussion.[7]

The problem of finding a single word is not accidental, or a quibble on method. The lack of an accepted term indicates a chronic failure in political discourse, the chasm between theory and practice; for the order I am considering is not nameless because unimportant, or absent from our history. In fact, each highest form of political community succeeded because this order informed and stiffened it invisibly. The Greek democracy was not doctrinaire. There is no theorist of Athenian democracy, no proponent of a doctrine. All the major political theorists of Hellas formed their ideal systems as alternatives to the real order, admittedly fallible, that was stimulating their investigations. Thucydides, Plato, Aristotle—"oligarchs" all. It is true that there are some democratic speeches put in the mouths of Herodotean and Euripidean characters. But the speculative recommendations of democracy are very few; perhaps the most famous is the speech Thucydides invented for Pericles, a boast ironically voiced under the shadow of defeat. The Roman Empire actually professed a spurious theory, maintaining the façade of a republic. Medieval theory tried to redeem feudal and merchant practice but acted merely as a component force working for balance.[8] England is notoriously the producer and product of a kind of unconscious constitution. And America, after the *furor ideologicus* had passed that lifted the colonies on the wings of war, based its Constitution on an unashamed profession of compromise. The political ideal of *The Federalist* elevates compromise to a principle of harmony. It is one of the major attempts to articulate an Order of Convenience.

Do these preliminary remarks mean that politics must simply be opposed to theory; in the foolish modern word, "anti-intellectual"?[9] No. But the Order of Convenience must be built on a basic truth that is even more scandalous to modern ears: the particular aim of the state is not to achieve justice, and certainly not to dispense it. In the words of Newman, "satisfaction, peace, liberty, conservative interests [are] the supreme end of the law, not mere raw justice as such."[10] This, of course, does not mean that the state is to be unjust, or free of the imperatives of the moral law. The state, like the family, like the corporation, like the labor union, is bound by the laws of morality that are incumbent on all human endeavor, corporate as well as individual. In carrying out its function, the state must act with justice. But its specific aim is not to enforce justice as such. The family, too, must observe right order—the child obeying, the parent avoiding undue laxity or severity; husband and wife helping each other, yet observing measure in their demands upon each other. This due measure, this order of right, is achieved by the observance of justice; yet the formal aim of the family is not sheer justice as such. Its aim is to give birth and education to new members of our race, to recruit partners in the human adventure. Only when this purpose is clearly understood can the order of claims and the areas of just activity be discerned in the life of the family.

In the same way, the state must observe justice in its activities; but its aim is more limited, more concretely specified. And unless that aim is made clear, there is no way of knowing what justice is for the state; politics becomes an instrument for seeking every kind of good thing, for bringing ideal justice itself down to earth. We have seen the theocratic consequences of such an undertaking. These consequences make the rule of what Newman called "raw justice" the source of every tyranny that is not sheer outlawry, and the permanent temptation of every state. The nineteenth-century liberals found something evil in power itself, as if tyranny customarily advanced by some brutal and naked appeal of its own nature. But every truly powerful system of oppression was shaped by an ideal that can recruit talent, can use other energies than the thirst of a few for the acme of human rule. When ideal justice is set before the community as its political end, the only efficient path towards that ever receding goal is the marshaling of force in the state. All tyrannies give legitimacy to oppression by making it a transitional period through which men must pass on their way to Utopia, a kind of induced labor that is to bring forth the new order. So it was with the despots who had to "establish divine right," so with the Terror, so with the Utilitarian acceptance of the "growing pains" of industrialism, so with the dictatorship of the proletariat.

I do not mean to minimize, no conservative can, the effects of original sin in the life of society; but the most heartbreaking, and politically far-reaching, of these effects is not the drive of sheer evil, but the misguided and desperate grasping after good—the enthusiasms, heresies, crusades that can mobilize human generosity. The optimistic Liberal does not recognize that society is ultimately hurt less by individuals who catch at instant advantage than by the messiahs who undertake great missions with long-range planning, ingenuity, patient endurance, and conviction of ultimate triumph. We are witnessing the scale of this menace in the fiery spread and intensity of the Communist vision.[11]

The talk of "power" as a constant factor everywhere to be minimized is as self-defeating as the quantitative approach to freedom (something everywhere to be increased). The two views are, in fact, reverse sides of a single coin. Power arms itself for the long pull, invades the mind, and gives structure to human effort, not when it is a spasm leading to dissolution, but when it is summoned up by a false god, with rights over the whole man and all men. Nero is personally more despicable, but politically less destructive, than Robespierre or Lenin.[12]

But if the state is not to be founded on an ideal order of justice, what is its basis? Obviously, the real order—the order of man's needs. The individual only finds his natural fulfillment in society. As Aristotle pointed out, even language is a convention, a "coming together." Language is itself society. And all man's other achievements involve a similar social opportunity for the individual's self-expression. But if there is a society, there must be a state. As a necessary physical regimen keeps the individual alive, so there must be a regime, an order, a discipline in society. That regime is the state.

The fallacy of the rationalists is that they begin the construction of their political models with the isolated reason of the individual. They make the pure autonomy of the individual clash and, finally, merge with the autonomy of a just order. But man does not start with a formed and pure freedom. Man "free" of society is man free of air; free, that is, to suffocate. The rationalist pits the individual against an abstract order of justice in the state, instead of tracing the spontaneous growth and grouping of social forms that give the individual a field for expression and activity. The state appears, apocalyptically, in such theories, bringing justice "new-born" into prior chaos. But in the real order, the state arises from a hierarchy of social organizations, of groups formed to fill particular needs. The state stabilizes this spontaneous social expression. It answers a natural demand for unity. It cannot initiate such unity, or carve countries out of the map by legislative fiat. Although it is a commonplace that man is a "social animal," the rationalist theories contradict this commonplace. For if the state arises out of man's social instinct, then the state destroys its own roots when it denies free scope to the other forms of social life. The state, when it is made the source of justice, must be equally and instantly available to all citizens; and, in achieving this, in sweeping away the confusion of claims raised by families, economic orders, educational conventions, codes of conduct, natural gradations of privilege, the Liberal leaves society atomized, each man isolated, with all the weight of political power coming unintercepted upon him.[13] The higher forms of organization do not grow out of and strengthen the lower, but counter and erase them. This is what has happened under the Order of Justice from the time when Plato pitted the state against the family to the modern breakdown of divided jurisdiction in the centralized state. As usual, Rousseau follows the logic of this position to its fated end:

> Where, however, blocs are formed, lesser associations at the expense of the broader one, the will of each of these associations comes to be general with respect to its members and particular with respect to the state. . . . If, then, we are to have a clear declaration of the general will, we must see to it that there are no partial societies within the state, so that each citizen forms his own opinions.[14]

By this route, the Liberal state arrives, everywhere, at contradiction: though the state is instituted to assure the development of personality, societies that embrace the rationalist ideal are marked by a cult of impersonality. Plato attempted to erase the distinction between the sexes. The French and Russian revolutions came up with titles meant to attack titles: "Citizen" in one case, "Tovarich" in the other. Since political justice conditions all of a man's life in such societies, men rejoice in the reduction of persons to a minimal legal status and equality. In such communities, loyalty to the state is expressed as duty towards abstract justice, not as patriotism.

For the realist, on the other hand, the state, by disciplining a particular society, expresses the character of that society, protects its spontaneity and symbolic self-confrontation at all levels of life, draws on the society's specific resources, and commands a loyalty that is personalized as patriotism. How does the state accomplish this? How complement the multiple, spontaneous, or consanguineous forms of social coherence? As all things complement: by supplying what is lacking. Other social groups than the political have a positive bond of mutual affection or defined and positive interest. This is their strength, but it circumscribes their appeal. Only those qualify to take part who share the interests of a family or a class, of a school of thought or a creed. But conflicts of interest arise in the common area of life in which these activities take place. The task of adjudicating these conflicts by a shared code, and of including all the strata of society in a single frame of minimal order, must be entrusted to an agent of order with force at its disposal. This agency circumscribes a larger community than the partial groupings; it is not voluntary from moment to moment; it can enforce its judgments in the name of the very social forces that become obstreperous. The state is necessary because the other, overlapping social forms extend across a field of human activity that no one of them can circumscribe. Thus the end of the state is the orderly advancement and discipline of society as the necessary ground of human activity. And the necessary, basic condition for the formation of a state is a shared good that must be protected if all social and individual effort is to thrive. That is why Newman calls a common possession the basis of the state.[15]

The state, as extending throughout all other levels of social solidarity, must have a certain neutrality towards them all, and as the order-enforcing agent, it must take upon itself a certain negative, punitive function. This neutral and negative aspect of the state will be perverted, and become a positive push—as life-giving, rather than life-preserving—if the other forms of spontaneous activity wither; or if the state officials try to use their power to call up a positive vision of their own; or if politics is considered the all-inclusive area of man's achievement of excellence. To continue the comparison of individual regimen to social regime, such a society is like the health crank, who expends all his energy on the achievement of an ideal physical equilibrium, not using the body's forces for the essentially human tasks.

To prevent this usurpation on the part of the state, every society that is long-lived or successful finds ways of limiting the action of political force. The disciplinary agent of society is itself disciplined by society; the rulers are ruled. This system of checks is worked out by each community, but it is based on the general truth that the state's role is to enforce equity and order, rather than justice and charity. The free agencies of society must preserve their function by circumscribing the state's role in the totality of social activity. This fact has been instinctively recognized by all those theorists who, after talking about ideal forms of government, recommend a mixture of forms, striking a balance between all possible ruling forces in the state. This roundabout descent from the ideal to the real is clumsy. The true form of society is not to be found in a mixture of pure components, but in the particular aim and energy of each real community.

Each society must form a unique *constitution*, an "agreed station" of components, growing out of the resources it can command. The ideal state—of a justice or a freedom defined outside any particular human context—is as meaningless as some uniform ideal of individual fulfillment. Is monarchy, aristocracy, or democracy the best form of government? Such a question simply breeds further questions: Best for what society? And what kind of monarchy, or democracy? These questions are as hopeless as similar ones would be in the case of an ideal life for individuals. Is it better that man be an artist or philosopher, monk or martyr, doctor or teacher, worker or statesman? And if he is a doctor, should he engage in research, psychology, or compassionate work among the poor? If an artist, should he write or paint in an austere or demonstrative style? To attempt an abstract answer to these questions is to deny the mystery of individuality, the secret springs of motive, that make up the human fact of freedom. As ever, rationalism leads to sterile paradox, to an ideal freedom that is a denial of freedom. Calhoun rightly says:

> the great and broad distinction between governments is,—not that of the one, the few, or the many,—but of the constitutional and the absolute.[16]

And what is meant by a constitutional government? According to Calhoun, it is that government in which all the free forms and

forces of society—or as many as possible—retain their life and
"concur" in a political area of peaceful co-operation and compromise. According to Newman, it is that society in which the character of those "concurring" is best allowed for and given scope for
development:

> As individuals have characters of their own, so do races. . . .
> Moreover, growing out of these varieties or idiosyncrasies, and
> corresponding to them, will be found in these several races, and
> proper to each, a certain assemblage of beliefs, convictions, rules,
> usages, traditions, proverbs, and principles . . . tending to some
> definite form of government. . . . It is something more than law;
> it is the embodiment of special ideas, ideas perhaps which have
> been held by a race for ages, which are of immemorial usage,
> which have fixed themselves in its innermost heart, which are in
> its eyes sacred. . . . They are the creative and conservative in-
> fluences of Society; they erect nations into States, and invest
> States with Constitutions.[17]

Absolutism, or despotism, is a sheer thrust of force across the grain
of these free and preservative influences, a defiance of the spontaneous life that checks government even as it impels it forward.
A constitutional regime gives both *life* and *limit* to government;
it maintains a system that rules even society's rulers. The force
exercised by despots may be, and often is, the assertion of an ideal,
but of an ideal unrooted, unembodied in the flesh and substance of
society. It is, literally, a ghostly thing seeking to haunt or possess
the body politic by unnatural forces. For this reason, the answer to
Lincoln's question must be that no nation *can* long endure if it is
only "dedicated to a proposition." It must be dedicated to a people,
to its particular human possibilities, since

> that must be pronounced no State, but a mere fortuitous col-
> lection of individuals, which has no unity stronger than despot-
> ism, or deeper than law.[18]

One cannot simply ask whether a thing is just (as abolition of
slavery is just, whether in fifth-century Athens, first-century

Rome, or nineteenth-century Richmond); whether it is desirable (as better education of the young is desirable); whether it is moral (as sexual continence is moral). In politics one must ask at the same time, always, whether it is constitutional. Should the state act, and if so to what extent, with what precautions, and following what precedents; in conjunction with what tempering and expanding activity on the part of spontaneous organizations? If these questions are not asked, if the state enters the private area of morals, then censorship and orthodoxy give the political guardian a divine character. There is no limitation of the state but by the single test of constitutionality.

The constitution is not always, and is never merely, a written document.[19] It is the "shared situation" of society, that continuous arrangement whereby men preserve their common stake in a political regime. It is composed of all the influences that make a state continue to express the character of its people; that recruit and give room for the development of talent; that develop the resources of personality through society. Newman even wrote that "bribery" (*i.e.*, the buying of titles and offices), after it had been systematized as a recognized and efficient part of the British government's balanced operation, was part of the English constitution; and therefore to be used as a tool of the community, provided no specific act of immorality is committed, like the breaking of an oath.[20] In the same way, a society that is basically tribal in organization must have a state that is based on the tribes. Otherwise, the society has no way of meshing with its political order, of making its character felt, of maintaining identity while it grows towards a different mode of articulating itself, politically. Such a society proves the

> inexpediency of suffering the tradition of Law to flow separate from that of popular feeling . . . there ought to be a continual influx of the national mind into the judicial conscience; and, unless there was this careful adjustment between law and politics, the standards of right and wrong set up at Westminster would diverge from those received by the community at large, and the Nation might some day find itself condemned and baffled by its own supreme oracle. . . .[21]

As an instance, the "democratic" regimes being established in Africa, over inchoate areas arbitrarily defined as nations, perfectly exemplify Calhoun's maxim that the only realistic division of governments is into constitutional and absolute. These "democracies," imported from a Hellenic-Christian tradition of many centuries' growth, and imposed on stray parts of the tribal labyrinth of Africa, are not based on any real consensus. So-called popular support and "nationalism" do not express the genius of Africa itself, of any real nation. The native groups who "express their will" so simply with the marking of a ballot have merely expressed a hope that Western material comforts will magically be made theirs by this method. The result is an absolutism—an enlightened one, it may be claimed, but surely an absolutism. The term "democracy" means little or nothing in such a context; whereas other forms of government, today condemned out of hand as "dictatorships," may have a very effective constitutional system.

Does this mean that society must settle, always, for what it has, never push out towards higher achievement; must it forswear leadership in order to avoid loss of "constitution," treat all hope of better things as a temptation to visionary absolutism?

On the contrary, a constitution fosters not only liberty but leadership. In an integral community, the leaders really lead; they are followed. There is no chasm between the masses and the intelligentsia. One of the principal ironies of modern democracy is that egalitarian doctrine has driven a greater wedge between thinkers and the populace than most systems of privilege ever did, so that it seems almost necessary that "clerks" be traitors. The interplay of various groups within accepted tradition makes talent serve the community, not seek a false elevation by institutionalizing rebellion. When a nation has no tradition to appeal to but a "tradition of revolution," it has confessed bankruptcy; it can no longer marshal the potentials of the populace to serve the common stake, the constitution. When artists and philosophers and churchmen cannot find a meaningful area of mutual enrichment, then politicians must supply the social cohesion *ex nihilo*, and enforce it by militant centralization of power. In this situation, the boasts of broad franchise or democratic ritual do not give substance to man's liberty. For liberty is not the product of mechanical instruments like the electoral process.[22]

In modern democratic myth, man's freedom is given him entire at birth, a thing solid and circular in its perfection, but shattered and dispersed as time goes on. To prevent the final dissolution of all freedom, men form polities by chipping off a piece of liberty and surrendering it to the state, which is thus constructed out of the surrendered quantities of individual rights. The art of constructing a just state consists in finding how to sacrifice the thinnest possible slices of individual "sovereignty," and the most uniform, so that all these contribute to the central storehouse of national sovereignty. But man's freedom is not whole nor homogeneous. It is as complex as man himself, since it makes him man.

First, there is the basic freedom which consists in possession of a will. This will can never be taken away, or tampered with at its source. It can be killed, but only by killing the man, or reducing him to a subhuman level. Even in prison, the will is free so long as it exists.

Second, there is the last fulfillment of liberty, the state of continual choice that uses and never abuses freedom. This, according to Christian teaching, is the freedom of man at rest in his eternal reward. But according to authoritarian state systems, it is also a political ideal. All such systems imply, or, if pushed to logic, assert that man's freedom is freedom to do good. As Rousseau put it, the state forces man to be free.

In a third sense, freedom means the condition that encourages and allows for the active exercise of the will. This condition is achieved by education, by surroundings that stimulate and nurture free choice, by social discipline that gives man a peaceful area of movement. This is the freedom to which political discipline makes essential contributions. It is the freedom of a nation; not given by the state, but protected by it. Those who isolate a particular "political freedom" from the rest of man's self-extension into social institutions are usually reduced to the worship of various absolutes—the franchise, a widespread press, a public education—without regard to the genius of the groups and individuals finding common ground and seeking expression in the particular society. These absolutes can be as imprisoning as the authoritarian systems.[23] Plato says that freedom for "lead men" consists in obedience to the "gold men," the modern Liberal insists that freedom for the Congolese consists in an electoral and parliamentary system not geared to mesh with regional, tribal, emotional and intellectual differences or difficulties. The result in both cases is a union of chaos and compulsion, both impinging on the real exercise of freedom.

There is a fourth definition of freedom—this one spurious—as a mere lack of outside compulsion. But freedom is a spontaneity towards several alternatives, a principle of action. To define it as a lack is absurd. This leads to the ideal of the "open society," in which definite intellectual and cultural molds are avoided or broken, throwing the individual back on his own resources and responsibility at each step of his life. The ideal society, it is suggested, would be a kind of Great Books Club in which each person chooses his favorite historical and intellectual milieu, or browses among them all with an ultimate choice in mind. Such a society is impossible. There would be no agreed language, no common terms for contracts, no shared understanding of the way to get work done, no possibility of educational discipline. That is, there would be no society.[24] *Identity* would disappear, first in the society, then in the individual.

Freedom is not a mere lack; it is an urge to extend one's self by the exercise of choice, and unless there is a defined and delimited self, no extension is possible. There is no range of choice or reach of possibilities unless man operates from an established base of some sort. Unless a society can retain and enrich its identity, it does not admit the possibility of human fulfillment within its continuity, or even the luxury of revolt. All rebels would hate a genuinely open society; there would be nothing to rebel against. Tradition, what Burke calls "prejudice," is necessary to give freedom range in the real order, just as an individual, with all his limitations, is the necessary vehicle for the free will itself. And so, by another route, we find that freedom and order are correlates; and that rationally limited freedom is the partner of a humanly limited order, the limits being set by man's effort to achieve a fully human life under each society's historical conditions. The attempts at an absolute freedom recoil, logically and in experience, towards a political absolutism. Freedom must be concrete because man is; freedom is man.

Only the Order of Convenience, of enlightened expedience, of prejudice mobilized towards improvement, can give the practical art of politics a combination of flexibility and stability. The Order of Convenience can take the findings of the great political theorists and use them, without incurring the results of mistaken metaphysics. It can learn from Plato the importance, to society, of education and morality, without making the state a New Jerusalem of the intellect. It can take from Aristotle a realistic grasp of social psychology, of the uses of property, of moderation in reform, without making the state prior in right to the individual. It can learn from Rousseau the need for constant adjustment of political forms to the structure of society, without basing all forms on an explicit and rational "contract." Perhaps most significant of all, this kind of politics can return to the real genius of natural-law theory. It will recognize the laws of nature, not as dictates for an ideal life, but as the structure of reality calling, at each moment, for a real response, individual and social. It will seek "the common good," not as some ideal scheme of order, or quantitative accumulation of individual goods, but as the real life of the "commonalty," of community in all its mutually enriching forms. This true politics of the natural law is, as a modern exponent of that obscured system reminds us, rooted in a metaphysics vastly different from the eighteenth-century definition of Nature. Taking the American Republic as a concrete example, John Courtney Murray writes:

> Its basis was not the philosophic rationalism that called itself Enlightenment, but only a political pragmatism more enlightened than the Enlightenment ever was, because it looked to the light of experience to illuminate the prudential norms necessary to guide it in handling a concrete social reality that is vastly complicated.[25]

The political realist also preserves the virtue of justice, by assigning it its true place in the life of the state. This justice is primarily a matter of equity and procedure, of the fair enforcement of the constitution. This is not a role as inspiring or ambitious as justice plays in the states aiming at an ideal order. It is primarily a matter of fair rules for the free development of a society's particular impulses, the virtues of an umpire or a policeman; and, under threat of foreign aggression, the virtues of a watchdog. In fact, the disappointment of idealists, when faced with this system, is violent. Even Lord Acton, the moralist of liberty, considered Newman's politics "immoral"; and Augustine's attack on the *just* state of Plato has largely been ignored, or dismissed as a "deplorable lapse" in an otherwise great thinker.[26] But this recognition of the state's limited function is the means for freeing man in his extra-political and supra-political roles.

The Greeks sundered man from the hieratic order of politics, secularizing the state by an exercise of reason. But the order of reason, in the final theorists of Hellas, became as strict a political regimen as the religious state had been. Christianity completed the secularization of the state by placing man's goal on the other side of time, distinguishing, finally, the things of God from the things of Caesar. This duality, approached variously under the understandings and misunderstandings of the Two Cities or the Two Swords, led Christian wisdom to define and defy political absolutism. "Two there are," wrote Gelasius I to Anastasius I, "by which this world is ruled on title of sovereign right"—the area of priestly ministration, that is, of the individual soul and its divine freedom; and the order of kingly authority, that is, of temporal peace, establishing the condition in which men can discern and exercise their ultimate freedom.[27]

The effects of this new, and final, secularization were farther-reaching than the establishment of religious freedom. Once the state lost its primacy as an interpreter of the eternal order, it lost the claim by which it cowed all intermediate societies—the family, the free organizations of groups in which man seeks the answer to his own mysteries. As John Courtney Murray says, in a chapter called "Are There Two Or One?", "this comprehensive right [of the Church] asserted within the political community requires as its complement that all the intrapolitical sacrednesses (*res sacra in temporalibus*) be assured of their proper immunity from politicization."[28]

Although the medieval limitation on the state arose out of the state's recognition of the Church's mission, the Christian ordination of man has left a sacredness about the individual soul that has survived the breakup of a single center for Christendom. The

modern state, in its best manifestations (like the American Constitution), retains the secularization paradoxically created by
Christianity's other worldliness. The state must be agnostic, if
nothing else, about the possibilities and final goal of the individual;
and allow the human adventure to proceed, not pre-empting the
place of that unknown City that may be calling man. Thus the apparently mincing ideal of the state that shocks Liberals is the
charter of freedom for the spirit of man. By foregoing the in-
spirational political theories, man taps other and more enduring
sources of inspiration. Such are the virtues of convenience. For
"convenience," in its older English usage, meant consonance,
especially the correspondence of things with thought. The convenient state has constant reference to man, and is adjusted to his
real endeavors. It is the meeting of political institutions with the
mystery and activity of man, a standing-together (constitution)
of political discipline and the individual discipline of exercised
freedom.

It would be useless to claim that the term "conservative" always
means, or should mean, the advocacy of such a convenient state.
As we have seen, the "divine right" and providential branch of conservatism belongs rather with the proponents of an Order of Justice.
But I think it is true that the really great conservatives were not
believers in the sacredness of the *status quo*. What distinguishes
them—look at Burke and Johnson, Burckhardt and De Tocqueville, Randolph and Calhoun, Adams and Newman—is a pungent
sense of reality, of man's real needs and achievements. The great
conservatives were not powerful, with personal stock in the *status
quo*; they were, almost all of them, the foes of current fads, of
enthusiasms that commanded the power centers of their day as
Liberalism has swept the world in our time. The caricature of the
conservative as a mere lover of his own person and privilege will
not stand. If you want to find the jealous embrace of attained
power, go to the Liberal ideologue, who must have total power
in order to achieve his total reform, his rapid creation of Utopia.
Go to Pericles, to Caesar, to Robespiere, to Bonaparte; to Lenin,
or Mao Tse-Tung, or Castro; go, for that matter to Wilson and
Franklin Roosevelt. The conservative is typically moderate,
skeptical, critical. He forms a permanent opposition to that per-

manent new theory or new regime that promises escape from the hard human realities.

To say that the enduringly important conservatives of the past were believers in a politics of convenience is to imply that the conservatism offering most to the future will be of this same kind; and I think the implication is a sound one.

Empirical Observations

CHAPTER TEN

The Morality of Free Enterprise

JOHN CHAMBERLAIN

WHEN Brent Bozell argues[1] against Frank Meyer's contention that freedom is the "condition of a virtuous society," he is speaking a truth that would hold only for a race of martyrs. For it takes a rare individual to follow the dictates of his own choice of virtue if the whole machinery of the state—the courts, the police, the army—happens to be against it. A Thoreau will go to jail rather than pay taxes to a government engaged in an unjust war—but how many Thoreaus do we have with us at any given moment?

True, a state may be controlled by a church which, by revealed truth, may be presumed to possess an absolute standard of virtue. But the church-run state is no guarantee of a virtuous society. Men, as the authors of *The Federalist Papers* insisted long ago, are not angels, and even bishop-statesmen in history have been guilty of great monstrosities of behavior. Borgia Popes are possible, and the Word from the Burning Bush sometimes gets completely distorted when passed along.

The state being what it is, a mechanism of control that shares in the innate viciousness, or the original sin, of average mankind, it should follow axiomatically that the less power it has, to exert compulsion on human choices between good and evil, the less likelihood that it will be able to impose on people a total mistake. The surest way to limit state power is to keep it separate from the people's livelihoods. The power to enforce absolute evil on a population becomes tremendous—and tremendously tempting—

when the entire economic apparatus of a nation becomes an integral part of its machinery of rule. When the state possesses the power to deny bread to a man's family, even potential martyrs will hesitate to go against its edicts.

To be sure, economic freedom is no guarantee of virtue. But, as Frank Meyer has put it, "a free economy is . . . necessary in the modern world for the preservation of freedom"—and this, as we have said, is the condition of virtue for anyone but the bravest of the brave. But if economic freedom is no guarantee of virtue (only good men can guarantee that), it nevertheless manages to establish a state of affairs in which the virtuous can turn thumbs down on an evil business practice. But when economic freedom is limited, virtue becomes more difficult. Whenever the state impinges on economics, corruption ensues almost automatically. Sometimes the corruption comes at the instigation of businessmen themselves. At other times the corruption is forced on both consumers and producers by a set of planning officials who have their own predilection to original sin, chiefly the sin of overweening pride.

The first type of corruption is the one which Marxists commonly attribute to *laissez faire*. But it is not *laissez faire* when a businessman tries to use the state to get a special advantage for himself; indeed, it is its precise opposite. It may be true, as Adam Smith once said, that when two or more businessmen get together, their natural tendency is to conspire among themselves to raise prices. But to make a conspiracy effective there must be state co-operation in the creation and maintenance of a monopoly. The value of the Sherman Anti-Trust Act does not reside in the efforts of the Department of Justice to ferret out and prosecute wrongdoing. No, the value of the anti-trust legislation is that, as long as it is on the books, no combination of businessmen can bring suit in a court of law against their recalcitrant brothers for breaking agreement to fix a price or accept a quota or limit one's sales to a given geographical area. The anti-trust laws permit the maverick to break the line—and in a free society you may be sure there will always be a plentiful supply of mavericks in any trade.

The post-Civil War period, the "Gilded Age," figures heavily in our history textbooks as the era of our most rampant business corruption. But all the classic instances of this corruption involve the use of state power. It was not *laissez faire* when the Big Four of the Central Pacific Railroad, Collis P. Huntington, Leland Stanford, Mark Hopkins, and Charles Crocker, wangled from $16,000 to $48,000 a mile from the Federal government to lay their tracks across the California Sierra and the Nevada desert to Utah. The Big Four set up a construction company of their own and paid the United States taxpayers' money into their own pockets for building fees, thus placing themselves advantageously on two sides of a bargain. This was corruption—but it was with the necessary connivance of the state. The Union Pacific organizers, building westward from a site near Omaha in Nebraska to meet the Central Pacific, followed the same sort of corrupt practice with the creation of the Crédit Mobilier building corporation. Again, the Crédit Mobilier was not an instance of *laissez faire*; it was a device set up by a chosen beneficiary of government. If the free market had been left to build the railroads, the corruption of Crédit Mobilier would have been virtually impossible.

By its seizure of taxpayers' money to subsidize the favored businessmen of the Central and Union Pacific and other western railroads, the government drained the post-Civil War economy of the Eastern seaboard of much working capital. Surely this contributed to the Depression of 1873. When Commodore Vanderbilt heard of the collapse of one government-supported railroad venture in the West, he remarked, "Building railroads from nowhere to nowhere at public expense is not a legitimate business." The Commodore's use of the word "legitimate" bespoke a sound conception of natural, as against positive, law. As one who had had to bribe hold-up men in state legislatures to stay off his back when he was pursuing the *naturally* legitimate business of building railroads with his own money to go from somewhere to somewhere, the Commodore knew that the state, when brought into economic matters, is a prime engineer of corruption.

During the late nineteenth century the railroad rebate figured as a source of corruption. A case can be made for rebates given for an assured regularity and a guaranteed volume of shipments. When a discount is standard for everybody under stated terms, no one can object. But when the Rockefeller-controlled South Improvement Company exacted "drawbacks" from the Pennsylvania Railroad on rates paid by competitors for their oil shipments, it amounted to using a power conferred by the State of Pennsylvania to dip into the competitors' tills. This was legalized theft. The State of Pennsylvania, which had allowed its offending creature, the railroad, to exercise the government-conferred legal power of eminent domain to establish its right of way in the first place, quite properly objected when it was presented with evidence of the railroad's grant on "drawbacks." The South Improvement Company had manifestly corrupted the Pennsylvania Railroad, a utility that had been granted privileges on the plea that it was there to serve the public without favoritism.

The long history of the Gilded Age may be spangled with instances of corruption, but the crimes cannot be laid to free competition or to the *laissez-faire* capitalism espoused by Adam Smith. Today, when the state's hand is in practically everything, businessmen try to get the state mechanism on their side without thinking that the power to confer is also the power to control and, eventually, to destroy. Everybody takes the short view. When Hans Isbrandtsen tried to revive the American whaling industry, for example, short-sighted United States lard producers at once moved on Washington to kill off the promised competition from whale oil. Isbrandtsen's own whale ship was indubitably American-owned; so the whale oil it produced was not legally subject to tariff. Unfortunately, however, Isbrandtsen made the innocent mistake of shipping some of the American-produced oil back to the United States from the Antarctic whaling grounds by a foreign owned tanker. This enabled his whaling ship to remain on the Antarctic cruising grounds for a much longer period. But it also enabled the domestic lard producers to enter a specious plea that transport on a foreign-owned vessel had turned Isbrandtsen's American-produced whale oil into a commodity subject to a high tax. Despite this and other annoyances, Isbrandtsen persisted in the whaling business. But by forcing a tax on whale oil, the American lard producers, as the story is told by Isbrandtsen's biographer James Dugan, "set off an inexorable chain reaction. Norwegian whalers, priced out of the American market, sold their oil to German margarine manufacturers. German consumers, who had been eating American lard on their bread, now bought margarine instead. In two years United States lard exports to Germany fell from 500 to 100 million pounds." Thus the corruption of government by favor-seeking businessmen who had only contempt for *laissez-faire* principles backfired. It was a clear case of the come-uppance that is the inevitable long-term penalty of following an evil course.

The ring-around-the-rosy of attempted legal suppression of one's competitors goes on and on and on. The trucking companies, who ought to be happy that no Interstate Commerce Commission regulates their rates, move to get the government to ban railroad mergers. The railroads, which need the mergers in order to achieve the savings that will allow them to survive, quite rightly object to the trucking companies' attitude. But then, with a magnificent dis-dain for logical consistency, the railroads turn right around and lobby against the use of coal-slurry pipe lines by the coal com-panies. The coal companies are properly outraged by this effort to deprive them of a cost-cutting method of transport. But they, in turn, object when the quotas on imported residual oil are relaxed. When everybody gets his own handout or special privilege by corrupting the government into making things difficult for his competitors, the advantages will all be cancelled out. But every-body will be paying his share of the cost of maintaining the government bureaucracies that regulate and oversee the dispensa-tion of the special favors. Nobody stands to win but the bureau-crats, who will gain the morally iniquitous privilege of living off the high costs of the rest of the population.

When businessmen try to use the seizure of government mecha-nisms to channel special favors to themselves, they can hardly ob-ject when labor unions follow suit. But the truly *laissez-faire* businessman has a right to protest when a government-sheltered, industry-wide union succeeds in imposing a settlement on him which, if he were permitted to make his own uncoerced bargains with workers, he would never have to accept. The legal exception of unions from the anti-trust laws is an egregious example of cor-rupt favoritism on the part of government.

The type of corruption that is forced on consumers and pro-ducers alike by the Planning State has already reached the United States in the field of electric power. Here the taxpayer, who is everybody, has his substance taken by legal theft to subsidize cer-tain special power users. Connecticut pays for the Tennessee Valley Authority in Tennessee and Alabama. The TVA, in turn, is exempted from the taxes that are paid by private power companies, which are kept from growing by a legally sanctioned deprivation of funds that belong to them by every precept of natural, as against positive, law.

The worst depredations of the Planning State, however, have taken place abroad. And the more "total" the planning, the more vicious the crimes that are committed in its name. In Castro's Cuba, innocent democrats have been deprived of their equity in companies merely because certain stockholders had been supporters of the fallen dictator Batista. In Nazi Germany, Goering enriched himself by simple fiat, taking what rightfully belonged to others. In Soviet Russia, some four million peasants, not all kulaks by any means, were casually murdered by the mechanism of a state-induced famine in order to force collectivization on Russian agriculture. In Red China a similar murder by artifical famine is practiced as a matter of state policy. These things are not ordinarily labeled "corruption." But they certainly come under the heading of corruption in any older dictionary.

As Hayek has pointed out in his classic *The Road to Serfdom*, the corruption induced by planners inevitably takes on gangster aspects. For it takes men with the morality of monsters and the hides of pachyderms to accept jobs that involve riding roughshod over dissenting individuals. An overriding Plan can admit of no exceptions and must be managed by the rigid enforcement of a statistical punch-card operation. This means coercing people to work where the Plan says they must work. And it means compulsion on the consumer to take what the planner thinks is good for him. No sensitive man, alive to the quivering differences in individuals, could make himself part of any such planning operation. So, as Hayek says, "the worst get on top"—and they are the sort of men who do not scruple to use force to stay on top.

In England, which happens to have a lot of sensitive people even when they call themselves Socialists, the government drew back from total planning when it became apparent that the police would have to be called in to enforce state allocation of labor power. When the "control of engagements" was given up because of its threat to "liberties of the subject," England saved itself from the ultimate in corrupt practice. What, after all, is more corrupt than the compulsion of a man to labor against his will in a place and for a master whom he has not chosen? This sort of thing used to be called slavery.

To return to Frank Meyer's epigrammatic statement that "freedom is the condition of a virtuous society." It is the "condition" of virtue when applied economically because it allows the consumer to discipline the businessman into following the path of rectitude as a prerequisite of getting the business. With the consumer standing ready to give or withhold patronage, the producer must behave because it is what pays him his long-term profit.

As Mr. Meyer puts it, "a free economy can no more bring about virtue than a state-controlled economy." But a free economy is of vital importance in maintaining the political freedom under which a continuing state of evil can be resisted. And if the consumer is a good human being who knows quality and service and a good price when he sees them, he can force virtue on even the most amoral businessman.

CHAPTER ELEVEN

The Challenge of Crisis

PRELIMINARY THOUGHTS ON A CONSERVATIVE DEFENSE DOCTRINE

STEFAN T. POSSONY

I

A DECLARATION of faith is not a policy. "Faith" in politics smacks of literature and wonderland. Instead of utopianism, we need purposes and specific objectives which can be attained. Platonism in politics is useless, and little more than escapism on the part of those who cannot think of practical tasks and those who prefer to talk rather than to act.

Policy, to be effective, must reflect a sense of direction. On the basis of desired trends, it must be responsive to *real* trends. If trends and purposes do not converge, we must comprehend the causes and meaning of the divergence and analyze whether—and how— the trends can be deflected to coincide with our goals.

As a next step, purposes must be reviewed with a sense of realism. This means that facts are acknowledged even when they do not fit preconceived notions, and that factual interrelationships are interpreted objectively, and in their entirety, and not on the basis of selective evidence.

The realist clearly distinguishes the past as well as the future from the present. The realistic conservative conceives of the future neither as an idealization of the past nor as a utopia of perfection. By extrapolating from trends affecting the variables; by acknowledging the endurance of the constants; by basing forecasts upon the behavior of the constants and variables; and by differentiating the essence of his purposes from appearances and historically conditioned interpretations, he will propose specific policies. He will insist that these policies must be pursued flexibly, but only so long as the forecasts prove correct; and then only to the extent that events bear out the anticipations which served as the basis for the orginial recommendation.

Realism also means that political programs or decisions must be aimed at common-sense solutions of concrete problems; that the application of doctrinaire thinking to problem solving is rejected; and that "problems" and "solutions" must not be conceived in so broad or so abstract a framework that the problems never can be concretized and the solutions never achieved.

In their weak moments, conservatives often dream of a utopia derived from a romanticized idealization of a particular historical period. But conservatives also have their strong moments—and then they fight against abstractions, halos, and illusions. When he has his feet on the ground, the effective conservative is an idealist because he emphasizes political morality, rights, and duties, and because he evaluates the accomplishments of a given state and social order on the basis of cultural, ethical, and human values. He also is an empiricist because he measures by the *full* time dimension of human experience and discounts generalizations derived from short-lived experiences.

The conservative may disagree with specific policies and even with the over-all policies, or trends, that dominate an entire period. He may be opposed to institutions, especially state institutions committed to revolutionary purposes. He will not, I hope, interpret in a literal sense Hegel's dictum that what is real also is reasonable. But if he reflects upon the matter, he will realize that no policy, however objectionable, is entirely capricious or lacking in sense. If he applies realism to conservatism itself, he probably will discover that foolish policies have often been adopted because the conservative has been unable to formulate realistic alternatives. Revolutions occur when evolution collapses; and this happens, almost invariably, when conservatives lose their sense of reality and act upon political dogmas which they have learned by rote. Don Quixote was not a conservative; he was a fool.

The central contention of conservatism has been that, before building something new, the values that have been created must be conserved. I take it that in the United States the foremost conservative commitment is to defend—and improve—our constitutional government, our laws and our system of order; the social and economic institutions on which our civilization is built; and the Bill of Rights, which is the basis of our human relationships and freedoms. The conservative is not committed to preserving our morality, institutions, laws, and procedures precisely as they now are, let alone to upholding their abuses, but he is committed to the notion that reforms must be accomplished by Americans through constitutional process, and neither through revolution nor imposition by a foreign conqueror.

As one of the major means of attaining a free society and individual liberty, the conservative is committed to upholding a free-enterprise, property-based economy. The right to own property is an inalienable human right. Yet the commitment to free enterprise is largely instrumental and therefore not absolute. Nevertheless, it is extremely strong because conservative purposes can hardly be implemented through a centrally managed economy.

The conservative does not believe that the end justifies the means. He specifically rejects the notion that brutality and immorality, or unrestrained state power, are effective, let alone preferred means. Basing himself upon historical experience, he knows that radical or criminal means never lead to the accomplishment of humane purposes and that usually such means become ends in themselves in a power struggle for the sake of power. He believes that realistic and concrete objectives can be reached safely, at the least human and economic cost, through evolution and development. Ends which cannot be attained step by step through "moderate" means are *ex hypothesi* utopian or fraudulent.

The American conservative is committed to defending the United States and its social order aginst the threat of Communism, including take-over by infiltration and revolution and including the political and physical destruction of the United States by nuclear weapons. This task involves the defense of our allies and friends, particularly those who are imbued with the notions of constitutional government. It implies further that free institutions must be defended and the scope of freedom must be enlarged gradually throughout the world, including the Soviet Union and the countries subjugated by Communists.

By 1963, few conservatives would deny that defense against Communism or the elimination of the Communist threat has become the foremost national task. Unfortunately, however, many conservatives misconstrue the nature of this threat, are overimpressed by subsidiary problems, and oppose policies that are almost mandatory, because they do not fit historical precedents or their preconceptions about the scope of government.

There is a basic difference between American and European conservatives: The American conservative is very close to a position which, about a hundred years ago, was described as "Manchester liberalism"; he is a man advocating minimal government and, *tout court*, governmental abstention from the economy. This type of conservative thinking is derived from the young and liberal John Stuart Mill, but in listening to some self-styled conservatives, I am reminded more often of Bakunin than of any other author. The European conservative does not want an oversized state, but he wants an effective and strong state. He desires the highest efficiency of the state within the spheres of its responsibility. He opposes the anti-state notions of liberalism and anarchism and considers the state not only to be indispensable, but by its very nature—which is to care for the community as a whole—the most significant of all social and political institutions. A well-conceived and effectively run state, which is based on law and precludes arbitrariness and oppression, is a good, not a bad, institution. Hence the idea that checks and balances must be used to cripple the state is an absurd extension of the correct notion that abuses and usurpations of power must be prevented.

Unlike the statist or absolutist, the conservative recognizes that there are limits to the effectiveness of state action; that the state must not assume functions which are more effectively discharged by other institutions or by individuals; and that the state is not an end in itself but a mere *instrument* in the service of society. Tyranny must be prevented just as much as impotence, if only because the latter leads to the former. The state needs to be neither more nor less powerful than required by a given situation. A rational conservative therefore will assume that the "true measure" of the state will not be static but will rise or fall with the challenges posed by reality.

My specific contention is that many conservatives are inclined to advocate unworkable defense policies, partly because, like many Liberals, they profess to see a threat of militarism; partly because, in their own version of persecution mania, they sense a dark plot to socialize the United States through massive armament efforts; and partly because the organization, size, and rising costs of defense appear to them to be destructive of free society. When their attention is called to the fact that a society which would be defeated or destroyed can hardly remain free, they either argue that a society which arms itself to the teeth in order to withstand nuclear attack will, by necessity, lose its freedom anyway; or they rationalize the threat and "eliminate" it by verbal sophistry.

Let us look at some hard facts:

1. Since the advent of long-range aircraft, intercontinental missiles, submarine-launched missiles, and orbital vehicles, the United States is no longer immune to direct attack. It no longer possesses the option of taking as much or as little of any war as accords with its desires, and it no longer can decide unilaterally to what extent and at what speed it cares to mobilize its resources. Previously, the United States was four to seven thousand miles removed from the decisive battlegrounds. At present, the battle zone includes North America, and it is very likely that the United States will become the Flanders of a future world conflict. Thus, the United States has lost one of its greatest strategic assets—its isolation.

2. In modern war, the old distinctions between civilians and soldiers, or between the battlefield and the peaceful hinterland, no longer apply. War threatens every woman and child just as much as every soldier and every civilian worker, and every hamlet as much as every armaments plant and military base. Nuclear weapons have transformed the United States, with all its people and cities, its industries and transport systems, into a highly vulnerable target complex. Nuclear attack can damage seriously, and possibly destroy, our resources and jeopardize the health and survival of a large fraction of the American people. War affects the entire society. Consequently, a society which cannot wage and

survive military conflict cannot endure. Thus, a second asset has been lost—our invulnerability.

3. The combination of fast, long-range delivery means with nuclear firepower provides would-be aggressors with surprise-attack capabilities unparalleled in history. American strategy can no longer be geared to the assumption that we can enter war un-armed and still win. Our preparedness must be responsive to the danger that the *first* battle may be decisive and that it may co-incide with the *last* battle. Thus, a third asset has been lost—long warning time.

4. Industrial capacity henceforth must be geared to winning or at least surviving the first battle as a prerequisite of preserving any portion of our strengths. Strong forces-in-being must be created and maintained in constant and instant readiness. Thus, a fourth asset has been lost—our freedom to use resources for civilian purposes and to provide for defense only if and when this is clearly necessary, after the occurrence of war. Previously, the United States economy was geared to defense in about one year out of ten; henceforth, it must support defense on a permanent basis.

5. Defense and armaments must be predicated on the realiza-tion that weapons require constant modernization. Technological progress is extremely rapid. It depends, in part, on research pro-grams and budgets; i.e., on deliberate decisions. But technology is also something of an impersonal force; new discoveries often re-sult from accidents or are by-products of routine scientific investi-gations and industrial-product improvements. In its broad stream, technology is evolutionary, characterized by a steady accumula-tion of knowledge; but there frequently occur "revolutions" that derive from new fundamental insights into the laws of nature and from engineering "break-throughs." Both types of "quantum jumps" inevitably lead to new types of weapons.

a. In antiquity, the weapons cycle lasted hundreds of years. Even during the nineteenth century, the life span of a particular weapon was counted in decades. At present, it often takes only five and not more than ten years before a weapons system becomes obsolescent or obsolete, and must be replaced by the "next gen-eration." For example, the B-17 heavy bomber was replaced in succession by the B-29, the B-36, and the B-52, which in turn will be replaced by a supersonic long-range heavy bomber. The development from the B-17 to the B-52 lasted about twenty years; presumably the B-52 will be discarded by 1970, or earlier: a cycle of nine years, or less, not counting "submodels" (like the B-52H), which often involve substantial changes.

b. In addition to the heavy bomber, there emerged missile delivery systems, which within about ten years after inception will have progressed from the Atlas via the Titan to the Minuteman, a three-year cycle, except that older models can be continued in service for many years.

c. This is by no means the whole story: There was a parallel development in medium bombers, in fighter bombers, in medium- and short-range missiles, and in submarines. And there is the beginning of a similar cycle in spacecraft.

d. Other things being equal, a military force whose armaments are tuned to a faster weapons cycle will defeat a force geared to a slower cycle. Moreover, the force with the faster cycle can be victorious without broad quantitative superiority.

Thus, the United States lost a fifth asset: It can no longer depend upon last-minute imports of weapon technology from abroad.

6. Modern weapons systems incorporate ever higher energy levels. The horsepower incorporated in delivery means increased within fifty years by a factor of five thousand to fifty thousand. Firepower, within less than twenty years, increased by twenty to thirty million. Speed, range, altitude, endurance, payload, versatility, in brief all performance characteristics without exception, have been progressing by significant jumps. To handle these enormous and growing energy requirements, new metals and materials and entirely new production processes must constantly be developed. The energy progression is greater, for example, than the advance from human feet via the bicycle to the large automobile and even the DC-7; yet military technology must perform such a progression every five to ten years. It is entirely unlikely that technological progress will slow down in the foreseeable future. Hence, the costs of defense will rise, and not merely because of inflation. Thus, the sixth asset—low-cost defense—is gone.

The specific threat to the United States is not posed by abstract technology or by an imaginary opponent, but by concrete nuclear warheads and bombs that would be carried in Soviet missiles, planes, and submarines from bases in the Communist bloc to targets in the United States. The enormity and growth of this threat are not fully realized. It is not understood that once the Soviet Union had acquired nuclear weapons and long-range means of delivery, an entirely new leaf was opened in the history of the United States.

There are some who detect a gigantic bluff in the Communist armaments program. A few have doubted the existence of Soviet nuclear weapons and missiles, and many have derided Soviet space accomplishments. The "doubting Thomases" imply that they know more than the heads of states, prime ministers, and defense secretaries of the leading NATO countries, the directors of the American and British nuclear programs, the Joint Chiefs of Staff, NATO commanders in chief, the commanders of SAC and ADC; and the technical committees of the United States Congress. But there is no reason to assume that these "doubting Thomases" really know what they are talking about, especially since most of them never had access to genuine information. The Soviet fifty-megaton shot and the missile firings into the Pacific probably resolved the "doubt" in favor of the Western intelligence services.

There may be an argument about quality, numbers, deployments, and readiness of Soviet weapons. There is room to dispute the extent of the Soviet capability to mount an intercontinental surprise attack. There can be disagreement about the date when the Soviet military establishment will be ready for full-fledged nuclear war. There is no question but that the Soviets try to exaggerate their strengths and fool us about the rapidity of their buildup. There is no denying that estimates of relative Soviet power have been inflated and misused in election campaigns. More importantly, there is a campaign to demoralize the American people on the grounds that the Communists have become unconquerable.

However, exaggerations are not combatted by underestimations and amnesic wishing away. Despite the exaggerations of their bluff, the Soviets *are* building modern weapons systems; they *are* making enormous and rapid progress, and the threat posed by them to the United States—and the rest of the world—*is* growing without let-up. Whether this threat is a little larger or a little smaller, a little earlier or a little later, such doubts do not substantially modify the American security problem. If we cannot manage at all times to hold against the Communists an overbearing counterthreat—

and this means superior forces-in-being—then victory will go to them by default.

Those who underestimate the Soviet threat have an image of "Russia" as it was before World War I. They mistake a country which for about seventy years has been under intense industrialization, for a peasant economy. They ignore the very substantial scientific resources which the Bolsheviks inherited and developed. They exaggerate American technological superiority and the industrial difficulties encountered by the Soviets in mass production of modern weapons. Consequently, they have a distorted image of the basic balance of strength between the Soviet Union and the United States.

Soviet military strength has a base broader than just the Soviet Union. Eastern European resources, espionage through which Western technological know-how is transplanted behind the Iron Curtain, and trade allowing the Soviets to copy Western equipment, sometimes with improvements, are significant components of Soviet power. By contrast, the West is handicapped because scientific and technological developments behind the Iron Curtain may remain hidden or are discovered late, and because many Western technological resources are used for the good life and not for defense. Substantial technological resources potentially available to NATO have remained outside Western defense programs.

It is a widespread illusion that their planned economy prevents the Soviets from achieving rapid technological growth. A centrally planned economy is unsuited to improving the standard of living and is ineffective in serving the requirements and desires of consumers. But it offers many advantages for war preparation. A military economy is characterized by the fact that there is a monopolist consumer, the general staff. It is therefore poor economics to assume that a country, because it has poor living standards, cannot have excellent weapons. Moreover, in a regulated economy, compression of consumption is more feasible as an aid to large-scale armament than in a free system.

A planned economy is, relatively speaking, most effective in those branches where, as in heavy industry and armament industry, production rests on a few large plants and involves a simple distribution system. Furthermore, the Soviet type of economy offers obvious advantages for the allocation of manpower and for the financing and management of large, high-priority research programs. Their planned economy exhibits considerable disadvantages across the board, and perhaps the Communists would be an even greater threat if they did not own a Communist economy. But as it is, the Soviets are entirely capable of giving us a good run for our money.

Incidentally, modern technologies can readily be adopted by backward economies. Sometimes it is even easier for them to go in for ultramodern equipment; they are breaking new ground and do not need to worry about write-offs, recapitalization, and relocations. The Japanese proved this point quite convincingly in World War II.

Thus, the comfortable theory that the Communists must rely on subversion and upheaval as their only practical means of conquest, and the contention that they do not really possess a genuine option for war, are wishful thinking. There is a phony Lenin quote to the effect that the best way to defeat the United States would be to force it into bankruptcy through armaments. Lenin never said it; he could have said it, in fact, only if he had shared the economic convictions of Senator Taft. In that case, we could sleep very soundly.

There is an internal and an external threat. If any Communist strategist harbored illusions that the United States could be toppled through internal aggression alone, he would be kicked out as a "rightist deviationist." The internal threat to the survival of the United States as a political and physical entity is significant *only* because it is tied to the external threat, from which, as a threat, it is derived, and to which it makes a partial, though significant contribution. It does not require much familiarity with Communist doctrine to understand that in the Communist mind the external and internal threats are dialectically intertwined,—as in fact they are in strategic reality.

As to the notion that the Communists are not really aiming at nuclear war, it can be easily documented that the contrary is correct. For example, Marshal Rodion Malinovsky, Minister of Defense, speaking in October, 1961, to the Twenty-second Party Congress, made it perfectly plain that a future war would be fought primarily with nuclear rocket weapons and would be initiated by surprise attack. He left no doubt, as Khrushchev has never left any doubt, that war will be avoided only if the United States surrenders. The Communists are indeed supreme realists. They understand far better than some illusionary conservatives that the United States, the main roadblock to their final success, can be eliminated only through nuclear weapons and military victory. Once this is understood, it may be admitted readily that the United States is threatened also by internal aggression aimed at weakening its defense posture.

In the contest between the United States and the Soviet Union, the Communists enjoy several advantages:

1. The United States has allowed them the initiative in selecting the time of attack by renouncing any first-strike intention. Consequently, we can retaliate only with those forces which are left over *after* the initial hostile strike; yet they would be able to apply their full power against American forces and targets. Their relatively free choice of timing also permits them to optimize their relative posture in terms of weapons quality and quantity. These facts mean that the military ruble goes strategically a far longer distance than the defense dollar.

2. Their centralized decision-making structure, and the high priority given to preparation for war, allow them to cut technical and industrial lead-times to a minimum. The Soviets have not always been able to beat American lead-times, and they often pay the penalty of excessive haste. Nevertheless, their weapons cycles tend to be shorter than ours, and they have been gaining steadily in the quality race. Where they had trouble catching up, as in the nuclear area, they have succeeded through psychological strategy in delaying our program while they have accelerated theirs. The test-ban treaty is a psychological ploy to overtake the United States in the nuclear field.

3. Soviet budgetary policies, their willingness to allocate relatively larger outlays to basic and applied research, and to the industrial defense effort as a whole, as well as their unwillingness to underfinance and "stretch out" military programs, provide them with advantages so obvious that they need not be labored.

What do these facts spell out for the United States?

First, it is imperative to take away from the Kremlin the certainty that Soviet forces will be allowed by the United States to strike the first blow. If the United States wants to survive *and* to avoid being forced into a preventive war, it must maintain a broadly superior military force financed by a substantial budget.

Second, to keep pace with the threat, our forces and budgets will have to be increased gradually and perhaps in spurts. This situation does not change even if the Soviet armament effort, for economic reasons, temporarily sags.

Third, the present military budget of about sixty billion dollars is too low and sooner or later may have to be increased.

Fourth, American research and development programs are too small and too diffused, inadequately geared to strategic needs, and unnecessarily divorced from European talent and resources. Basic research also is lagging. These programs are not oriented towards winning the technological race for the free world.

Fifth, the American weapons cycle must be shortened. Hence political and strategic decision making must be speeded up, and industrial management must be streamlined.

Sixth, this enormous effort must be continued indefinitely. There is no short cut through "arms control" and compromise by negotiation. Perhaps the Soviet Union will develop more peacefully than is predictable today; perhaps technological revolutions will change the strategic situation. We can *hope* for such turns of fortune; but we must *plan* for the continuation and aggravation of the crisis.

At this point, the following argument may be advanced: Granted that the defense effort must be gigantic, it remains nevertheless desirable to keep governmental expenditures to a minimum. Is it then not wise to pare military programs to the most "austere" level compatible with security? This was essentially the concept which Secretary of Defense Louis Johnson sold to President Truman and which Secretary of the Treasury George Humphrey sold to President Eisenhower. I consider this concept to be useless.

In the first place, it is a platitude, since obviously no one is going to buy more armaments than necessary. In the second place, this concept avoids the real problem which is to define the assumptions and methods through which irreducible minimal armament levels can be determined objectively. In practice, this concept has shown itself to be destructive, inasmuch as time and again it has eliminated promising research, slowed weapons cycles, reduced necessary support systems, cut armaments levels, lowered the enlistment rate, played into Soviet hands (e.g., the Sputnik success), and by logical extension, induced us to risk various disarmament adventures. This concept precludes gradual and systematic build-up and arbitrarily imposes "ceilings," which, *after* the opponent has made an unexpected advance (he always does), are quickly abandoned. Subsequently, costly crash programs are instituted. In the end this concept costs us more and gives us less security than the concept that we always should stay ahead of the Communists, quantitatively and qualitatively, and hence should think in terms of curves rather than levels and ceilings.

A variant of the "pare-down" solution stipulates that the military must be forced to discard old weapons systems more rapidly. But "old" weapons systems can be given up only gradually, depending on the *de facto* rate of modernization. *If we want to avoid lapses in security, we must provide for the overlapping in time of old and new weapons.* We cannot throw away the old before the new systems are ready for use.

Is "unification," designed to eliminate "duplication," the hoped-for panacea?

Savings through merging of functions are possible, but, as should be clear to a conservative, basic reorganization must be gradual, lest it become disruptive. "Unification" is applicable, and indeed attractive, to several support functions and to staff and command. But combat forces cannot be merged—this would make as much sense as combining the carburetor with the battery. Each weapons system is a "force," whatever it may be called. It always will remain organizationally necessary to group similar weapons systems together in over-all "forces," known as Army, Navy, and Air Forces. More, rather than fewer, presumably "competitive" weapons systems must be anticipated.

Hence the need for intermediary organizational echelons between the supreme command and the field forces will grow; organizational complexity cannot be overcome by short cuts and panaceas. Reorganization is day-by-day routine, and substantial reorganization may be necessary to preserve, in the face of expanding technology, that degree of cohesion and responsiveness without which command cannot be effective. But an organizational scheme predicated on the notion that the intermediate levels, which accomplish most of the noncombat functions, can be eliminated, is impractical. There is nothing sacrosanct about a triple military establishment; we might find it advisable, for example, to add space and guerrilla establishments to the Army, Navy, and Air Force. But as long as we fight on land, at sea, and in the air, the triple setup remains a prerequisite for the unification of combat forces under unified or joint field commands. "Service rivalry" sometimes was beneficial, sometimes harmful, and I hold no brief for it. But I do not believe that the imposition of "unified" thinking or of a "single" doctrine would enhance our security. It may just make mistakes more costly.

II

With these factors in mind, the question is: How can the defense effort be run without destroying the very basis of our society? We must be clear that if this effort were managed ineffectually, our society would be destroyed. But if we are effective and efficient, and arm successfully, it can enhance our way of life. To the extent that we achieve and subsequently maintain broad technological superiority, accomplish shorter weapons cycles, and improve our decision-making and command structure, the economic pressures of defense can be alleviated; at the same time a higher level of security can be achieved. Since confidence usually stimulates investment and since confidence depends upon a feeling of security, notably a conviction that war is unlikely and, if it were to come, would not be cataclysmic, American victory in the technological race probably would enhance American economic growth.

The defense effort must be managed by the government. Hence "big government" is unavoidable. Let us not forget that the size of the government has purely instrumental meaning and that a small government is a means, not an end. If our over-all ends demand large-scale defense, we must reconcile ourselves to the inescapable requirement of sustaining large Federal programs. But this does not mean that we have to buy an omnipotent state, that we must abandon constitutional government or allow the government to assume functions unsuited for public management. Nor need we tolerate the bureaucracy's undermining our free institutions or restricting the contributions of the "private sector."

An American defense effort can be productive only if it is run within the spirit of the free-enterprise system and if it takes full advantage of the specific strengths of our economy. Here I would make a number of proposals:

1.   Under present renegotiation practices, the profit incentive is almost eliminated from defense contracts. Procurement and R&D contracting trends have been undermining competition and have led to an ever greater and unnecessary concentration of technological resources in government hands. If defense contractors were allowed adequate profit margins, write-offs, and liberal tax advantages for research and experimentation, the technological basis could be broadened. There should be tax incentives which would result in restoring ample endowment funds to the universities, in order to reverse the stream of research which went from the universities to the government. It may be added that many corporations could display greater initiative in fostering research for defense.

2.   The elimination of socialist types of legislation seems mandatory. For example, the Atomic Energy Act established an entirely unnecessary socialist monopoly which has hamstrung progress, notably in civilian nuclear applications. Similarly, policies of "pro-capitalist socialism," such as arbitrary quotas on oil imports, are of very questionable value. Our patent legislation deserves a hard look, including the provision that inventions made by government employees become an entirely free commodity. The *gratis* utilization of American patents by hostile powers must be prevented. Our much overrated anti-trust legislation often is applied capriciously and frequently inhibits greater efficiency in corporate operations and a proper division of labor in research. There is also the problem of subsidies, which run to over seven billion dollars. Some of those cannot be avoided, but most were designed as temporary aids and have become inexcusable in a prosperous growth economy.

3.   Proper currency management is equally mandatory. This is one area where the impact of socialist thinking has been critically destructive of strategic purposes; many foreign aid programs result in little more than a weakening of the dollar. A conservative must, of course, favor investments abroad as a means of achieving economic development; in the end progress abroad will stimulate

progress at home. But uneconomic investments do not contribute anything to anybody. By undermining the dollar, they undermine the economic strength of the United States. A weakening of our economy would soon affect other countries and might lead to a reduction of military strength. Unrealistic aid programs have inflationary effects, depress the flow of local investment, and sometimes encourage "nationalization." Directly and indirectly they discourage the gradual evolution of free economies in the underdeveloped areas.

4. Trade policy must be adjusted to conform to strategic criteria. The notion that trade as such is good and, in any shape or form, contributes to peace is illusory. If we trade with Communists through their trade monopoly, we can be sure that we are contributing to their strength. Trade must serve to enhance the economic posture of the free world and of countries which are at least potentially friendly. Some risks undoubtedly will have to be taken, and some compromises and *quid pro quos* will be inevitable. But trade and, above all, commercial credit should not be used to aggravate our security tasks.

5. Politics must be taken out of United States interest and discount rates. If we want to stimulate growth, we must stimulate investment first. Our interest (and profit) rates are artificially depressed; hence investment and growth are lagging. A more realistic interest rate also would tend to restrain consumption.

6. The ratio between consumption, investment, and armament, which presently prevails in the United States, probably is unsound. A slowdown in the *growth* of consumption may become necessary, and there is nothing intrinsically bad about stabilizing consumption. This can be achieved without discriminatory legislation through sales taxes, differential corporate taxes, tax credits, commodity specifications, etc. and also by making it more attractive for individuals to invest. If consumption increases are postponed and investments funneled into armament industries and foreign countries, the money which the consumer cannot spend on himself should not be lost to him forever. Defense emergencies are no reason to deny property rights. Instead of taxing the consumer to the hilt, he should have alternative options for investment. Tax rebates or reductions could be granted to investors in risk ventures, and instead of making presents of American tax money to foreign

nationals, the person who is forced to invest should get advantages, at least future advantages, out of the transaction. The economic growth of the underdeveloped countries would accelerate if foreign aid gradually were superseded by investment and by contractual arrangements between American and foreign firms.

7. It seems to me that a different approach to the bookkeeping of our military budgets also is in order. At present, every military expense is considered a loss and therefore is paid from tax revenue. Most military expenditures, like unused insurance policies, are losses, but not all are. We do not usually consider education a loss, but when a soldier is being trained and educated by the armed forces, we book it as an expenditure. Many of the inventions without which our modern economy never would have come into existence originated in, or were made practical by, the military services, including, in varying degrees, radio, television, a dependable automobile engine, aircraft, computers, and several medical advances. Our investments in nuclear energy, which to date have total something like forty billion dollars, are listed as a loss; yet this invention has given the United States—and the world—a new fuel which will have economic importance at least equal to that of coal. Most of these forty billions were spent on "insurance," but, through a fraction of this sum, heretofore practically valueless rock was appreciated to a potential value of many trillions of dollars. This, of course, is not the only economic gain which we ultimately will realize from nuclear energy. But why must we paralyze our thinking by assuming that this sort of national investment is a loss to our economy? And why, incidentally, must the investment be exclusively from taxes?

8. Better distribution of defense costs among the major allies is a method of reducing the burden on each partner. We have not pushed this very far, because it involves sharing of nuclear "secrets" (which the Soviets already for the most part possess). The development of the Common Market facilitates an imaginative application of the common-defense concept to economics. For example, the burden of such costly programs as anti-missile defense and space must by no means be carried by the United States exclusively. NATO-wide economic co-operation also could improve joint investment programs in the underdeveloped countries.

All these are examples to illustrate the point that the task is not to bewail the rising costs of defense but to devote attention to the reform of the American economy.

With this point out of the way, the foremost economic defense problem is to reform the tax system. There is no technical difficulty in running a huge defense program in a free economy, *provided* proper methods of financing are employed. Inflation must be rejected, of course. Hence, the choice is between loans and taxes. If defense costs rise, a tax increase on the basis of the present unfair and fundamentally bad tax legislation would be disastrous for every branch of the economy. A tax reform, if skillfully conceived, could alleviate the tax burden *and* ultimately yield higher revenue.

Tax reform is the foremost concrete measure which conservatives should advocate. But how to go about it? Undoubtedly, a tax reform, especially if it is as drastic as it should be, will produce a temporary deficit. Because there is a tendency to look with horror at the national debt of the United States, the discussion usually stops here. Obviously, a high debt is undesirable, requires the annual payment of huge amounts of interest, and complicates the management of currency. Nevertheless, it is sometimes preferable to borrow money than to tax. A real tax reform cannot be carried out unless we are willing to finance it through a ten to twenty billion dollar loan. Such an addition to the national debt would be no benefit, but if this is the price that has to be paid for the enormous advantage of acquiring a workable tax system, such a loan would be a most economical debt. Of course, any tax reform must be accompanied by a simultaneous reduction of civilian government expenditures.

Are we not overimpressed by red ink? Surely, no corporation ever looks exclusively at its debts and completely forgets about its assets. The property owned by the government of the United States, figured extremely conservatively, constitutes assets worth twice the national debt. There is no reason why we should hold on to many of these possessions. It would be advisable to sell industries to private management and thus add to the tax revenue instead of using tax income to keep them going.

There is opposition to the income tax, and proposals have been made for its repeal. In my judgment, this tax has many undesirable features, but the primary question is: given the rising defense outlay, what would take the tax's place? I have seen calculations showing that the return of Federal-run businesses to private corporations would save just about the personal income tax revenue, provide additional indirect savings, and produce added revenue from corporate and excise taxes. As a result, the government would, or could, achieve a surplus and reduce the national debt.

Enormous sums are poured down the drain. State and local government in 1959 lost 1.3 billion dollars in water, transportation, insurance, and housing but made 250 million dollars in power and liquor: a loss of over one billion, not counting the "invisible" loss of the tax revenue which private management would achieve. There is no earthly reason why governments should be engaged in these activities, why they should not be turned over to tax-paying private management.

The hospital bill for all government runs to 3.6 billion dollars, not counting "compulsory charities." Much of the free service given to veterans would be insurable; perhaps two billion could thus be saved, without hurting the veterans.

Publicly owned electric-power utilities would, if in private hands, produce about 500 million dollars of tax revenue, but they now *cost* the taxpayer about 600 million, a loss of 1.1 billion; the public, in addition, loses about 500 millions of income which would be distributed if the power were generated privately.

Another example: the governments pay about 600 million for parks and recreation, but it should be easy to break even in this activity or make a profit. The loss in this venture alone is about one billion dollars, at a minimum.

There is an unnecessary postal deficit of almost 800 million dollars. Sugar subsidies and excise taxes, together with government-induced overpayments for raw and refined sugar, cost the consumer about 360 million a year.

If agriculture were putting its fair share into the national kitty (i.e., paying 9 per cent of the tax revenue, corresponding to its position in the American economy), it would pay taxes totaling about 7 billion dollars. Actually, the federal government pays about 8 billion dollars to agriculture and recoups only 1.5 billion, plus perhaps 2 to 2.5 billion in tax revenue from farm-related industry and farm labor. At a minimum, the actual fiscal loss attributable to agriculture is about 4 billion dollars. In addition, owing to price supports, the consumer probably overpays about 4 billion dollars for farm products. This is about the same amount the government pays to get rid of the surplus on the world market. In the first round we double the price in the United States, and in the second round we halve it abroad; both operations are paid for by the taxpayer. God only knows what the true costs of the agricultural programs are, but the out-of-pocket losses are certainly not below 10 billion annually. The true economic loss is at least 15 billion and may be over 20 billion dollars per year.

We are running this fantastic program for the benefit of 1.5 million marginal farmers. If we were to pay those farmers outright $5,000 per farm and year for doing nothing, or even allow them to make any additional profit they can, we would be saving 2.5 billion dollars for the fiscal year. Or we might withdraw all subsidies and supports and make agriculture a tax-free profession; this at least would cut the useless and costly circulation of funds through the bureaucracy. Despite all the direct and indirect subsidies, the income of one-fourth of the full-time farmers is depressed—*and* the United States is about to become a net importer of agricultural products. Occasional wheat deals, to help maintain Khrushchev in power, do not change the basic trend.

The government's economic operations more and more resemble those of the *ancien régime* before 1789. It is clear that if the government were eliminated from business, tax revenue would no longer be needed to underwrite nonprofitable economic programs. Instead, those activities which by nature are "business" and not strictly administration and welfare could be made lucrative and would yield rather than consume tax revenue. At the same time, though many financial sanctuaries and privileges sustaining this crazy system would be eliminated, the public would have a good deal more disposable income.

But nonbusiness state expenses should not be sacrosanct either. The government contribution to education is over fifteen billion dollars; much of this—at least five billion, I would guess—is a useless expenditure because low-IQ students derive no benefits from a twelve-year "education." Furthermore, much of the expense is wasted quality-wise,[1] and technological improvements in teaching, which might reduce educational costs, are introduced only slowly or not at all.

Additional billions could be saved if the various government insurance programs gradually were placed on a business basis; further, service could be improved *and* the social value of the programs enhanced.

With respect to defense, too, savings could be made by monetizing, to some extent, services and logistics for dependents, such as laundries, barbers, canteens, local transportation, base maintenance, housing, etc. (Care would have to be taken, however, not to create monopolies through licensing.)

Sometimes, because bureaucracy is not capable of operating flexibly, it cannot take advantage of price fluctuations and changes. Thus, we could have saved considerably if space heating for our forces in Europe had been switched, by 1950 or so from coal to oil. There are hundreds of examples of this kind.

The armed forces are holding thirty billion dollars worth of industrial property, most of which is on a stand-by basis and never will be used. Depreciation and maintenance of these facilities swallow up, unnecessarily, one or two billions a year. These plants and this equipment should be sold to private corporations or, if obsolete, scrapped.

Similarly, a great part of what is alleged to be defense responsibilities could be turned over to corporate management. Presumably, the functions of the General Services Administration also could be entrusted to private firms; or that Administration itself might be incorporated.

Thus, through monetizing and reasserting the market principle in *all* spheres of economic activity, we would be able to finance defense and yet accentuate growth and cut taxes. By all means, let us have temporary tax-financed "shock absorbers" to facilitate the transition.

However, the question still would be whether enough would be saved to eliminate the income tax, which accounts for half of the Federal tax revenue. We must also ask whether almost exclusive reliance on corporate and excise taxes is advisable in any case. It is evident that progression rates can be scrapped, that double taxation can be eliminated, that rates can be lowered, etc. It strikes me that the data—with their double countings and hard-to-calculate interconnections—are too uncertain to allow, at this time, firm recommendations for the blanket repeal of any type of tax.

There is an elementary first step, and that is to oblige the government to publish adequate statistics on its business activities, to adopt bookkeeping compatible with corporate practices, and to calculate exactly the gains and losses of the government's business operations. On this basis, the spinning off of governmental business ventures should be initiated in earnest and without delay.

As a second and parallel step, I would recommend that conservative economists figure out efficient methods of transition to permit government reform without unnecessary friction and upheaval. Those parts of the population who are affected directly must be enabled to adjust gradually to the new conditions.

Economic reform is a matter of strategy. Unless we have a proper concept which reflects all the data and unless we proceed by evolution, we shall not get anywhere.

In the strictly political area, there is a crying need for better understanding of strategic and armaments problems and of the disadvantages of socialistic management. This is largely a matter of education and public opinion, and I will refrain from discussing this point further.

Within the government, there is a need for organizational provisions allowing faster decision making on strategic challenges and on the adoption of weapons systems, improved institutions for the waging of the cold war, and better co-ordination across the board with our allies. The informational flow to Congress is most inadequate and requires improvement. In the long run, a democracy cannot work if the legislature is not privy to crucial information and if the government uses the classification system in a selective manner to influence votes.

Such organizational reforms as here illustrated can be made without technical difficulty and without undermining the constitutional character of our government; quite the contrary. The difficulty, so far, has been that the need for these reforms has not been felt.

Constitutional democracies are entirely capable of defending themselves, and of doing so without abandoning their political and economic systems. Democracies, in fact, have proved themselves to be better equipped for fighting wars than dictatorships. The history of Switzerland provides us with the most illustrative and pertinent example. This conservative democracy has always been capable of maintaining substantial military forces; it has preserved, for generations, a largely free economy; it has never compromised its constitutional processes or the democratic nature of its government; yet each Swiss citizen serves in the army, first on full-time assignment and subsequently, for many years, on part-time assignments. In two world wars, Switzerland was deemed by Germany to be too formidable an opponent to attack. Thus, the crowning glory of this constitutional-democratic strategy has been that Switzerland, through proper attention to defense, preserved its peace.

The Swiss really are a nation in arms. Every American has the Constitutional right to bear arms, but this is a forgotten tradition. An enlargement of National Guard and reserves forces and the institution by new legislation of voluntary service for a few hours weekly—for example, to man air defenses or perhaps do something about the shelter program—would boost United States deterrence of Soviet attack immeasurably. Community-wide collections for the purchase and maintenance of arms are another possibility. There definitely is plenty of room for voluntary defense actions outside the government. If the citizens were to insist on their *personal right* to self-defense, government paternalism would be checked, and defense would be strengthened.

Conservatism must do better than propose solutions that are applicable in good international weather only. It must mature into an all-weather philosophy of government. If conservatives were to view defense with less "concern" and approach the problem in a constructive spirit, who knows but that we might find the solutions for which free peoples and free men are searching?

CHAPTER TWELVE

Notes Towards an Empirical Definition
of Conservatism

RELUCTANTLY AND APOLOGETICALLY GIVEN BY

WILLIAM F. BUCKLEY, JR.

I AM asked most frequently by members of the lecture audience
two questions, to neither of which have I ever given a satisfactory
answer. The first is asked by those who share my feeling that the
world is in crisis and the nation imperiled: "What can I do?" I
don't know, and haven't the stomach to contrive an aphoristic answer. The second question, asked alike by friendly and hostile
listeners, is: "What is conservatism?" Sometimes the questioner—
guarding against the windy evasiveness one comes to expect from
lecturers—will add, "preferably in one sentence." On which occasions I have replied: "I could not give you a definition of Christianity in one sentence, but that does not mean that Christianity is un-
definable."

Usually that disposes of the hopes of those who wish a neatly
packaged definition of conservatism which they can stow away in
their mind, alongside (or replacing?) the definitions of astrology,
necrophilia, xenophobia, and philistinism. Those who are obstinate
I punish by giving, with a straight face, Professor Richard Weaver's definition of conservatism as "a paradigm of essences towards
which the phenomenology of the world is in continuing approxi-
mation"—as noble an effort as any I have ever read. The point is, of

course, that we are at that stage dangerously close to mere verbal gambiting. I have never failed, I am saying, to dissatisfy an audience that asks the meaning of conservatism.

Yet I feel I know, if not what conservatism is, at least who a conservative is. I confess that I know who is a conservative less surely than I know who is a Liberal. Blindfold me, spin me about like a top, and I will walk up to the single Liberal in the room without zig or zag, and find him even if he is hiding behind the flower pot. I am tempted to try to develop an equally sure nose for the conservative, but am deterred by the knowledge that conservatives, under the stress of our times, have had to invite all kinds of people into their ranks, to help with the job at hand, and the natural courtesy of the conservative causes him to treat such people not as janissaries, but as equals; and so, empirically, it becomes difficult to see behind the khaki, to know surely whether that is a conservative over there doing what needs to be done, or a radical, or merely a noisemaker, or pyrotechnician, since our rag-tag army sometimes moves together in surprising uniformity, and there are exhilarating moments when everyone's eye is Right.

I have, after all, sometimes wondered whether I am myself a true conservative. I feel I qualify spiritually and philosophically; but temperamentally I am not of the breed, and so I need to ask myself, among so many other things, how much it matters how one is temperamentally? There are other confusions. Whittaker Chambers, for instance, distinguished sharply between a conservative and a "man of the Right." "You," he wrote me, on resigning as an editor of *National Review*, "are a conservative, and I know no one with better title to the word. But I am not one, never was. I call myself, on those occasions when I cannot avoid answering the question, a man of the Right." I reflected on that letter, needless to say, as would you if you were the editor of a journal from which Whittaker Chambers had just withdrawn, and remarked an interesting thing, that in the five-year history of the journal, Chambers was the only man to resign from its senior board of editors explicitly because he felt he could no longer move within its ideological compass; and yet he never wrote a piece for us (or in the last dozen years of his life, that I know of, for anyone else), that was out of harmony with the thrust of *National Review's* position.

Oh yes, people withdraw, and write and denounce you, and

swear green grass will never grow over your grave, on account of this or that offensive article or editorial or book review; but these losses are merely a part of the human attrition of outspoken journalism. They prove nothing, in our case, that has anything to do with ideological fecklessness. What I am saying is that notwithstanding the difficulty in formulating The Conservative Position, and the high degree of skepticism from our critics before *National Review* was launched, *National Review's* position was, I believe, instantly intelligible, from the very first issue. *He would probably say that anyway,* (the skeptic will charge) *it being in his and the journal's interest to say so.* But I make that statement on empirical grounds, as I propose to make others in this essay on the meaning of conservatism, which will reason *a posteriori* from the facts to the theory—and which will be based exclusively on my own experiences as editor of *National Review.* Since I shall not allude to it again, let me say so now, unambiguously, that this essay is about the experiences of *National Review* and their bearing by the processes of exclusion on a workable definition of contemporary conservatism. I do not by any means suggest that *National Review* is the only functioning alembic of modern conservatism; merely that it is the only one whose experiences I can relate with any authority, and that its experiences may be interesting enough to be worth telling.

Roughly the same group of men, representing the same vested interests in certain ideas and attitudes, continue to be the major participants in *National Review.* The magazine found instantly, and expanded, an audience which seemed intuitively to grant and to understand the happy eclecticism of the magazine's guiding ideas; while the critics, whose delighted line at the beginning was one or another variant on the theme, "This country needs a conservative magazine, and having read *National Review*, we *still* say what this country needs is a conservative magazine," finally, except for the bitter-enders, gave up, and began to refer to *National Review* as, plain and simple, a "conservative journal." Others, who as I say refuse to give up, will continue to refer to it only after a ritualistic pejorative: "the McCarthyite *National Review*," "the ultrarightist *National Review*," etc. But it being so, that in language the governing law is usage, it is by now predictable that those who feel Peter Viereck or Clinton Rossiter or Walter Lippmann are the true architects of American conservatism are bound to enter the ranks of eccentricity, like the right-wing gentlemen who, because they continue to insist on referring to themselves as "liberals," have difficulty communicating with the rest of the world, which for two generations now has understood liberalism to mean something else, beginning, roughly, from the time Santayana observed that the only thing the modern liberal is concerned to liberate is man from his marriage contract.

I

Since this is to be an empirical probe, based, apologetically, on my personal experience as editor of *National Review*, I shall speak about people and ideas with which *National Review* has had trouble making common cause. In 1957, Whittaker Chambers reviewed *Atlas Shrugged*, the novel by Miss Ayn Rand wherein she explicates the philosophy of "objectivism," which is what she has chosen to call her creed. Man of the Right, or conservative, or whatever you wish to call him, Chambers did in fact read Miss Rand right out of the conservative movement. He did so by pointing out that her philosophy is in fact another kind of materialism, not the dialectical materialism of Marx, but the materialism of technocracy, of the relentless self-server, who lives for himself and for absolutely no one else, whose concern for others is explainable merely as an intellectualized recognition of the relationship between helping others and helping oneself. Religion is the first enemy of the objectivist, and after religion, the state—respectively, "the mysticism of the mind" and "the mysticism of the muscle." "Randian Man," wrote Chambers, "like Marxian Man, is made the center of a godless world."

Her exclusion from the conservative community was, I am sure, in part the result of her dessicated philosophy's conclusive incompatibility with the conservative's emphasis on transcendence, intellectual and moral; but also there is the incongruity of tone, that hard, schematic, implacable, unyielding dogmatism that is in itself intrinsically objectionable, whether it comes from the mouth of Ehrenburg, or Savonarola—or Ayn Rand. Chambers knew that specific ideologies come and go, but that rhetorical totalism is always in the air, searching for the lightning rod of the ideologue-on-the-make; and so he said things about Miss Rand's tone of voice which, I would hazard a guess, were it the tone of anyone else's voice, would tend to make it, *eo ipso*, unacceptable for the conservative:

> ... the book's [*Atlas Shrugged's*] dictatorial tone ... is its most striking feature. Out of a lifetime of reading, I can recall no other book in which a tone of overriding arrogance was so implacably sustained. Its shrillness is without reprieve. Its dogmatism is without appeal ... resistance to the Message cannot be tolerated because disagreement can never be merely honest, prudent, or just humanly fallible. Dissent from revelation so final can only be willfully wicked. There are ways of dealing with such wickedness, and, in fact, right reason itself enjoins them. From almost any page of *Atlas Shrugged*, a voice can be heard, from painful necessity, commanding: 'To a gas chamber—go!' The same inflexibly self-righteous stance results, too, in odd extravagances of inflection and gesture ... At first we try to tell ourselves that these are just lapses, that this mind has, somehow, mislaid the discriminating knack that most of us pray will warn us in time of the difference between what is effective and firm, and what is wildly grotesque and excessive. Soon we suspect something worse. We suspect that this mind finds, precisely in extravagance, some exalting merit; feels a surging release of power and passion precisely in smashing up the house."[1]

As if according to a script, Miss Rand's followers jumped *National Review* and Chambers in language that crossed the i's and dotted the t's of Mr. Chambers' point. (It is not fair to hold the leader responsible for the excesses of the disciples, but this demonstration by Miss Rand's followers—never repudiated by Miss Rand —suggested that her own intolerance is easily communicable to other Objectivists.) One correspondent, denouncing him, referred to "Mr. Chambers' 'break' with Communism"; a lady confessed that on reading his review she thought she had "mistakenly picked up the *Daily Worker*"; another accused him of "lies, smears, and cowardly misrepresentations"; still another saw in him the "mind-blanking, life-hating, unreasoning, less-than-human being which [sic] Miss Rand proves undeniably is the cause of the tragic situation the world now faces ..."; and sumimng up, one Objectivist

wrote that "Chambers the Christian Communist is far more dangerous than Chambers the Russian spy."

What the experience proved, it seems to me, beyond the inac-
ceptability of Miss Rand's ideas and rhetoric, is that no conservative
cosmology whose every star and planet is given in a master book of
co-ordinates is very likely to sweep American conservatives off
their feet. They are enough conservative, and anti-ideological, to
resist totally closed systems, those systems that do not provide for
deep and continuing mysteries. They may be pro-ideology enough
to resist such asseverations as that conservatism is merely "an attitude of mind." But I predict on the basis of a long association with
American conservatives that there isn't anybody around scribbling
into his sacred book a series of all-fulfilling formulae which will
serve the conservatives as an Apostles' Creed. Miss Rand tried it,
and *because* she tried it she compounded the failure of her ideas.
She will have to go down as an Objectivist; my guess is she will go
down as an entertaining novelist.

II

The conservative's distrust of the state, so richly earned by it,
raises inevitably the question, how far can one go? This side, the
answer is, of anarchism—that should be obvious enough. But one
man's anarchism is another man's statism. *National Review*, while
fully intending to save the nation, probably will never define to the
majority's satisfaction what are the tolerable limits of the state's
activity; and we never expected to do so. But we got into the problem, as so often is the case, not by going forward to meet it, but by
backing up against it.

There exists a small breed of men whose passionate distrust for
the state has developed into a theology of sorts, or at least into a
demonology; to which they adhere as devotedly as any religious
fanatic ever attempted to adhere to the will of the Lord. I do not
feel contempt for the endeavor of either man. It is intellectually
stimulating to discuss alternatives to municipalized streets, as it is
to speculate on whether God's wishes would best be served if we
ordered fried or scrambled eggs for breakfast on this particular
morning. But conservatives must concern themselves not only with
ideals, but with matters of public policy, and I mean by that something more than the commonplace that one must maneuver within

the limits of conceivable action. We can read, and take pleasure in, the recluse's tortured deliberations on what will benefit his soul— Bernanos' *Diary of the Country Priest* was not only a masterpiece; it was also a best-seller. And we can read with more than mere amusement Dr. Murray Rothbard's suggestion that lighthouses be sold to private tenants who will chase down the beam in speed boats and collect a dollar from the storm-tossed ship whose path it illuminates. Chesterton reminds us that many dogmas are liberating, because however much damage they do when abused, it cannot compare with the damage that might have been done had whole peoples not felt their inhibiting influence. If our society seriously wondered whether or not to denationalize the lighthouses, it would not wonder at all whether to nationalize the medical profession.

But Dr. Rothbard and his merry anarchists wish to *live* their fanatical anti-statism, and the result is a collision between the basic policies they urge, and those urged by conservatives who recognize that the state sometimes is, and is today as never before, the necessary instrument of our proximate deliverance. The defensive war in which we are engaged cannot be prosecuted by voluntary associations of soldiers and scientists and diplomats and strategists, and when this obtrusive fact enters into the reckonings of our state-haters, the majority, sighing, yield to reality; while the small minority, obsessed by their antagonism to the state, would refuse to give it even the powers necessary to safeguard the community. Dr. Rothbard and a few others have spoken harshly of *National Review*'s complacency before the twentieth-century state in all matters that have to do with anti-Communism, beading their litanies about the necessity for refusing at any cost to countenance the growth of the state. Thus, for instance, Mr. Ronald Hamowy of the University of Chicago complained about *National Review* in 1961 ". . . the Conservative movement has been straying [far] under *National Review* guidance, leading true believers [the words were not capitalized in the text] in freedom and individual liberty down a disastrous path . . . and that in so doing they are causing the Right increasingly to betray its own traditions and principles."[2]

And Mr. Henry Hazlitt, reviewing Dr. Rothbard's *magnum opus, Man, Economy, and State* (Van Nostrand), enthusiastically for *National Review*, paused to comment, sadly, on the author's "extreme apriorism," citing, for instance, Dr. Rothbard's opinion that libel and slander ought not to be illegalized, and that "even black-mail 'would not be illegal in the free society. For blackmail is the receipt of money in exchange for the service of not publicizing certain information about the other person. No violence or threat of violence to person or property is involved.' . . . when Rothbard wanders out of the strictly economic realm, in which his scholar-ship is so rich and his reasoning so rigorous, he is misled by his epistemological doctrine of 'extreme apriorism' into trying to sub-stitute his own instant jurisdprudence for the common law prin-ciples built up through generations of human experience."

"Extreme apriorism"—a generic bull's-eye. If *National Review's* experience is central to the growth of contemporary conservatism, extreme apriorists will find it difficult to work with conservatives except as occasional allies helping to storm specific objectives. They will not be a part of the standing army, rejecting as they do the burden of reality in the name of a virginal anti-statism. I repeat I do not deplore their influence intellectually; and tactically I worry not at all. The succubi of Communism are quite numerous enough, and eloquent enough, to be counted upon to put their ghastly presences forward in effective protest against the marriage of any but the most incurable solipsist to a set of abstractionist doctrines whose acceptance would mean the end of any human liberty. The virgins have wriggled themselves outside the mainstream of Amer-ican conservatism. Mr. Hamowy, offering himself up grandly as a symbol of the immaculate right winger, has joined the Committee for a Sane Nuclear Policy.

III

We ran into the John Birch Society, or more precisely into Mr. Robert Welch—we have always distinguished between the two. Mr. Welch's position is very well-known. Scrubbed down, it is that one may reliably infer subjective motivation from objective result; e.g., if the West loses as much ground as demonstrably it has lost during the past fifteen years to the enemy, it can only be because those who made policy for the West were the enemy's agents. The *ultima ratio* of this position was the public disclosure —any three-hundred-page document sent to hundreds of people can only be called an act of public disclosure—that Dwight Eisen-hower is a Communist. (To which the most perfect retort—was it

Russell Kirk's?—was not so much analytical, as artistic: "Eisenhower isn't a Communist—he is a golfer.")

In criticizing Mr. Welch we did not move into a hard philosophical front, as for instance we did in our criticisms of Miss Rand, or of the neo-anarchists. Rather we moved into an organizational axiom, the conservative equivalent of the leftists' "Pas d'ennemi à gauche." The position has not, however, been rigorously explicated or applied. Mr. Welch makes his own exclusions: for instance, Gerald L. K. Smith, who, although it is a fact that he favors a number of reforms in domestic and foreign policy which coincide with those favored by Mr. Welch (and by *National Review*), is dismissed as a man with an *idée fixe*, namely, the role of the Perfidious Jew in modern society. Many right wingers (and many Liberals, and all Communists) believe in a *deus ex machina*. Only introduce the single tax, and our problems will wither away, say the followers of Henry George. . . . Only expose the Jew, and the international conspiracy will be broken, say others. . . . Only abolish the income tax, and all will be well. . . . Forget everything else, but restore the gold standard. . . . Abolish compulsory taxation, and we shall all be free. . . . They are called nostrum peddlers by some; certainly they are obsessed. Because whatever virtue there is in what they call for, and some of their proposals strike me as highly desirable, others as mischievous, no one of them can begin to do the whole job, which continues to wait on the successful completion of the objectives of the Committee to Abolish Original Sin. Many such persons, because undue emphasis is given to their pandemic insight, the linch pin of social reconstruction, are dissatisfied with *National Review*. Others react more vehemently—our failure to highlight *their* solution has the effect of distracting from its unique relevance, and so works positively against the day when the great illumination will show us the only road forward. Accordingly, *National Review* is, in their eyes, worse than merely useless.

The defenders of Mr. Welch who are also severe critics of *National Review* are not by any means all of them addicts of the conspiracy school. They do belong, however inconsistently, to the school that says that we must all work together—as a general proposition, sound advice. Lenin distinguished between the sin of "sectarianism," from which suffer all those who refuse to co-operate with anyone who does not share their entire position, right down to the dependent clauses; and the sin of "opportunism," the weakness of those who are completely indiscriminate about their political associates.

The majority of those who broke with *National Review* as the result of our criticisms of Mr. Welch believe themselves to have done so in protest against *National Review's* sectarianism. In fact I believe their resentment was primarily personal: they were distressed by an attack on a man who had ingratiated himself with them, and towards whom their loyalty hardened in proportion as he was (so often unfairly) attacked. When an attack rose from their own ranks, their bitterness ran over; and now it is widely whispered that *National Review* has been "infiltrated."

The questions we faced at *National Review* were two. The first, to which the answer was always plainly no, was whether Mr. Welch's views on public affairs were sound. The editors knew from empirical experience that they were not. Enough of us had recently been to college or were in continuing touch with academic circles to know that the approaches to the internal security, and to foreign relations, that have been practiced by successive administrations after the Second World War are endorsed by the overwhelming majority of the intellectuals of this country, and that therefore any assumption that only a Communist (or a fool, as Mr. Welch allowed) could oppose the House Committee on Un-American Activities, or favor aid to Poland and Yugoslavia, must deductively mean that the nations' academies are staffed, primarily, by Communists (or fools). It is not merely common sense that rejects this assumption, but a familiarity with the intricate argumentation of almost the entire intellectual class (who, of course, are not fools, at least not in the sense in which Mr. Welch uses the word).

The second question then arose, whether it was necessary explicitly to reject Mr. Welch's position as an unrealistic mode of thought; and that had to be answered by asking whether at the margin it contributed or not to the enlightenment of right-wing thought. The answer was not as obvious as one might suppose. Ironically, the assumptions that reason will prevail and that logic and truth are self-evident—the constituent assumptions of those who believe that that syllogism is correct which says *A*) We were all-powerful after the war, *B*) Russia is now as powerful as we are, therefore *C*) We willed the enemy's ascendancy (the essence of

Mr. Welch's methodology)—argued in favor of leaving Mr. Welch alone. Thus might one reason, if he believed that the truth will triumph: if Mr. Welch merely succeeds in drawing people's attention, which otherwise would not be drawn, to public events, to read about them and think about them—then those people, though introduced to public concern by Mr. Welch, will by the power of reason reject, upon examination, Mr. Welch's specific counsels; and graduate as informed members of the anti-Communist community.

But reason is *not* king (and many of those who have shrunk from Mr. Welch have done so less because on reflection they repudiate his analysis, than because public scandal of a kind has in fact attached to discipleship in a movement dominated by a man with a very special set of views which reality rejects). And so it seemed necessary to say what one hoped would be obvious: that the Welch view is wrong; that it is wrong irrespective of the many personal virtues of Mr. Welch, and wrong irrespective of how many people who were otherwise politically lethargic, are now, thanks to Mr. Welch, politically animated.

In consequence, *National Review* was widely criticized for "throwing mud" at Mr. Welch (a curious way to refer to the act of throwing at Mr. Welch his own statements!); and some battle lines (and some necks) were broken. Whom did we actually alienate? A body of people? A body of thought? I tend to think not, for the reasons I have suggested. If we alienated those who genuinely believe in *pas d'ennemi à droite*, why do these same people (a) applaud Mr. Welch's exclusion of Gerald L. K. Smith and (b) proceed to exclude us? It is no answer to the latter inconsistency that the penalty of turning against someone on your side excuses the turning away against the offender; and Mr. Welch, while failing to be consistent on point (a) above, *was* consistent in respect of (b): aside from a few aggrieved references to *National Review*'s naiveté, and to the Communists' need of conservative front men to implement the smear of the John Birch Society, he has not, as yet anyway, excluded us from the anti-Communist community.

For this reason I tend to put down our encounter with Mr. Welch as having no philosophical significance in an empirical probe of the contemporary locus of American conservatism—except to the extent it can be said that *National Review* rejects what goes by the name of the conspiracy view of history. Most of the followers of

Mr. Welch who broke with *National Review* on account of our criticisms of him showed themselves, by the inconsistency of their own position, to have acted primarily out of personal pique—to which, of course, they are entitled. But perhaps this brief analysis is relevant, if only because it explains why *National Review's* noisiest collision did *not* serve any great purpose in the construction of an empirical definition of conservatism.

IV

A few years ago Mr. Max Eastman, the author and poet, wrote sadly that he must withdraw from the masthead of *National Review:*

> There are too many things in the magazine—and they go too deep—that directly attack or casually side-swipe my most earnest passions and convictions. It was an error in the first place to think that, because of political agreements, I could collaborate formally with a publication whose basic view of life and the universe I regard as primitive and superstitious. That cosmic, or chasmic, difference between us has always troubled me, as I've told you, but lately its political implications have been drawn in ways that I can't be tolerant of. Your own statement in the issue of October 11 [1958] that Father Halton labored 'for the recognition of God's right to His place in Heaven' invited me into a world where neither my mind nor my imagination could find rest. That much I could take, although with a shudder, but when you added that 'the struggle for the world is a struggle, essentially, by those who mean to unseat Him,' you voiced a political opinion that I think is totally and dangerously wrong . . .

Can you be a conservative and believe in God? Obviously. Can you be a conservative and not believe in God? This is an empirical essay, and so the answer is as obviously, yes. Can you be a conservative and despise God, and feel contempt for those who believe in Him? I would say no. True, Max Eastman is the only man who has left the masthead of *National Review* in protest against its pro-religious sympathies, but it does not follow that his deed was eccentric; he, after all, was probably the only man on *National Review* with that old-time hostility to religion associated with evangelical atheism; with, e.g., the names of Theodore Dreiser, Upton Sinclair, Henry Mencken, and Clarence Darrow, old friends of Eastman. If one dismisses religion as intellectually contemptible, it becomes difficult to identify oneself wholly with a movement in which religion plays a vital role; and so the moment came when Max Eastman felt he had to go, even while finding it difficult to answer the concluding observation I made to him: "I continue to feel that you would be at a total loss what to criticize in the society the editors of *National Review* would, had they the influence, establish in America."

Mr. Eastman's resignation brought up an interesting point, to which I also addressed myself in my reply to my old friend.

> You require [I wrote] that I take your letter seriously, and having done so I must reproach myself, rather than you. For if it is true that you cannot collaborate formally with me, then it must be true that I ought not to have collaborated formally with you; for I should hate for you to think that the distance between atheism and Christianity is any greater than the distance between Christianity and atheism. And so if you are correct, that our coadjutorship was incongruous, I as editor of *National Review* should have been the first to spot it, and to act on it. All the more so because my faith imposes upon me more rigorous standards of association than yours does.

I know now, four years after this exchange of letters, that my point here, that the reciprocal of the proposition that a God-hater cannot associate fully with a Christian, is not in fact true—for reasons that are not easy to set down without running the risk of spiritual or philosophical condescension. But the risk must be taken, and I choose the Christian rather than the secular formulation because although the latter can very handily be made, see, *e.g.*, Eric Voegelin's "On Readiness to Rational Discussion",[3] it remains debatable in a way that the Christian formulation does not. The reason why Christian conservatives can associate with atheists is because we hold that above all faith is a gift, and that therefore there is no accounting for the bad fortune that has beset those who do not believe, or the good fortune that befell those who do. The pro-religious conservative can therefore welcome the atheist as a

full-fledged member of the conservative community even while
feeling that at the very bottom the roots do not interlace, so that
the sustenance that gives a special bloom to Christian conservatism
fails to reach the purely secularist conservatism. Voegelin will argue
on purely intellectual grounds, taking as his lesson the Socratic
proposition that virtue can be taught, but only if virtue is defined
as knowledge. Socrates defined knowledge, Voegelin reminds us,
as transcendental cognition, as, in fact, requiring the ability to see
far enough into the nature of things to recognize transcendence, a
view he elaborated in the *Protagoras,* the *Statesman,* and the *Laws.*
The God hater, as distinguished from the agnostic (who says
merely that he doesn't know), or simply the habitual atheist (who
knows there is no God, but doesn't much care about those who
disagree), regards those who believe in or tolerate religion as
afflicted with short-circuited vision—which is the result of a combination of intellectual defectiveness and psychological immaturity,
and leads to the use of analysis and rhetoric which Max Eastman
"can't be tolerant of."

The agnostic can shrug his shoulders about the whole thing, car-
ing not whether, in his time, the conflict between the pro-religious
and anti-religious elements within conservatism will be resolved—
there are so many other things to do than think about God. "Are
you anything?" a lady flightily addressed at her dinner table a
scholarly gentleman and firebrand conservative who had always
managed to nudge aside questions, or deflect conversational trends,
that seemed to be moving into hard confrontations involving religion. He smiled. "Well, I guess I'm not *nothing*"—and the conversation went on pleasantly. Max Eastman *is* nothing; and he can
no more resist the opportunity to incant his nonbelief than the holy
priest can resist the opportunity to proselyte: and so the tension.

Mr. Eastman, like many other programmatic conservatives, bases
his defense of freedom primarily on pragmatic grounds. Mr. Erik
von Kuehnelt-Leddihn once remarked that Friedrich Hayek's
Constitution of Liberty seemed to be saying that if freedom were
not pragmatically productive, there would be no *reason* for freedom. It appears to be the consensus of religious-minded conservatives that ordered freedom is desirable quite apart from its
demonstrable usefulness as the basis for economic and political association. The research of the past ten years on Edmund Burke

would seem to have liberated him from the social pragmatists by whom he had been co-opted. Not to stray too far from the rules of this discussion, I cite a poll a few years ago which showed that the great majority of the readers of *National Review* think of themserves formally as religious people, suggesting that conservatism, of the kind I write about, is planted in a religious view of man.

Though as I say, only a single resignation has been addressed to *National Review* in protest against the magazine's friendliness to religion, there is much latent discord, particularly in the academic world, centering on the question not so much of whether God exists or doesn't (only a few continue to explore the question consciously, let alone conscientiously, and most of the latter are thought of as infra dig)—but on the extent to which it is proper to show towards religion the intellectual disdain the God haters believe it deserves. Russell Kirk was not allowed inside the faculty of a major university in which, *mirabile dictu*, conservatives (specifically, libertarians) had control of the department . . . because of his "religiosity." The Mt. Pelerin Society, an organization of free-market economists and laymen, has recently trembled over inscrutable personal issues, but somewhere, in the interstices of the strife, there is a hardening of positions relating to religious differences, or differences over religion, which sometimes express themselves, loosely, in arguments between "traditionalist" and "libertarian" conservatism.

Though I say the antagonism is here and there seen to be hardening, I have grounds for optimism, based not merely on *National Review's* own amiable experiences with all but the most dedicated atheists, but on the conviction that the hideousness of a science-centered age has resulted in a stimulation of religious scholarship and of all those other instincts, intellectual and spiritual, by which man is constantly confounding the most recent wave of neoterics who insist that man is merely a pandemoniac conjunction of ethereal gasses. The atheists have not got around to answering Huxley's self-critical confession, that neither he nor his followers had succeeded in showing how you can deduce Hamlet from the molecular structure of a mutton chop.

I repeat what is obvious to the reader, that these are merely notes, though not I hope altogether desultory, suggesting where are some of the confines of contemporary conservatism, the walls it runs up against, and bounces away from. The freeway remains large, large enough to accommodate very different players, with highly different prejudices and techniques: from Frank Meyer, with his metaphysics of freedom, to Russell Kirk, with his traditionalist preoccupations; from Brent Bozell with his vision of the church-centered society to Garry Wills and his insuperable wall of separation; from Willmoore Kendall and Ernest van den Haag with their emphasis on the consensual society to Milton Friedman and the Open Society—the differences are now tonal, now substantive; but they do not appear to be choking each other off. The symbiosis may yet be a general consensus on the proper balance between freedom, order, justice, and tradition.

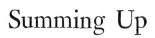
Summing Up

CHAPTER THIRTEEN

Consensus and Divergence

FRANK S. MEYER

IN THE first chapter of this book I attempted to demonstrate both the roots of the divergence between the traditionalist and the libertarian emphases within the contemporary American conservative movement and the common ground of their consensus. The contributors were deliberately chosen as the clearest and ablest exponents of the two tendencies. The reader himself will have to judge whether the book as so assembled confirms the judgment of the opening chapter: that the consensus is a great deal more fundamental than the divergence; that, as against the prevalent Liberalism of the first six decades of the century, contemporary American conservative thought shares a common set of values; and that these values are derived in their essentials from the values held in common by the Founding Fathers.

I should like, however, in conclusion, to indicate what seem to me the major mutual attitudes and underlying principles held by all the writers for this book—attitudes and principles, which, despite specific divergences, they hold in common not only among themselves, but also with the men and women in every walk of life who make up the rapidly growing conservative movement. These basic agreements, I would submit, are demonstrated again and again, in spite of the particular and often rather opposed theses of the writers (even when those theses seem as eccentric to the central conservative position as F. A. Hayek's "Why I Am Not a Conservative" or Willmoore Kendall's critique of the Bill of Rights, a charter which is venerated by the overwhelming majority of American conservatives).

That consensus can perhaps best be summarized by contrasting its basic assumptions, as demonstrated throughout this book (no less than in such a practical political document as Senator Goldwater's *The Conscience of a Conservative*), with the basic assumptions of Liberalism:

1. However varied their religious commitments, the contributors all accept, implicitly or explicitly, the existence of an objective moral order based on what Eric Voegelin has called "the constitution of being"—that is, the existence of immutable standards by which human conduct should be judged.

This conservative acceptance of hard truths imbedded in reality clashes directly with the Liberal dependence upon the instrumental as the foundation and justification of political theory and practice. The Liberal's faith is in "democracy" (the rightness of whatever is desired by 50 per cent of the population plus one), or in "progress" (the rightness of the direction in which events have been and are moving and, therefore, the rightness of whoever has the power to move them), or in "enlightened up-to-date experts" (the rightness of the intellectual fashions of the age) . . . or in a combination of all three.

2. For all of the contributors, the human person is the necessary center of political and social thought. Whether their stress is upon his freedom and his rights or upon his responsibilities and his duties, it is in terms of the individual person that they think and write. They affirm the primacy of the person in contradistinction to contemporary Liberalism, which is essentially concerned with collectivities ("the people," "minorities," "new nations"), instrumentalities for the submergence and manipulation of the persons who make them up. Whether conservatives conceive the fulfillment of the person primarily in terms of individual autonomy or in terms of community, they reject the ideological concept of collective entities; those to whom community is the predominant concept think not in terms of collectivities, but in terms of a rich interpenetration of personal relationships, based upon tradition and confirmed by living generations.

3. This is seen most clearly in the contrast between the conservative and the Liberal attitudes towards the state. While there

is great divergence among conservatives as to the degree to which the state must be limited, they all share, in contrast to contemporary Liberals, a distaste for the use of the power of the state to enforce ideological patterns upon human beings. However much they may differ on the modes by which, and the extent to which, the power of the state should be limited, they are in full agreement that it is but one institution among many and that when its role is aggrandized in the fashion of the twentieth century it becomes dangerous beyond measure.

4. The "planning" of human life, so characteristic of the Liberal *ethos*, is anathema to every one of the contributors. That instrumental outlook in which human beings are conceived as faceless units to be organized and directed in accordance with the blueprints of the social engineer, can be held only when men ignore the separate integrity of each human person as a focus of value and the existence of immutable moral laws not susceptible to ideological reconstruction.

Whether the concentration of conservatives is on the importance of the free-enterprise economic system and the strict limitation of the state as guarantee of the freedom of persons from the plans of the social engineer, or on the living multiplicity of the community arising from the rich tradition of a civilization, the libertarian and the traditionalist emphases within conservatism alike reject the centralized power and direction necessary to the "planning" of society.

5. The spirit of the Constitution of the United States as originally conceived pervades these pages: the limitation of government to its proper functions; within government, tension and balance between local and central power; within the Federal government, tension and balance between the co-ordinate branches. As opposed to the Liberal disdain for the rights of the states before the Federal government, and the Liberal apotheosis of the Executive within the Federal government, conservatives, irrespective of whether their emphasis is upon tradition and order or upon liberty, unite in their veneration of the ordered liberty conceived and executed by the Framers of the Constitution.

6. Throughout the book, sometimes explicit, sometimes implicit, runs a devotion to Western civilization and an awareness of the necessity of defending it against the messianic world-conquering intentions of Communism. Whether (again) our heritage is

valued primarily because it *is* our tradition or because it is en-
visioned as a matrix of freedom unparalleled in historical experience,
there is here no hint of that scorn for one's own, taking the form of
a vague internationalism, which characterizes the Liberal outlook
and which has paralyzed our resistance to Communist aggression
these past decades.

   This, then, I see as the consensus arising from these essays. The
divergencies can be simply summarized as the degree of emphasis
placed by the various writers upon the relative importance for the
good society of moral tradition and freedom; upon the extent to
which, on the one hand, the sanctions of state and community or,
on the other hand, *peitho*, the persuasion of moral and intellectual
authority functioning through free individual persons, should be
emphasized. The most libertarian of the contributors agree upon
the necessity of the maintenance of a high moral tone in society;
those most concerned with order and tradition respect the moral
liberty of the individual person and reject the centralizing state
and egalitarian reduction of the person to a statistic in social planning—the deep-etched stigmata of contemporary Liberalism.

   Returning to our starting point, I would maintain that this book
demonstrates that there exists a common understanding, despite
sharp differences of emphasis, a consenus amid divergence, of the
same quality as that which united those who created the Constitution and the Republic.

Notes to Chapter Four

   1. I want to emphasize that my use of the word "libertarian" signifies the
chemically pure form of classical liberalism, with all of its metaphysical
implications. The term is sometimes used in a different sense to identify
those who insist on limited government and political freedom, without im-
plying acceptance of the anti-religious philosophy here associated with it. I
have used the authoritarian-conservative-libertarian terminology in order to
establish a recognizable continuum of ideas and intend no derogation of "libertarians" of the second sort. Indeed, I believe many of the people who call
themselves "libertarians" would accept the position I describe as "conservative," with its dual emphasis on freedom and moral authority. To the extent
they do, I trust my terminology will not obscure the fact that the argument of
this essay is not an attack on such "libertarians," but a vindication of them.

Notes to Chapter Five

   1. Lord Acton, who is often thus misquoted, has in fact very intelligently said: "Power *tends* to corrupt, and absolute power corrupts ab-

solutely." *Historical Essays and Studies* (London, 1907), p. 504. [My emphasis.]

2. P. Gaxotte, *Thèmes et variations* (Paris, 1957), p. 26.

3. *Ibid.*

4. See W. Eucken, Grundsätze der Wirtschaftspolitik (Bern-Tübingen, 1952), S. 194.

5. W. Röpke, "Der wissenschaftliche Ort der Nationalökonomie," *Studium Generale*, Juli, 1953.

Notes to Chapter Six

The quotation at the head of the chapter is taken from Acton, *The History of Freedom and Other Essays* (London, 1907), p. 1.

1. This has now been true for over a century, and as early as 1855 J. S. Mill would say (see my *John Stuart Mill and Harriet Taylor* [London and Chicago, 1951], p. 216) that "almost all the projects of social reformers of these days are really *liberticide.*"

2. B. Crick, "The Strange Quest for an American Conservatism," *Review of Politics*, XVII (1955), 365, says rightly that "the normal American who calls himself 'A Conservative' is, in fact, a liberal." It would appear that the reluctance of these conservatives to call themselves by the more appropriate name dates only from its abuse during the New Deal era.

3. The expression is that of R. G. Collingwood, *The New Leviathan* (Oxford: Oxford University Press, 1942), p. 209.

4. Cf. the characteristic choice of this title for the programmatic book by the former British Prime Minister Harold Macmillan, *The Middle Way* (London, 1938).

5. Cf. Lord Hugh Cecil, *Conservatism* ("Home University Library" [London, 1912]), p. 9: "Natural Conservatism . . . is a disposition averse from change; and it springs partly from a distrust of the unknown."

6. Cf. the revealing self-description of a conservative in K. Feiling, *Sketches in Nineteenth Century Biography* (London, 1930), p. 174: "Taken in bulk, the Right have a horror of ideas, for is not the practical man, in Disraeli's words, 'one who practises the blunders of his predecessors'? For long tracts of their history they have indiscriminately resisted immprovement, and in claiming to reverence their ancestors often reduce opinion to aged individual prejudice. Their position becomes safer, but more complex, when we add that this Right wing is incessantly overtaking the Left; that it lives by repeated inoculation of liberal ideas, and thus suffers from a never-perfected state of compromise."

7. I trust I shall be forgiven for repeating here the words in which on an earlier occasion I stated an important point: "The main merit of the individualism which [Adam Smith] and his contemporaries advocated is that it is a system under which bad men can do least harm. It is a social system which does not depend for its functioning on our finding good men for running it, or on all men becoming better than they now are, but which makes use of men in all their given variety and complexity, sometimes good and sometimes bad, sometimes intelligent and more often

stupid." (*Individualism and Economic Order* [London and Chicago, 1948],
p. 11).

8. Cf. Lord Acton in *Letters of Lord Acton to Mary Gladstone*, ed. H.
Paul (London, 1913), p. 73: "The danger is not that a particular class is
unfit to govern. Every class is unfit to govern. The law of liberty tends
to abolish the reign of race over race, of faith over faith, of class over
class."

9. J. R. Hicks has rightly spoken in this connection of the "caricature
drawn alike by the young Disraeli, by Marx and by Goebbels" ("The
Pursuit of Economic Freedom," *What We Defend*, ed. E. F. Jacob [Oxford:
Oxford University Press, 1942], p. 96). On the role of the conservatives
in this connection see also my Introduction to *Capitalism and the Historians* (Chicago: University of Chicago Press, 1954), pp. 19ff.

10. Cf. J. S. Mill, *On Liberty*, ed. R. B. McCallum (Oxford, 1946), p.
83: "I am not aware that any community has a right to force another to
be civilised."

11. J. W. Burgess, *The Reconciliation of Government with Liberty*
(New York, 1915), p. 380.

12. Cf. Learned Hand, *The Spirit of Liberty*, ed. I. Dilliard (New York,
1952), p. 190: "The Spirit of liberty is the spirit which is not too sure
that it is right." See also Oliver Cromwell's often quoted statement in his
Letter to the General Assembly of the Church of Scotland, August 3,
1650: "I beseech you, in the bowels of Christ, think it possible you may
be mistaken." It is significant that this should be the probably best-re-
membered saying of the only "dictator" in Bristish history!

13. H. Hallam, *Constitutional History*, ed. "Everyman" (1827), III, 90.
It is often suggested that the term "liberal" derives from the early nineteenth-century Spanish party of the *liberales*. I am more inclined to believe
that it derives from the use of the term by Adam Smith in such passages
as *Wealth of Nations* (London, 1904), II, 41: "the liberal system of free
exportation and free importation" and p. 216: "allowing every man to
pursue his own interest his own way, upon the liberal plan of equality,
liberty, and justice."

14. Lord Acton in *Letters to Mary Gladstone*, p. 44. Cf. also his judgment of Tocqueville in *Lectures on the French Revolution* (London, 1910),
p. 357: "Tocqueville was a Liberal of the purest breed—a Liberal and
nothing else, deeply suspicious of democracy and its kindred, equality,
centralisation, and utilitarianism." Similarly in the *Nineteenth Century*,
XXXIII (1893), 885. The statement by H. J. Laski occurs in "Alexis de
Tocqueville and Democracy," in *The Social and Political Ideas of Some
Representative Thinkers of the Victorian Age*, ed. F. J. C. Hearnshaw
(London, 1933), p. 100, where he says that "a case of unanswerable power
could, I think, be made out for the view that he [Tocqueville] and Lord
Acton were the essential liberals of the nineteenth century."

15. As early as the beginning of the eighteenth century, an English ob-
server could remark that he "scarce ever knew a foreigner settled in England, whether of Dutch, German, French, Italian, or Turkish growth, but

became a Whig in a little time after his mixing with us" (quoted by G. H. Guttridge, *English Whiggism and the American Revolution* [Berkeley: University of California Press, 1942], p. 3).

16. In the United States the nineteenth-century use of the term "Whig" has unfortunately obliterated the memory of the fact that in the eighteenth it stood for the principles which guided the revolution, gained independence, and shaped the Constitution. It was in Whig societies that the young James Madison and John Adams developed their political ideals (cf. E. M. Burns, *James Madison* [New Brunswick, N. J.: Rutgers University Press, 1938], p. 4); it was Whig principles which, as Jefferson tells us, guided all the lawyers who constituted such a strong majority among the signers of the Declaration of Independence and among the members of the Constitutional Convention (see *Writings of Thomas Jefferson*, Memorial ed. [Washington, 1905], XVI, 156). The profession of Whig principles was carried to such a point that even Washington's soldiers were clad in the traditional "blue and buff" colors of the Whigs, which they shared with the Foxites in the British Parliament and which was preserved down to our own days on the covers of the *Edinburgh Review.* If a socialist generation has made Whiggism its favorite target, this is all the more reason for the opponents of socialism to vindicate the name. It is today the only name which correctly describes the beliefs of the Gladstonian liberals, of the men of the generation of Maitland, Acton, and Bryce, the last generation for whom liberty rather than equality or democracy was the main goal.

17. Lord Acton, *Lectures on Modern History* (London, 1906), p. 218 (I have slightly rearranged Acton's clauses to reproduce briefly the sense of his statement).

18. Cf. S. K. Padover in his Introduction to *The Complete Madison* (New York, 1953), p. 10: "In modern terminology, Madison would be labeled a middle-of-the-road liberal and Jefferson a radical." This is true and important, though we must remember what E. S. Corwin ("James Madison: Layman, Publicist, and Exegete," *New York University Law Review*, XXVII [1952], 285) has called Madison's later "surrender to the overweening influence of Jefferson."

19. Cf. the British Conservative party's statement of policy, *The Right Road for Britain* (London, 1950), pp. 41-42, which claims, with considerable justification, that "this new conception [of the social services] was developed [by] the Coalition Government with a majority of Conservative Ministers and the full approval of the Conservative majority in the House of Commons. . . . [We] set out the principle for the schemes of pensions, sickness and unemployment benefit, industrial injuries benefit and a national health scheme."

20. A. Smith, *Wealth of Nations* (London, 1904), I, 432.

21. *Ibid.*

Note to Chapter Seven

1. "The Restoration of Tradition," *Modern Age*, Vol. 5, No. 2 (Spring, 1961).

Notes to Chapter Nine

1. An example of this simplistic reading of Scholastic theory is Robert M. Hutchins' *Saint Thomas and the World State*, Aquinas Lecture (Milwaukee, Wis.: Marquette University Press, 1949). Hutchins argues that the principle of *autarkeia* makes the entire world—now so interdependent and threatened with mutual annihilation—the smallest possible unit for a just political constitution. "Saint Thomas" is pictured as demanding this, though there is, in the lecture, no recognition of the limits put on the principle of *autarkeia* by revelaton or philosophical realism.

2. This doctrine of divine legitimacy was diluted, in certain forms of eighteenth- and nineteenth-century "conservatism," to the view that Providence invariably manifests itself in the history of states, sanctioning established power. Whatever is, is good; the *status quo* is sacred. Burke, and even Tocqueville, tread on or near this dangerous ground whenever they invoke Providence; and Professor Russell Kirk, in his *The Conservative Mind*, seems to say that one denies the existence of a divine Providence by maintaining that its workings are mysterious, not readily traced in the achievement of political power.

3. J. J. Rousseau, *Social Contract*, trans. Willmoore Kendall (Chicago, 1954), I, 6.

4. *Ibid.*, II, 6; Cf. II, 3.

5. It is necessary to distinguish between the *consensus* which must exist to give union to a polity, and the *orthodoxy* exacted by rationalist systems. A consensus, as the word's form indicates, is a meeting of several views on common ground; an orthodoxy is the reduction of all views to a single view. Consensus implies compromise, establishing a minimal ground of agreement on which to base political organization. Orthodoxy goes to the roots of metaphysical and religious awareness and demands a "right view" on these things, not merely a *modus vivendi*. (The contemporary word for this is "ideology," according to the fine anger and bad etymology of John Adams, "the science of idiocy.")

6. The "conservative" belief in a manifest (as opposed to mysterious) Providence is not normally classed with the ideal systems of the Liberals, but it should be. The theological naïveté of such "conservatism" makes the real world ideal, so that "the King's Justice" *is* justice.

7. Burke and Cardinal Newman use the term for their concept of government, but not with sufficient regularity to make it the leading characterization of their descriptions. (Cf. the Rivington *Burke*, VI, p. 257: "They [the French] build their politics, not on convenience, but on truth.")

8. In the current idealization of medieval society, for instance, it is largely forgotten that the Scholastic theologians were virtually unanimous in condemning the guilds as centers of monopoly power. See the important collection of texts in Raymond de Roover's "The Concept of the Just Price: Theory and Economic Policy," *Journal of Economic History* XVIII (1958).

9. Conservatives are generally distrustful of speculatist's rules for the

practical science of politics; as artists are skeptical about the "rules" of academic aestheticians. In both cases, the distrust has been amply justified. In politics, conservatives often find their allies are religious thinkers, artists, and orators rather than the philosophers. Burke had the wisdom to cast his reflection (with an eighteenth-century consciousness of the importance of genre) in the form of orations and letters—a thing ignored by those who now make Burke the giver of a law or the founder of a school.

10. "Who's To Blame?" *Discussions and Arguments* (London: Longmans, 1907), p. 351. The state is to seek "such a justice . . . as may not be inconsistent with the interests of a large conservatism" (p. 350).

11. The Liberal often speaks of replacing selfishness with principle as the final solution to human problems—not seeing that principle, codes and creeds, moral fervor, and fanaticism can be devouring flames. Cf. Ronald Knox's *Enthusiasm*.

12. The modern Liberal lost the fear of power as he came to exercise it; but the "individualist" branch of American conservatism retains it, along with Acton's unfortunate dictum. (What "absolute power" and "absolute corruption" are supposed to mean in the mouth of an historian, no one can say.)

13. Rousseau, *op. cit.*, II, 12: "each citizen should be completely independent vis-à-vis each of the others, and as dependent as can be vis-à-vis the city."

14. *Ibid.*, II, 3. Rousseau applies, in the modern world and in a totalistic way, the historically conditioned techniques for replacing clan law that are analyzed by Aristotle in the *Politics*: democracy was advanced in Hellas, we are told, when men saw that "private cults should be reduced to a minimum or transformed into public ones, and every device is to be explored for throwing everyone together with everyone as much as possible, for shattering other, older loyalties." (*Pol.* 1319b24-27).

15. *Historical Sketches*, I, p. 161: "a society is a collection of individuals made one by their participation in some common possession." The common possession may be race, religion, language, or shared historical experience, as well as possession of a naturally defined area of the earth. Newman's definition should be compared to Augustine's realistic way of defining the state (*City of God*, XIX, 24): "A political community is a gathering of rational creatures united by the things for which they have a shared love. Acton, in one of his file-card aphorisms, remarked that "Liberty is the creation of property, not religion." This is true only if Newman's and Augustine's wide concept of property,—as some good thing shared, commanding a fixed loyalty from the community at large—be accepted; and only if a religion refusing to give to Caesar what is God's can be considered, at the political level, such a "property."

16. *A Disquisition of Government* (New York: Appleton, 1853), p. 37.

17. "Who's To Blame?" pp. 315-16.

18. *Ibid.*, pp. 351-52.

19. American society offers a special situation, since it brought a high degree of political wisdom into a new and unsettled area. To make up for the lack of checks and balances of native growth, the American Constitu-

tion aimed more specifically at an internal balancing of governmental activities than was necessary in communities of more gradual growth. This gives to the written Constitution of America a force and focal position that would not normally belong to a state's explicit political charter. The American Constitution *is* the American tradition, reaching back to Europe and articulated through an extraordinary act of conscious statesmanship; and departure from it is the more dangerous because the country has little other tradition to give it form.

20. "Who's To Blame?" pp. 351-52.

21. *Ibid.*, p. 349.

22. John Courtney Murray, S. J., *We Hold These Truths* (New York: Sheed and Ward, 1960), p. 208: "the totalitarianizing tendency is inherent in the contemporary idolatry of the democratic process. . . . What is urged is a monism, not so much of the political order itself, as of a political technique. The proposition is that all the issues of human life— intellectual, religious, and moral issues as well as formally political issues— are to be regarded as, or resolved into, poitical issues and are to be settled by the single omnicomptetent political technique of majority vote."

23. One of Acton's numberless file cards, studied by Herbert Butterfield, contains the statement that the real conflict acted out in the course of the French Revolution was "the great struggle between liberty and democracy"—not between monarchy and democracy, tradition and liberty, but between man's desire to be free and the doctrinaire channels into which this thrust was guided and expended.

24. Even Ernst Cassirer, in arguing for the moral unity of Rousseau's work, admits contradiction on the "literal" level in Rousseau's concept of an open society as the milieu for education: "From the very outset, the work stands outside the conditions of human society. It releases the pupil from every kind of relationship to human society; it places him, as it were, in a vacuum. The walls of this prison close in on him ever more confiningly . . . to lead him back to the simplicity and plainness of nature. But is it not the height of unnaturalness thus to hide the existing order of things from the child? And furthermore, is this attempt not doomed to failure from the outset? . . . At decisive turning points of spiritual and ethical development, such external aid is required and employed—we may recall, for example, the conversation between Emile and the gardener, which is designed to convey and to make comprehensible to Emile the first idea of property. Thus the fanatical love of truth, which was to guide this system of education, ends up by degenerating into a curiously complicated system of deceptions, of carefully calculated pedagogical tricks" (*The Question of Jean-Jacques Rousseau,* trans. Peter Gay (New York: Columbia, 1954).

25. Murray, *op. cit.*, p. 164.

26. Cf. *Letters of Lord Acton to Mary Gladstone* (London: Macmillan, 1905) for Acton's "deep aversion" (p. 243) to the "sophist, the manipulator, not the servant, of truth" (p. 70). A. J. Carlyle called Augustine's denial of the concept that the state's characteristic attribute is justice "a deplor-

able error for a great Christian teacher" (*Social and Political Ideas of Some Great Mediaeval Thinkers*, ed. F. J. C. Hearnshaw (London, 1923), p. 51).

27. Murray, *op. cit.*, p. 209: "Christianity has always regarded the state as a limited order of action for limited purposes, to be chosen and pursued under the direction and correction of the organized moral conscience of society, whose judgments are formed and mobilized by the Church, an independent and autonomous community, qualified to be the interpreter of man's nature and destiny." Cf. Acton, *The History of Freedom and Other Essays* (London: Macmillan, 1907), p. 205: "In the Jewish as in the Gentile world, political and theological obligations were made to coincide; in both, therefore,—in the theocracy of the Jews as in the *politeia* of the Greeks, —the State was absolute. Now it is the great object of the Church, by keeping the two spheres permanently distinct,—by rendering to Caesar the things that are Caesar's, and to God the things that are God's—to make all absolutism, of whatever kind, impossible."

28. Murray, *op. cit.*, p. 203. For a psychological presentation of the fact that liberty arises from creatively divided loyalties, *cf.* T. S. Eliot's discussion of religion in *Notes Towards a Definition of Culture*.

Note to Chapter Ten

1. "Freedom or Virtue," *National Review*, XIII, 10 (Sept. 11, 1962), 181-87.

Notes to Chapter Eleven

1. Recently, I read an astounding remark: "To really democratize the class structure, it may be necessary to reduce the level of education which middle and upper-class British youth receive before reaching the university; but is this too great a price to pay for an open and equalitarian society?" (*The New Leader*, November 21, 1960, p. 18.) On that sort of basis, which is the opposite of what the supposedly egalitarian Communists are doing, the security of the United States would collapse from inanition within one generation.

Notes to Chapter Twelve

1. Several years later, in the *New Individualist Review*, a graduate student in philosophy, a disciple of Hayek, von Mises, and Friedman, analyzed the thought and rhetoric of Miss Rand and came to similar conclusions. Miss Rand, he wrote, is "hate blinded," "suffocating in her invective." See Bruce Goldberg, "Ayn Rand's 'For the New Intellectual,'" *New Individualist Review*, Nov., 1961, p. 29.

2. *New Individualist Review*, Nov., 1961, p. 3. On behalf of *National Review* I answered (in part): "The American conservative needs to proceed within the knowledge of history and anthropology and psychology; we must live in our time. We must indeed continue to cherish our resentments against such institutionalized impositions upon our prerogatives as social security. But we must not, if we are to pass for sane in this tormented world, equate as problems of equal urgency, the repeal of the social security

law, and the containment of the Soviet threat. The problem of assigning priorities to the two objectives is not merely a problem of intellectual discrimination, but of moral balance."

3. As essay in *Freedom and Serfdom, An Anthology of Western Thought* (Dordrecht, Holland: D. Reidel Co., 1961).

Contributors

William F. Buckley, Jr., is Editor-in-Chief of *National Review* and author of *God and Man at Yale*, *McCarthy and His Enemies* (with L. Brent Bozell), *Up from Liberalism*, and *Rumbles Left and Right*. His weekly newspaper column, "On the Right," and his lecturing and writing have gained him recognition as one of the leading spokesmen of American conservatism.

John Chamberlain is the author of *Farewell to Reform*, *The American Stakes*, *MacArthur 1941-51* (with Gen. Charles Willoughby), *The Roots of Capitalism*, and *The Enterprising Americans*. He now writes the daily syndicated column, "These Days." He has been associated with the *New York Times* (for which he wrote the daily book column for many years), *Life*, *Fortune*, *Barron's*, *The Wall Street Journal*, *Scribner's*, *Harper's*, *The Saturday Review*, and *National Review*.

M. Stanton Evans is the Editor of the *Indianapolis News* and author of *Revolt on the Campus* and *The Fringe on Top*.

F. A. Hayek, until recently Professor of Social and Moral Science at the University of Chicago, is now at the University of Freiburg. He was formerly Professor of Economics at the London School of Economics and at Vienna. His many books include *Prices and Production*, *The Pure Theory of Capital*, *The Road to Serfdom*, *Individualism and Economic Order*, *The Counter-Revolution of Science*, *The Sensory Order*, *The Constitution of Liberty*.

Willmoore Kendall is a Senior Editor of *National Review*. For many years on the faculty of Yale, he has also been Visiting Professor of Political Science at Georgetown University and Stanford University. He has recently gone to the University of Dallas to become Chairman of a new Department of Political Science and Director of the Institute of Studies in the American Political Tradition. He has served as Chief of the Latin American Division of the Office of Reports and Estimates of the Central Intelligence Agency and head of the American Republics Division, Office of Intelligence Research, Department of State. He is the author of *John Locke and the Doctrine of Majority Rule*, *Democracy and the American Party System* (with Austin

Ranney), and *The Conservative Affirmation.* He is a frequent contributor to the *American Political Science Review,* the *Midwest Journal of Political Science,* and the *Journal of Politics.*

Russell Kirk is the author of *Randolph of Roanoke, The Conservative Mind, A Program for Conservatives, Academic Freedom, Beyond the Dreams of Avarice.* He contributes widely to journals in the United States, Canada, and England and writes a syndicated column.

Frank S. Meyer is a Senior Editor of *National Review* and Editorial Advisor of *Modern Age.* He is the author of *The Moulding of Communists* and *In Defense of Freedom: A Conservative Credo.*

Father Stanley Parry, C.S.C., teaches political science at the University of Notre Dame, where he has been Chairman of the Department since he took his doctorate at Yale. Recently he has given up administrative work to devote his time to teaching and writing, including the completion of a book on Johannes Althusius. He has contributed to the *Review of Politics, National Review,* and *Modern Age.*

Stefan T. Possony is the Director of International Studies, the Hoover Institution, Stanford University. Formerly Professor of International Relations at Georgetown University, he has lectured at the National War College, the Naval War College, and the Air University and has contributed numerous articles to military and general journals. He is the author of *Strategic Air Power, International Relations* (with Robert Strausz-Hupé), *A Century of Conflict,* and *A Forward Strategy for America* (with William R. Kintner and Robert Strausz-Hupé).

Wilhelm Röpke has been Professor of Economics at Jena, Graz, Marburg, and Istanbul. He is now at the Graduate Institute of International Studies in Geneva. The author of some twenty books, including *Civitas Humana, The Social Crisis of Our Time, A Humane Economy,* and *Economics of the Free Society,* he has been widely credited as the inspirer of Ludwig Erhard's economic policies which produced the West German "economic miracle."

Stephen J. Tonsor is Associate Professor of Intellectual History at the University of Michigan. He contributes to many scholarly journals, including *The American Historical Review,* the *Journal of the History of Ideas, Victorian Studies,* and the *Anglican Theological Review.*

Garry Wills is Assistant Professor of Classics at Johns Hopkins University. He is the author of *Chesterton: The Man and the Mask* and is a regular contributor to *National Review.*